THE FATHERS
OF THE CHURCH

A NEW TRANSLATION

VOLUME 22

THE FATHERS OF THE CHURCH

A NEW TRANSLATION

EDITORIAL BOARD

ROY JOSEPH DEFERRARI
The Catholic University of America
Editorial Director

MSGR. JAMES A. MAGNER
The Catholic University of America

BERNARD M. PEEBLES
The Catholic University of America

MARTIN R. P. MCGUIRE
The Catholic University of America

THOMAS HALTON
The Catholic University of America

ROBERT P. RUSSELL, O.S.A.
Villanova University

WILLIAM R. TONGUE
The Catholic University of America

HERMIGILD DRESSLER, O.F.M.
The Catholic University of America

REDMOND A. BURKE, C.S.V.
The Catholic University of America

SISTER M. JOSEPHINE BRENNAN, I.H.M.
Marywood College

FUNERAL ORATIONS

by

SAINT GREGORY NAZIANZEN

and

SAINT AMBROSE

Translated by

LEO P. McCAULEY, S. J.
JOHN J. SULLIVAN, C. S. Sp.
MARTIN R. P. McGUIRE
ROY J. DEFERRARI

With an Introduction on the Early Christian Funeral Oration by Martin R. P. McGuire

THE CATHOLIC UNIVERSITY OF AMERICA PRESS
Washington, D. C. 20017

NIHIL OBSTAT:

        JOHN M. A. FEARNS, S.T.D.
              Censor Librorum

IMPRIMATUR:

     ✠ FRANCIS CARDINAL SPELLMAN
        Archbishop of New York

August 15, 1953

Library of Congress Catalog Card No.: 67-28586

Copyright © 1953 by
THE CATHOLIC UNIVERSITY OF AMERICA PRESS, INC.
All rights reserved
Reprinted with corrections 1968

First Paperback Reprint 2004
ISBN 0-8132-1402-5 (pbk)
ISBN-13: 978-0-8132-1402-3 (pbk)

CONTENTS

INTRODUCTION

    The Early Christian Funeral Oration, by Martin R. P. McGuire vii

ST. GREGORY NAZIANZEN

    Introduction 3

    On His Brother, St. Caesarius, translated by Leo P. McCauley, S. J. 5

    On St. Basil the Great, Bishop of Caesarea, translated by Leo P. McCauley, S. J. 27

    On His Sister, St. Gorgonia, translated by Leo P. McCauley, S. J. 101

    On His Father, in the Presence of St. Basil, translated by Leo P. McCauley, S. J. 119

ST. AMBROSE

On His Brother Satyrus, translated by John J. Sullivan, C. S. Sp., and Martin R. P. McGuire

Introduction 159
First Oration 161
Second Oration: On Faith in the Resurrection . 197

On Emperor Valentinian, translated by Roy J. Deferrari

Introduction 263
Text 265

On Emperor Theodosius, translated by Roy J. Deferrari

Introduction 303
Text 307

INDEX 335

THE CHRISTIAN FUNERAL ORATION

THE CHRISTIAN FUNERAL ORATION is one of the most elaborate of Christian literary forms. It represents an attempt to adapt to Christian use a pagan Greek form with many hundreds of years of tradition behind it, a form which in itself is only one branch, but an important branch, of the literary genre known as the encomium. Beside the funeral oration, there arose also a closely related literary genre, the treatise on grief or consolation, which was often given an epistolary form. It was inevitable that the systematic, philosophical treatment of grief and consolation in such treatises should have an increasing influence on the content of the funeral oration. The Greek treatise on consolation impressed the Romans profoundly and many of its essential features passed into the Latin *consolatio*. Furthermore, the native Latin *laudatio funebris,* in its later form at least, could not escape the influence of the Greek encomium and of the Greek and Latin treatises on grief and consolation.

The Christian masterpieces presented in this volume reflect, then, a long, rich, and varied pagan literary tradition in East and West, and at the same time exhibit modifications and new elements which give them their specific Christian character. Before attempting to evaluate their form and content properly, it will be useful, therefore, if not necessary, to examine their background in some detail.

The Greek funeral speech developed out of the formal laudation or commemoration of those who had fallen in battle for their country. The famous funeral speech of Pericles as presented by Thucydides (*c.* 460-395 B.C.) is probably the earliest extant example. The fallen are collectively praised for their bravery. The State expresses its thanks to them for victory and preservation, public and private grief for them must be borne with dignity, and all, especially members of their families, must remember that their fellow citizens, sons, and brothers were mortal, and that in dying a beautiful death they have escaped the ravages of disease and the afflictions of old age.

Isocrates (427-329 B.C.), the great publicist and teacher of rhetoric, apparently was the first to compose a funeral oration on an historical individual. His speech on Evagoras of Cyprus, addressed to the latter's son Nicocles, and the *Epitaph* or funeral speech of the Attic orator Hypereides on his friend Leosthenes, in their form and content had considerable influence on the development of the funeral speech as a literary type. Consolation is furnished by the thoughts that the dead had enjoyed many advantages and blessings in life, that all men must die, that the present dead were fortunate in the time of their death, and that they escaped disease, sorrow, and other kinds of human misfortune. Hypereides adds the consolation to be derived from the thought of happiness in a future life for those who have honored the gods in the present life.

In the period after Alexander the Great the funeral oration was regarded more and more as a branch of epideictic oratory, and a special schema with a whole series of *tópoi* or commonplaces was elaborated for this as well as for other branches of the epideictic genre. Fortunately, we have extant the treatise on epideictic oratory[1] composed by the Greek rhetorician Menander in the third century A.D. This representative work gives us much precious information on the various kinds of encomia when the genre had reached its zenith, at least on the side of theory.

Menander divides encomia or eulogies into two main classes: the *basilikòs lógos* or 'royal oration,' for the living, and the *epitáphios lógos* or 'epitaph' for the dead. The latter is subdivided into four types:

(1) The pure encomium, which treats of one long dead, and is primarily concerned with praise.

(2) The epitaph, which has two forms: the first or general type, like the ancient funeral oration of Pericles; the second or particular type, dealing with a specific individual. The second type is concerned with an individual who has recently died, and usually combines praise with consolation and lament.

(3) The monody, a brief but intense lament.

(4) The consolatory speech, which is closely related to the monody, but places much more emphasis on consolation.

The schema of the typical *epitáphios lógos* may be presented as follows: (1) exordium; (2) encomium (laudation proper, combined with lament and developed under the following *tópoi* or commonplaces: family, birth, natural endowment, upbringing, education, life and occupation, with emphasis or moral qualities exhibited, achievements, fortune, and comparison with others, especially the great and famous); (3) final exhortation, and prayer.

The *epitáphios lógos* was much cultivated in the Greek schools of rhetoric and never with greater brilliance than in the second half of the fourth century A.D., when it was taught in theory and exemplified in practice at Athens, Constantinople, Antioch and other centers by such famous sophists

---

[1] For the Greek text of Menander, cf. Spengel, *Rhetores Graeci* III 327ff.

as Libanius, Himerius, and Themistius. Himerius was undoubtedly one of the principal teachers of Gregory Nazianzen in rhetoric at Athens. It is not surprising, then, to find the influence of the pagan encomium and its *tópoi* so marked in the first great Christian funeral orations. But before considering these in detail, we must first discuss briefly the development of the Greek treatise on consolation and the Latin *consolatio,* because of their close relationship with and influence upon the Greek and Latin funeral oration respectively.

Democritus of Abdera (*c*. 460-*c*. 370 B.C.), Plato (427-347 B.C.), Xenophon (*c*. 430-354 B.C.), Antisthenes (450-366 B.C.) and Diogenes of Sinope (400-325 B.C.), the founders of Cynic philosophy, Aristotle (384-322 B.C.), Xenocrates of Chalcidon, Plato's successor as head of the Academy (339-322 B.C.), and Theophrastus (*c*. 372-288 B.C.), Aristotle's successor in the Peripatetic School, had all dealt with the theme of death and the problem and means of consolation. It remained for Crantor (*c*. 335-275 B.C.), however, the pupil of Xenocrates, to write a treatise *On Grief* which was regarded throughout antiquity as the most comprehensive and model work of its kind. Crantor's treatise was cast in the form of a letter to a certain Hippocles on the death of his children, and both in form and content it exercised a great influence on all later works on the consolation theme in the Greek East and subsequently in the Latin West. There were other important writers, including the great Stoics, Zeno and Panaetius, but none was regarded as important as Crantor in this field. Panaetius, in fact, recommended that Crantor's treatise should be learned by heart. The theme of consolation also fell within the scope of the Cynic-Stoic diatribe from the time of Bion of Borysthenes (*c*. 325-255 B.C.), and the consolation equipped with a full complement of commonplaces became one of the important forms of that genre. All this earlier Greek literature on consolation had a marked influence on Cicero (*c.* 105-43 B.C.), Seneca (*c.* 5 B.C.-A.D. 65), and Plutarch (*c.* 46-120 A.D.).

The 'consolation' as a literary genre was introduced into Latin literature by Cicero. His first work, *On Consolation* (*De consolatione*), written to console himself on the death of his daughter Tullia, is lost. He has dealt, however, in detail with the theme of death and consolation in Books I and III of his *Tusculan Disputations* and it is thought that these books cover substantially the material which was presented in the lost treatise. Seneca's most important contributions to the genre are his *Ad Marciam de consolatione, Ad Helviam matrem de consolatione,* and *Ad Polybium de consolatione.* Of these, only the first deals with death, the other two being concerned with consolation on exile. Mention must be made here also of the relatively short but magnificent letter of consolation which Servius Sulpicius Rufus wrote to Cicero on learning of the death of Tullia.[2] There are a number of similar letters in Cicero, Seneca, and Pliny the Younger. The consolation was also cultivated very much as a more or less formal genre in poetry as well as in prose. On the Latin side, let it suffice to mention the consolation on death in Lucretius 3.830-1094, Horace, *Odes* 1.24 and 2.9, the consolatory elegies of Propertius and Ovid, the Pseudo-Ovidian *Consolatio ad Liviam,* the *Epicedia* of Statius, the elegies of Martial.

Closely related to the Latin consolation, and much earlier in date, was the native Roman *laudatio funebris*. It was an ancient Roman custom for a funeral speech to be given at the death of a member of a prominent Roman family by a kinsman or friend. Such funeral orations made a strong impression on the Greek writers Polybius (*Hist.* 6.53-54), Dionysius of Halicarnassus (*Rom. Antiq.* 6.17.2-6), and Plutarch (*Publicola* 9.7). Unfortunately, only brief descrip-

---
2 Cicero, *Epist. ad Fam.* 4.5.

tions, passing references,³ and scattered fragments have come down to us. The *laudatio funebris* was regarded as private in character. It was not published, but a copy was kept in the family archives. The *Agricola* of Tacitus, as a laudatory biography, probably reflects fairly well the essential features of the *laudatio funebris,* but at a time when it had definitely come under the influence of Greek rhetoric. Since it was essentially a eulogy, it corresponded more closely to the Greek *basilikòs lógos* than to the *epitáphios lógos*. Cicero has in mind the *laudatio funebris* as well as the panegyric in general when he describes its character thus: 'He who proposes to be the panegyrist of anyone will understand that he has in the first place to deal fully with the favours of fortune. These are the advantages of race, wealth, connexions, friendships, power, good health, beauty, vigour, talent and the rest of the attributes that are either physical or externally imposed: it must be explained that the person commended made a right use of these benefits if he possessed them, managed sensibly without them, if they were denied to him and bore the loss with resignation, if they were taken away from him; and after that the speaker will marshal instances of conduct, either active or passive, on the part of the subject of his praises; whereby he manifested wisdom, generosity, valour, righteousness, greatness of soul, sense of duty, gratitude, kindliness, or in short any moral excellence you please . . . '⁴

The commonplaces of the pagan Greek and Latin consolation literature as a whole have a monotonous similarity. Among them may be mentioned the following: Fortune rules all and one must always be ready to meet its blows; all men are mortal; to have lived virtuously, not long, is of prime

---
3 Cf. *Ad Herennium* 3.6.110ff.; Cicero, *De orat.* 2.11.46; *De invent.* 1.59; Quintilian, *Inst.* 3.7.10-18.
4 Cicero, *De orat.* 2.45-46, trans. Sutton (Loeb Classical Library).

importance; time cures all ills; death gives freedom from the ravages of disease, the evils of old age, and all other misfortune; the examples of others ought to give one comfort and courage; the dead no longer suffer grief or pain; many think that there is a happy life for the soul beyond the grave; reason must temper grief; displays of emotion are unmanly. These rather impersonal arguments based on reason became stereotyped. They have a philosophical coldness about them which, apart from Seneca's occasional emphasis on the warmth of family affection as a source of consolation, only becomes more marked with the repetition of centuries. In spite of their ineffectual character in many respects, they continued to be inculcated without essential change in the pagan schools of rhetoric until Christianity gave a new life to the traditional genres and commonplaces of consolation and added the incomparably superior means of consolation furnished by the Christian faith.

Christian consolation, whatever the literary vehicle of its expression, is based on the central doctrines of the Christian religion: belief in a personal God, the Creator of the world and of man, all-powerful but all-just and all-merciful, in the three Persons of the Trinity and their attributes, in the Incarnation of Christ the Second Person of the Trinity, and of the death of the God-Man on the cross as the supreme sacrifice for our redemption, in His resurrection as the Saviour of mankind and as Victor over sin and death, in the reality of the Eucharistic Sacrifice and the spiritual help and comfort to be derived from participation in it, in the Church as a divine institution, in the future life as the true life, in the communion of saints, in the resurrection of the body, in a last judgment, and in an eternal life of happiness in heaven or of punishment in hell. Furthermore, in the Psalms and Prophets of the Old Testament, and in the New Testament in its entirety,

Christians possessed a consolation literature of unique power and beauty and one enjoying unique authority as the Word of God Himself.

The Christian teachings on the resurrection of Christ and or the resurrection of the body occupy a central place in Christian apologetic and consolation. No Christian beliefs met with greater opposition or ridicule from the pagan milieu of early Christianity. After nearly two thousand years of the Christian tradition, it is difficult for us to appreciate the full significance of the great passage[5] in which St. Paul cites the resurrection of Christ as certain proof of the resurrection of the body and as the fundamental and certain proof also of the validity of the Christian faith, and then proceeds to answer in detail a number of questions raised regarding the possibility of the resurrection of the body and the nature of the body after its resurrection. It is not surprising, therefore, to find that belief in the resurrection and arguments to support that belief are emphasized in early Christian consolatory literature. The supporting arguments soon develop into a body of commonplaces which appear repeatedly in the various types of Christian writings. These commonplaces, moreover, are interwoven with those employed by the pagans as arguments for the immortality of the soul and taken over by the Christians to serve the same purpose. Thus, Clement of Rome (c. 30-100) in his *Epistle to the Corinthians* declares that the resurrection of Christ is the strongest proof of the certainty of our resurrection, and he employs arguments from nature to support this proof: the alternation of day and night, the living plant growing from the decayed seed in the ground, and the example of the phoenix springing again into life from its ashes. The last illustration was especially effective in antiquity, because the reality of the phoenix and its life cycles was widely believed. Athenagoras (fl. 177) in his work, *On*

---
5 1 Cor. 15.12-58.

the Resurrection of the Dead, shows that the resurrection is not only possible but necessary, drawing upon Pythagoras and Plato for the argument that an original whole, even after the separation of its parts, can be restored. Tertullian (d. after 200) deals with the resurrection in greater detail in his *On the Resurrection of the Flesh* and *On the Soul.* In addition to the authority of Scripture, he cites the pagan belief in the immortality of the soul and the arguments used to support it: the rising and setting of the sun, the phases of the moon, the fall and renewal of foliage, and the story of the phoenix. St. Cyprian (d. 258) in his *On Mortality* stresses the reward of eternal joys and the certainty of the resurrection. Lactantius (early 4th cent.) has a long section, 'On the Happy Life,' in his *Divine Institutes.* He considers the immortality of the soul the highest good, and he argues that God who created man has the power to restore bodies, however impossible this may seem under certain circumstances. In his exposition, he reviews critically the various pagan views and arguments in respect to immortality. It may be observed in passing that the most elaborate treatment of the phoenix in ancient literature is the poem *On the Phoenix* ascribed to Lactantius.

In the course of the three centuries, then, from the coming of Christ to the establishment of the Peace of the Church under Constantine, all the typical elements of Christian consolation were formulated and developed. The commonplaces of pagan consolation were utilized, but they were given a new life and a new meaning when combined with the infinitely more effective arguments drawn from Christian doctrine and the Scriptures. In this period the literary vehicle for consolation was the official or quasi-official letter, the homily, or the treatise. Consolation was thus presented in an incidental and general fashion, and largely as a part of Christian apologetic. But the Peace of the Church ushered in the golden age of Christian literature (*c.* 325-451). Almost all the great Fathers and ecclesiastical writers of that period were trained in the pagan schools of rhetoric—the ancient Church did not develop a program of formal higher education except in Scriptural studies—under the leading sophists of the time. They were intimately familiar by long training with all the canons and conventions of style in a period when stylistic ornament was an obsession and proficiency in its employment a mark of the highest prestige and glory. They could not entirely escape the literary interests and tastes of their environment. It was only natural, under the circumstances, that they should be zealous to use their literary training and talents in the service of their faith, and that in so doing they should adapt long-established pagan literary genres to their use. Hence the polished Christian dialogues, treatises, letters and letter-treatises, homilies, panegyrics, and funeral orations, to say nothing of the poetry of high quality in form and content, of the golden age of patristic literature. Consolation in this age finds formal expression in dialogues, treatises, letters, and funeral orations. It is the last genre which is our primary concern here.

Of the ancient Christian funeral orations we have extant, four by St. Gregory Nazianzen (*c.* 329-*c.* 390), four by St. Ambrose (339-397)—the second oration on Satyrus, however, is more properly a *consolatio*—and four by St. Gregory of Nyssa (d. 394). All the funeral orations of the first two Fathers are included in the present volume. Those of St. Gregory of Nyssa are omitted because they are somewhat inferior when considered as whole. They reflect the rhetorical exaggerations of the sophistic style to a greater degree and a much greater dependence upon and identity with pagan models.

St. Gregory Nazianzen was the pioneer in adapting the pagan funeral oration to Christian use. Therefore, it will be appropriate here to analyze briefly two of his funeral orations which may be considered most typical of the genre in its Christian Greek form, namely, the oration on his brother Caesarius, the first of his extant funeral orations, and that on his friend St. Basil, the masterpiece of Christian Greek funeral speeches.

The oration on St. Caesarius may be analyzed as follows: exordium—division of the subject (Ch. 1); encomium—ancestry and parentage (2-4); physical endowments (5); upbringing and education (6-7); occupation and achievements (8-10); life in Constantinople (10); struggle between Caesarius and Julian (11-14.); death and funeral (15); the orator addresses his dead brother directly (16-17); exhortation (18-21) and counsel (22-23); final exhortation and prayer (24).

A glance at the schema of Menander for the *epitáphios lógos* given above will indicate that the oration follows the general plan. However, apart from the Christian elements, there are some differences. There is almost a complete absence of lament; on the other hand, the description of the death and funeral is borrowed from the monody. The consolatory speech suggested the development of the thoughts on the brevity of human life and on the lot of the soul after death (16-17). The principal Christian elements are the Christian outlook throughout, the frequent Biblical quotations, the emphasis on spiritual rather than earthly goods, the emphasis on eternal happiness of the soul with God in heaven as its true home, the resurrection of the body, and the final solemn prayer to God.

But it is in the funeral oration on St. Basil that St. Gregory Nazianzen reveals his complete mastery of the genre and his originality in adapting it to a more independent and specifically Christian use. The analysis which follows is largely taken from Boulenger[6]: exordium—the orator explains his

---

6 F. Boulenger, *Grégoire de Nazianze* (Paris 1908) xxix-xxxi.

delay (1-2); encomium—ancestors of Basil (3); their piety and its proofs (4-8); his parents (9-10); physical endowments (10); praise of knowledge, education in Caesarea in Cappadocia and in Constantinople (11-14) and at Athens (14-24); his life as a priest, abuses in the hierarchy (25-27); his disgrace, persecution, and struggle, and his acts compared to Joseph's (28-36); his election as bishop and conception of the office (37-38); his administration of his church, attempts to establish unity in the Church, struggles against the emperor, the prefect, the judge, and against the bishops (38-59); his moral and intellectual qualities: poverty, austerity, celibacy, solicitude for the poor and sick, refutation of the charge of arrogance, his eloquence, his writings and teachings (60-69); comparisons with others: Adam, Enos, Henoch, Noe, Abraham, Isaac, Jacob, Joseph, Moses, Aaron, Samuel, David, Solomon (in wisdom only), Elias and Eliseus, Daniel and his companions, Jonas, the Machabees, St. John the Baptist (in detail), St. Peter, the sons of Zebedee, and St. Stephen (70-77); his death (78-79); funeral, lament, and counsel (80); praise of Basil for his holiness and pious acts (81); address to Basil and solemn prayer (82).

This oration, as the schema shows, is really an *epitáphios lógos,* but one in which the orator has made important modifications, from the viewpoint of the traditional form, in content, *tópoi,* and emphasis to suit his purpose. The pagan funeral oration is here transformed into a masterpiece of Christian eloquence in which the pagan elements do not assume undue importance, but are harmoniously subordinated to Christian use. Guignet well says: 'This oration represents admirably the intelligent independence which Gregory could exhibit towards the great rhetors of whom he was the spiritual son. Obviously, Gregory's method of composition cannot be understood if we neglect the models which he followed. Given the tyranny exercised in his time in all the domains of literature, we observe in this oration a splendid emancipation. For one who is familiar, on the one hand, with the rigidity of the sophistic teachings and, on the other, with the intellectual pattern so strongly impressed upon young minds in the workshops of the schools of rhetoric, the easy attitude of freedom which Gregory adopts towards their precepts constitutes a definite and real effort in the direction of newness and originality.'[7]

St. Ambrose introduced the Christian funeral oration into Latin literature most probably under the impulse given by his great contemporaries in the East, Gregory Nazianzen and Gregory of Nyssa. It would hardly seem accidental that his funeral oration on Valentinian and Theodosius and his first oration on his brother Satyrus should be the only known examples of the genre in ancient Christian Latin literature. Apart from his excellent rhetorical training in Latin, St. Ambrose had a much better knowledge of Greek than the great majority of his intellectual contemporaries. Hence, his funeral orations proper reflect an intimate acquaintance with the canons of Menander and other Greek theorists and practitioners in the field of rhetoric as well as the influence of the Latin *laudatio funebris* and *consolatio*. It should be emphasized, however, that St. Ambrose did not feel as closely bound by his pagan models as his Greek contemporaries. Furthermore, his funeral orations are more thoroughly permeated with Christian thought and with scriptural quotation, phraseology, and imagery, and they are distinguished as a whole by more marked personal tone and warmth of feeling. To give a concrete idea of their rhetorical structure, it will suffice to reproduce Rozynski's schema[8] of the first oration on Satyrus: exordium (1-6); general grounds for lament—My sorrow for the death of Satyrus is very great, because without him I

---
7 M. Guignet, *Saint Grégoire de Nazianze* (Paris 1911) 310.
8 F. Rozynski, *Die Leichenreden des hl. Ambrosius* (Breslau 1910) 18-19.

cannot live (14), I can no longer requite him for his benefits (19), in him I have lost all my joy, all my comfort, and every ornament of my life (33); special ground for lament—I weep for my brother, and rightly, because many virtues adorned him: fidelity in honoring God, an extraordinary prudence, and a noble eloquence (49), courage (50), self-control (56), a strict sense of rectitude, combined with kindness (62); end of lament—The recollection of all these special excellences of his now cause me great sorrow; I shall pine away with grief; grounds for consolation—In my sorrow I derive consolation from the favorable time of his death (68), the thought that we Christians should not mourn as pagans mourn (71), the thought that I have not lost my brother completely and the thought that my episcopal office will help much to alleviate my grief (77); conclusion—Receive my last farewell (78) and let me soon follow you (79); prayer (80).

This oration is classified by Rozynski as a consolatory speech, but it would seem rather to be a combination of this and of a monody. Furthermore, his attempt to fit the speech a little too rigidly into the schemata of Menander leads him to de-emphasize the central role given to the Christian elements in the oration, and especially the copious employment of Scripture.

An analysis of the structure of the so-called second oration on Satyrus shows that it is essentially a Christian *consolatio*. The commonplaces of the pagan genre are liberally employed, especially those dealing with death as a release from the troubles of this life and with the immortality of the soul. There are many resemblances in content and language to passages in the *Tusculan Disputations* of Cicero, but the chief Ciceronian source or influence was most probably his lost *De consolatione*. The central theme of the work, however, is the truly Christian consolation to be derived from an unquestioning and fervent belief in the eternal happiness of the souls of the just with God and in the certainty and reality of the resurrection of the body at the end of the world. In the course of his exposition, St. Ambrose draws heavily upon Scripture and in his application of passages of the Canticle of Canticles, St. Paul, and the Apocalypse especially he exhibits a mystic exaltation which in its glowing intensity reminds one of the Psalms of David and the Prophets of the Old Testament.

The translations in the present volume are based, in general, on the reprints of the old Benedictine editions available in Migne, *PG* 35-36, and *PL* 16. In the case of the orations of St. Gregory Nazianzen on St. Caesarius and St. Basil, and of the orations of St. Ambrose on Satyrus (I), Valentinian, and Theodosius, the new or revised texts published in the special editions listed in the bibliography were also utilized. The text of St. Ambrose is so badly reprinted in Migne that it was necesssary to check the text of the second oration on Satyrus, especially, against that of the original Benedictine text of 1686-1690.[1]

Scriptural quotations from the books of the Old Testament, except Genesis, are given according to the wording of Challoner's revision of the Douai Version. For Genesis and for the New Testament, the translations published under the auspices of the Confraternity of Christian Doctrine have been employed.

MARTIN R. P. MCGUIRE

---

[1] The translation of the funeral orations of St. Ambrose has been checked against the new critical edition of the Latin text edited by O. Faller, listed on p. xxii.

SELECT BIBLIOGRAPHY

Texts and Translations:

Grégoire de Nazianze. *Discours funèbres en l'honneur de son frère Césaire et de Basile de Césarée.* Texte grec, traduction française, introduction et index, par Fernand Boulenger (Paris 1908). (Textes et Documents, pour l'Etude historique du Christianisme publiés sous la direction de Hippolyte Hemmer et Paul Lejay 16).

S. Ambrosii Mediolanensis Episcopi de obitu Satyri fratris laudatio funebris, denuo edidit annotavit praefatus est D. Dr. Bruno Albers (Bonnae 1921). (Florilegium Patristicum 15).

Sancti Ambrosii Opera, Pars VII: Explanatio symboli, De sacramentis, De mysteriis, De Paenitentia, De excessu fratris, De obitu Valentiniani, De obitu Theodosii, rec. Otto Faller, S. J. (Vienna 1965). (Corpus scriptorum ecclesiasticorum Latinorum 73).

Sancti Ambrosii Liber de consolatione Valentiniani: A text with a translation, introduction and commentary, by Thomas A. Kelly, C.S.C. (Washington 1940). (Catholic University of America Patristic Studies 58).

Sancti Ambrosii Oratio de obitu Theodosii: Text, translation, introduction, and commentary, by Sister Mary Dolorosa Mannix, S.S.J. (Washington 1925). (Catholic University of America Patristic Studies 10).

Select Orations of Saint Gregory Nazianzen, trans. by Charles G. Browne and James E. Swallow (New York 1894). (A Select Library of Nicene and Post-Nicene Fathers of the Christian Church, 2nd ser. 7).

Des heiligen Bischofs Gregor von Nazianz Reden aus dem Griechischen übersetzt und mit Einleitung und Anmerkungen versehen, von Dr. Theol. Philipp Häuser (München 1928). (Bibliothek der Kirchenväter 59).

Some of the Principal Works of St. Ambrose, trans. by H. de Romestin et al. (New York 1896). (A Select Library of Nicene and Post-Nicene Fathers of the Christian Church, 2nd ser. 10).

Des heiligen Kirchenlehrers Ambrosius von Mailand Pflichtenlehre und ausgewählte kleinere Schriften, übersetzt und eingeleitet von Dr. Joh. Ev. Niederhuber, 3. Band (Kempten und München 1917). (Bibliothek der Kirchenväter 32).

Other Works:

B. Albers, 'Ueber die erste Trauerrede des hl. Ambrosius zum Tode seines Bruders Satyrus,' *Festgabe Ehrhard* (Bonn and Leipzig 1922) 24-52.

Sister M. Melchior Beyenka, O.P., *Consolation in Saint Augustine* (Washington 1950). (Catholic University of America Patristic Studies 83). Contains a good historical introduction on the development of the ancient consolation, pp. 1-30.

H. Dudden, *The Life and Times of St. Ambrose*, 2 vols. (Oxford 1935).

C. Favez, *La consolation latine chrétienne* (Paris 1937).

Sister M. Edmond Fern, *The Latin Consolatio as a Literary Type* (St. Louis 1941).

M. Guignet, *Saint Grégoire de Nazianze orateur et épistolier* (Paris 1911).

X. Hürth, 'De Gregorii Nazianzeni orationibus funebribus,' *Dissertationes philologicae Argentoratenses selectae*, Vol. 12 (Argentorati 1908) 1-160.

J. R. Palanque, *S. Ambroise et l'empire romain* (Paris 1933).

A. Puech, *Histoire de la littérature grecque chrétienne depuis les origines jusqu'à la fin du IVe siècle*, Tome III (Paris 1930).

F. Rozynski, *Die Leichenreden des hl. Ambrosius insbesondere auf ihr Verhältnis zu der antiken Rhetorik und den antiken Trostschriften untersucht* (Breslau 1910).

SAINT GREGORY NAZIANZEN

FOUR FUNERAL ORATIONS

Translated by
LEO P. McCAULEY, S. J., Ph.D.
Boston College

INTRODUCTION

CAESARIUS, WHOSE EARLY and untimely death is the subject of this funeral oration, was the younger brother of St. Gregory. Celebrated as a physician, he was highly esteemed by Emperors Constantius and Julian. While holding an imperial office in the province of Bithynia, he escaped death in the earthquake at Nicaea in 368, but shortly thereafter fell a victim to an unspecified disease. His remains were brought back to Nazianzus and interred in the family vault. On this occasion St. Gregory delivered the present oration in the presence of his parents.

The eulogy of Caesarius has the usual rhetorical divisions. The topics are amplified with all the richness cherished by the age. The embellishments of rhetorical art are present in full vigor. Noteworthy are the sections of the encounter between Caesarius and Julian (11-14), and the stirring, if lengthy, comparisons between this life and the life to come (18-23).

The exact date of the panegyric on St. Basil is uncertain. It was delivered at Nazianzus probably three years or a little less after the death of St. Basil on January 1, 379. The orator alleges as reasons for the delay his own ill health and the labors which engaged him at Constantinople. The extreme length of the speech suggests that it was not delivered in its present form. The speech follows the traditional rhetorical pattern. The orator presents in order, after a brief exordium, an account of the ancestors of Basil, his character, his education, his priesthood and his episcopate, his virtues, compares him with other great heroes of God, touches briefly on his death and burial, and concludes with the customary prayer. The oration has been admired by critics for its great power and beauty.

The date of the panegyric on Gorgonia cannot be determined exactly. We conclude from the oration itself that it was after the death of Caesarius in 369 and before the death of the elder Gregory in 374. The speech was probably delivered in Iconium in Lycaonia in the presence of Gorgonia's 'spiritual father' (22), Faustinus, then bishop of that city. It will seem surprising to us that the daughter of such pious parents should have postponed her baptism so long (20), though she must certainly have been baptized before the extraordinary incident involving her handling of the sacred Species (18). The eulogy is a noble and eloquent tribute to Gorgonia and marked with greater warmth of feeling than are his other funeral orations.

The oration on the death of his father was delivered by the younger Gregory at Nazianzus in Cappadocia early in 374. St. Basil the Great, who had been consecrated bishop by Gregory the Elder, was present, and the orator addresses the opening sections and one of the later sections (14) to his life-long friend. St. Nonna, mother of the orator, was also present, and the conclusion of the eulogy (42,43) is addressed to her. Gregory the Elder is presented as truly admirable in every way. The oration sketches his life and character, including the story of his conversion from heresy. So long a speech on the occasion of his father's death may seem a little out of place today. To many the panegyric may seem to lack genuine warmth of feeling, save perhaps in the sections dealing with his mother. An interesting sidelight on the ecclesiastical history of the time is the account of the election of the bishop of Caesarea (33-36).

ON HIS BROTHER, ST. CAESARIUS

PERHAPS YOU THINK, my dear friends, brethren, fathers —you who are dear to me in fact as well as in name— that I eagerly undertake this address, that it is my purpose to indulge freely in mourning and lamentation for the deceased, or to deliver a long and elegant discourse for the delight of men. Some of you are prepared to grieve and lament with me, to bewail your own sorrows in my sorrow— if any of you have been similarly afflicted—and to learn how to grieve through the sorrows of a friend; but others have come to gratify their ears and be entertained. They think we ought to make this sad event an occasion for display, as we were wont to do when we abounded in material wealth and sought honor in public speaking. But that was before we raised our eyes to the true and highest Word, and, in giving all to God from whom all comes, received God in place of all. Please do not entertain this view of us if you wish to regard us rightly. We shall not lament the departed more than is proper, since we do not approve of such excess in others, and we shall not bestow immoderate and unmerited praise. Yet, for an orator, a speech, and for one who particularly loved my speeches, a eulogy would be, if anything would, a dear and most personal gift. Nor would it be a gift only, but the most just of all obligations. But in our tears and admiration we must observe the law concerning such matters, and this is in full accord with our philosophy:[1] 'The memory of the just is with praises,'[2] and 'Shed tears for the dead, and like one suffering terribly begin your lament';[3] thus we are saved at once from insensibility and excess. Afterwards we shall show the weakness of human nature, and recall the worth of the soul, and offer the consolation due the mourners, and turn their grief from the flesh and temporal concerns to the things which are spiritual and eternal.

(2) Caesarius had for parents, to begin at the most fitting point, those whom you all know. Seeing and hearing of their excellent character, you emulate and admire it, and describe it to those who do not know it—if there are such—each taking a different phase, since no one individual could do so completely. It is not a task for a single tongue, however devoted and zealous one may be. Although they furnish many important topics for eulogy—I trust I do not seem excessive in honoring my own family—there is one characteristic which is most important of all and, as it were, their chief distinction, namely, their piety. I call them holy and venerable, and not less revered for virtue than for age, whose bodies are worn by time, but whose souls grow young for God.

(3) Our father was well engrafted from the wild olive into the cultivated olive, and so much did he share its richness that the engrafting of others and the care of souls was entrusted to him. Holding high office, and in a becoming manner, he presided over his people, a second Aaron or Moses, considered worthy to draw near to God and impart

---

[1] The term 'philosophy' (and its derivatives) is frequently employed in patristic Greek, as here, to designate the life of Christian perfection, with emphasis on ascetical practices and contemplation.
[2] Prov. 10.7.
[3] Eccli. 38.16.

the divine voice to those standing far off. He was gentle, not given to anger, of calm mien, warm in spirit, rich in externals, but richer still in what is hidden from the eye. Why should I describe one whom you know? Even if I should make an extended speech, I could not do justice to the subject and give an account satisfactory to the knowledge and demands of each of you. It will be better to allow your own thoughts scope than by my speech to mutilate the object of your admiration.

(4) Our mother, from the beginning and by virtue of descent, consecrated to God and receiving piety as a necessary heritage not for herself alone, but also for her children, was truly a holy mass from the holy first fruits of the dough. She so far increased and augmented it that some have expressed their belief—the assertion is bold, but I will make it—that not even her husband's perfection was any other's work than hers. And how wonderful it is that a greater and more perfect piety was bestowed as the reward of piety! Both were lovers of their children and of Christ. Yet it is a striking paradox that they were more devoted lovers of Christ than of their children. Their sole enjoyment in their children was that they be known as Christ's and called His. Their single definition of good children comprised virtue and kinship with the Chief Good. Compassionate and sympathetic, they rescued much treasure from moths and brigands and from the prince of this world, transferring it from their place of exile to their homeland, and storing up the glory of heaven for their children as their greatest inheritance. Thus they have anticipated a fruitful old age, equally honored for virtue and for years, full of days, both of those that abide and those that pass away. Neither has obtained first prize here on earth, only because each is kept from first place by the other. They have filled the measure of all happiness, with the exception of this final trial, or dispensation, whichever one thinks we ought to

call it. In my judgment, it is a dispensation, for now they have sent before them that son of theirs most in danger on the score of age. They may thus end their life in security and be brought to heaven with all their family.

(5) I did not mention these points because of a desire to eulogize them or because I am unaware that one could scarcely approach their worth though he devoted an entire discourse to their praise. My purpose was to show that in a way Caesarius owed his virtue to his parents. It should be no cause for marvel or incredulity if the son of such parents made himself worthy of such praise, but it would be indeed if he neglected the examples of his own relatives and looked to others. His early life was such as became one of noble birth and fair prospects. To be brief about his obvious qualities, his beauty and stature, his manifold grace, and his equability as shown in his voice—since we do not marvel at such gifts, however important they seem to others—I shall now proceed in my address to matters which it would be difficult to omit even if one wished to do so.

(6) While such was the character of our rearing and education at home, we were also thoroughly trained in the studies available in this city. In these he greatly excelled the majority in quickness and range of talent. How am I, without tears, to pass over these memories and to escape being convicted by my grief—contrary to my promise—of being unphilosophical? When the time came for leaving home, we were then first separated from each other. I devoted myself to the study of rhetoric in the schools of Palestine then flourishing, while he went to Alexandria, then and now, in reality as by fame, a workshop of all kinds of learning.

What am I to mention as first or greatest of his merits? Or by what omission shall I do least damage to my presentation? Who was more faithful to his teachers than he? Who more friendly to his comrades? Who better avoided evil companionship and association? Who devoted himself more to that of men of high character, those most renowned and distinguished from his own and from other countries? He knew well that these associations have an important bearing on virtue or vice. Wherefore, who was in greater honor with those in authority than he? Who in the entire city—though all individuals suffer obscurity because of its size—was more distinguished for moderation or more renowned for understanding?

(7) What field of learning was there that he did not penetrate, and that better than any one else as his specialty? Whom did he allow even to approach him, not only of his own circle and of his own age, but even of his elders and those longer engaged in their studies? He applied himself to all subjects as if they were but one, and to each as if there were no other. He overcame the naturally quick by industry, the habitually studious by mental acuteness; rather, he surpassed the quick in quickness, the industrious in industry, and on both scores those outstanding in both.

From geometry and astronomy and knowledge so dangerous for others, he selected what was useful, that is, from the harmony and order of heavenly bodies he learnt admiration for the Creator. What was harmful he avoided. He did not attribute all being and becoming to the motion of the stars, as do those who set up their fellow servant, creation, in opposition to their Creator. But he referred, as is reasonable, their motion, as all other things, to God. In arithmetic and mathematics, and in the marvelous art of medicine, which deals with constitutions and temperaments and the causes of diseases, so that, by the removal of the roots, their growths also may be cut off, who is so ignorant or contentious as to give him second place and not to be glad to be counted next after him and to carry away second prize? Nor is my statement unsubstantiated, but the regions of the East and

West, and wherever he afterwards visited, are signal monuments of his learning.

(8) When he had gathered all virtue and knowledge into his single soul, as a great merchant ship gathers all kinds of freight, he set out for his own city to share with others the fine wares of his learning. There, something quite remarkable occurred which is a special pleasure for me to recall, and, if briefly told, may not displease you. It was the maternal and loving prayer of our mother that, as she had sent off both of us, she would see us return together. The pair of us seemed, if not to others, at least to our mother, worthy of her prayers and glances when seen together, though we are now unfortunately separated. And so, through the will of God, who hears a just prayer and honors the love of parents for virtuous children, one of us from Alexandria, the other from Greece, one by land, the other by sea, returned by no forethought or agreement at the same time to the same city. The city was Byzantium, now the capital city of Europe. Here Caesarius soon after gained such fame that public honors, a distinguished marriage, and a seat in the Senate were offered him. A deputation was sent by public decree to the great emperor to petition that the leading city be adorned and honored with the leading scholar, if he had any concern that the city should really be first and worthy of its name, and that this distinction be added to all its others, namely, that it be embellished with Caesarius as physician and citizen; it was, to be sure, already flourishing and brilliant through its distinguished men in philosophy and other branches of learning.

But let this suffice. That occurrence seemed to others a mere blind and uncaused chance event, of which there are many examples in our lives, but to lovers of God it was very evidently nothing else than the work of God-loving parents gathering home their children from land and sea in fulfillment of their prayer.

(9) Let us not pass over an illustration of Caesarius' virtues, which may perhaps seem slight to others and unworthy of mention, but seemed to me then and now very important—if, indeed, fraternal love is praiseworthy. I shall not cease to place it in the first rank as often as I discuss his qualities.

The city wished to retain him by the honors I mentioned and refused to release him for any reason. Since I had great influence with Caesarius in all matters, I succeeded, taking the opposite view, in bringing about the fulfillment of our parents' prayer, our country's need, and my own desire. I took him as the associate and companion of my journey, and he preferred me not only to cities and peoples, and to honors and income, which were flowing to him in profusion from many sources or were to be expected, but almost to the emperor himself and his commands from the capital.

Thereafter I determined to devote myself to philosophy and to adapt myself to the higher life, shaking off all ambition like some hard master and severe disease. Or, rather, the desire was earlier; the life, later. Caesarius, however, offered the first fruits of his learning to his country and was admired in a manner worthy of his labors. But afterwards a desire of glory and of being a guardian of the city, as he persuaded me, took him to the court. This was not entirely pleasing to us and contrary to expectation—for I will declare to you that the least place with God seems better and more exalted than the first rank with an earthly king—but not at all blameworthy. For, as philosophy is the most important, it is likewise the most difficult of vocations. It is not an undertaking for the majority nor for any others except those called by the divine magnanimity, which gives its hand to those who have made a worthy choice. But it is no slight thing if a man who has embraced the second kind of life should lay claim to goodness and have greater esteem for God and his salvation than for earthly glory, and should set this before him as a stage or a sort of mask of many transient things in acting out the drama of this world, but should personally be living for God with that image which he knows he has received from Him and owes to Him as the giver. That, without question, was the purpose of Caesarius.

(10) He easily obtained the first rank among physicians. He merely revealed his learning, or, rather, a brief indication of his learning. Immediately he was numbered among the friends of the emperor and enjoyed the greatest honors. To those in power he offered the service of his art without charge. He knew that nothing can advance a man as can virtue and the reputation for noble actions. He far surpassed in reputation those to whom he was inferior in rank. Because he was beloved by all for his moderation, he was entrusted by them with what is most precious. He had no need of Hippocrates to administer the oath to him, and the simplicity of Crates was as nothing compared to his. To all he was more venerable than his rank warranted, being considered always worthy of his present great honors and judged worthy of greater honors to come. This was the view of the emperors themselves and of those who held positions next to them. The greatest marvel is that neither his fame nor the luxury surrounding him corrupted the nobility of his soul. Although he possessed many important honors, his own first claim to dignity consisted in being and being known as a Christian. All else, compared with this one fact, was for him mere childish games and trifles. All else was like parts played before others as on a stage quickly set up and dismantled, perhaps more easily destroyed than erected, as may be seen from the many vicissitudes of life and the rise and fall of prosperity. Piety alone is a personal good and truly abiding.

(11) This was Caesarius' philosophy, even in the courtier's cloak. In these thoughts he lived and died, showing and offering to God in the hidden man greater piety than ap-

peared in public. If need be, I shall omit all else, his succor of relatives in adversity, his disdain of vanity, his equality with friends, his boldness with rulers, his contests and discussions in behalf of truth in which he engaged with many, not only in the dialectic manner, but also with unusual piety and fervor. One fact, and that the best known, I shall tell in place of all these.

The emperor[4] of evil name was raging against us, and, having first become maddened against himself through his rejection of faith in Christ, he proved intolerable to others as well. Unlike the other fighters against Christ, he did not proclaim himself arrogantly for impiety, but concealed his persecution under the fiction of reasonableness, and, in the manner of the crooked serpent who possessed his soul, by all kind of machinations drew his unhappy victims into his own abyss. His first device and trick, in order to deprive us of honor in the contests—for that noble and magnanimous man begrudged even this to Christians—was to cause those suffering as Christians to be punished as criminals. The second was to give the name of persuasion, not tyranny, to this process, that there might be greater shame than danger involved for those who voluntarily yielded to impiety. Seducing some by bribes, some by dignities, some by promises, others by all kinds of honors which he did not confer in a royal but in a very slavish manner, in the sight of all, and alluring all by the witchery of his words and his own example, he made trial, after many others, of Caesarius himself. Alas for this madness and folly if he hoped to take Caesarius, a man such as he was, my brother and the son of these parents, for his prey!

(12) But to delay a little in my speech and to enjoy the narration, as the spectators at the marvelous happening, that noble warrior, fortified by the sign of Christ, and defending himself with His great Word, advanced upon a man expe-

---
4 Julian the Apostate.

rienced in arms and formidable in his skill of argumentation. Caesarius was not terrified at the sight, nor did he give any ground because of the flattery of his pride. He was an athlete ready to contend in word and deed against a contestant who was capable in both. Such was the stadium, and such the contender for piety. And masters of the contest were present: on one side Christ, arming His athlete with His own sufferings; on the other the dread tyrant, fawning upon him by the familiarity of his words and terrifying him by the weight of his power. The spectators on both sides, those who yet remained on the side of piety and those he had snatched from it, also were looking down to see how the contest inclined and who would conquer, and were in greater anxiety than they upon whom they gazed.

(13) Did you not fear for Caesarius that something unworthy of his zeal might befall him? Take heart. Victory is with Christ who overcame the world.[5] I should like above all, you may be sure, to present each single point of what was stated and proposed at the time—the discussion had some logical turns and niceties which are most pleasant to remember—but this would be wholly outside the scope of this occasion and this discourse. When Caesarius had foiled all his verbal subtleties and every hidden and open attempt, pushing them aside as child's play, he proclaimed in a loud and clear voice that he was a Christian and would so remain. Not even then was he finally dismissed. A strange desire possessed the emperor to be associated in and adorned with Caesarius' learning. On that same occasion he even uttered his famous cry in the hearing of all: 'O fortunate father, O unfortunate children!' For he deemed it proper to honor me also with association in dishonor, since he had known our learning and piety at Athens. Preserved for a second entrance into the imperial court, since justice fitly armed the emperor against the

---

5 Cf. John 16.33.

Persians, Caesarius returned to us a blessed exile, an unbloody victor, more renowned for his dishonor than for his glory.

(14) I judge this victory far more exalted and precious than the emperor's powerful hand and exalted purple robe and costly diadem. I am more uplifted by this narrative than if he had shared the entire empire with him. Accordingly, he lived in retirement during those evil times, and he did so according to our law. This bids us, when the occasion demands, to dare danger for the truth and not to betray piety through cowardice, but also, as long as it is licit, not to challenge dangers,[6] either through fear for our own souls or to spare those bringing danger upon us. When the gloom was dispelled, and a foreign land had delivered just judgment, and the glittering sword had overthrown the reprobate, and power had returned to Christians, why need I tell you with what glory and honor, or with what noble and numerous testimonies, and, as one bestowing rather than receiving a favor, he was again welcomed at court and his second honor succeeded his first? Time changed emperors, but Caesarius' reputation and primacy of place with them were untouched. The emperors were in rivalry as to which should have greater claim to Caesarius and deserve more to be known as his intimate friend. Such was Caesarius' piety, and such were the rewards of his piety. Let youths and men hear of it and let them press forward through the same virtue to the same distinction. 'For the fruit of good labors is glorious.'[7] Let them seek this zealously and consider it a part of true happiness.

(15) But there is another marvel concerning him which affords the strongest evidence of his parents' piety and his own. He was living in Bithynia, holding an office of great importance from the emperor, for he was controller of the imperial revenue and in charge of the treasury. The emperor intended

---
6 Cf. Matt. 10.23.
7 Wisd. 3.15.

this position to be a prelude to higher offices for him. When the recent earthquake occurred at Nicaea—and it is said to have been the worst ever recalled—it overwhelmed almost all the inhabitants and, along with them, destroyed the beauty of the city. He alone of the distinguished men, or together with very few, was saved from danger, sheltered in unbelievable safety by the falling ruins and suffering almost no ill effects from his peril. Yet it was enough to make him take fear as his teacher and guide to a more important salvation, and to devote himself entirely to his heavenly destiny. He shifted his service from transitory things and changed courts for his true advantage. This, then, was his intention and earnest prayer, as he persuaded me in his letters, when I had seized the occasion for an admonition. I had often admonished him before, when I was distressed that his nobility of nature should be devoted to inferior pursuits and his philosophic soul should be continually immersed in public affairs even as the sun is hidden by a cloud.

Although he survived the earthquake, he was not immune to disease, for he was human. His escape was peculiar to himself, his death common to others; the former was a sign of his piety, the latter of his nature. Moreover, consolation preceded our grief, so that, though shaken by his death, we might rejoice in the marvel of his former preservation. And now the noble Caesarius has been brought safely to us. His precious dust, his corpse, extolled with praise, has been sent home with hymns upon hymns, escorted to the altars of the martyrs and honored by the holy hands of his parents. His mother, clad in a bright robe, substitutes piety for sorrow, her tears subdued by philosophy, her lamentations quieted by the singing of psalms. He himself enjoys the rewards worthy of his newly made soul which the Spirit transformed by water.

(16) This, Caesarius, is my funeral offering to you. These are the first fruits of my oratory. You who often complained of

its concealment were destined to uncover it through its application to yourself. This is your adornment at my hands, and it is to you, I well know, the dearest of all adornments. It is not the soft flowing folds of silk, in which, even while alive, you did not delight after the manner of most men, since you were adorned with virtue alone; nor woven robes of transparent linen, nor outpourings of costly perfumes with their fragrance lasting but a single day, which you had long since left to the women's apartments, nor any other trifles or things valued by triflers, all of which this bitter stone would have concealed today along with your beautiful body. Away with pagan games and fables, whereby ill-fated youths are honored, garnering petty prizes from petty contests! Away with libations and first fruits and garlands and freshly plucked flowers, with which they honor the departed, following ancestral law and unreasoning grief rather than reason! My gift is a speech. Perhaps even future time will keep it, and it will continue to live and will not suffer the departed to be utterly gone, but will ever preserve our honored brother in men's ears and souls, setting forth more clearly than pictures the image of our beloved.

(17) Such, then, is our offering. If it is slight and less than his worth, yet what is according to our powers is pleasing to God. We have paid some of the debt, and we will pay the rest—surely all of us as long as we live—by offering honors and remembrance every year. But you, sacred and holy soul, may you enter heaven, may you rest in Abraham's bosom—whatever may be the meaning of this—may you behold the chorus of angels and the splendors and glories of blessed men. Or, rather, may you join the chorus and rejoice with them, smiling derisively from on high at everything here: so-called riches, cast-off positions, lying honors, illusions caused by our senses, the twists and turns of this life, the confusion and ignorance, as it were, of night battle, as you stand before the

great King and are filled with His light. May we now receive a slight emanation from it, such as appears in mirrors and riddles,[8] and may we hereafter obtain the fountainhead of Good itself, looking with pure mind upon pure Truth, finding, as a reward of our zealous labor for the good here below, that more perfect sharing and contemplation of the Good on high which the divinely inspired books and minds prophesy to be the end of initiation in our mysteries.

(18) What yet remains? Through words to offer consolation to the mourners. Powerful to those in grief is the remedy supplied by those who join in their grief. And those who have equal suffering are more effective in bringing consolation to those who suffer. To such, therefore, is our speech especially addressed. Regarding them, I should be ashamed if they should not be first in patience as in all other virtues. For, if they are greater lovers of their children than all others, let them also be greater lovers of wisdom and of Christ, pondering more deeply themselves on the passing from this life, and teaching their children. Or, rather, let them devote their whole life to the preparation for deliverance. But, if sorrow yet obscures your reasoning, and, like a kind of film covering the eye, does not allow you to see your duty clearly, come, you elders, receive a young man's admonition, and you parents, a son's; you who have admonished many and garnered experience by a long life, receive admonition from him who deserves to be admonished rather by those of your own age. Marvel not if I, a youth, admonish my elders. And if I can see anything better than gray hairs can, this, also, I give to you.

How much longer shall we live, honored elders, you who are drawing near to God? How long shall we suffer here? The whole life of mankind is not long when compared with the divine and eternal Nature, much less the remnants of life

---

8 Cf. 1 Cor. 13.12.

and the dissolution, as we might call it, of human breath and the end of our transient existence. By how much did Caesarius anticipate us? How long shall we yet bewail the departed? Are we not pressing on to the same destination? Shall we not soon be covered by the same stone? Shall we not soon be the same dust ourselves? Shall we gain anything in these few days except more evils, after seeing some, suffering some, or even perhaps committing others, being forced finally to pay the common and unalterable tribute to the law of nature, in following some and anticipating others, in bewailing some and being lamented by others, and in receiving from some the favor of tears which we have bestowed upon others?

(19) Such, brethren, is our life, we whose existence is so transitory. Such is the game we play upon earth: we do not exist and we are born, and being born we are dissolved. We are a fleeting dream,[9] an apparition without substance, the flight of a bird that passes, a ship that leaves no trace upon the sea.[10] We are dust, a vapor, the morning dew, a flower growing but a moment and withering in a moment.[11] 'Man's days are as grass: as the flower of the field, so shall he flourish.'[12] Beautifully has holy David meditated on our weakness. And again in the words: 'Declare unto me the fewness of my days';[13] and he defines the days of man as the measure of a span.[14] What would you say to Jeremias, who, complaining of his birth, even blames his mother, and that, too, for the failings of others?[15] 'I have seen everything,'[16] says Ecclesiastes. I have reviewed in my mind all human things, wealth, luxury, power, glory that is not stable, wisdom

---
9 Cf. Job 20.8.
10 Cf. Wisd. 5.10,11.
11 Cf. Osee 13.3.
12 Ps. 102.15.
13 Ps. 101.24.
14 Cf. Ps. 38.6 (Septuagint).
15 Cf. Jer. 15.10.
16 Eccle. 1.14.

that eludes us more often than it is mastered; again pleasure, again wisdom, often returning full circle to the same things, delights of the belly, orchards, numbers of slaves, a multitude of possessions, male and female table servants, singing men and singing women, arms, henchmen, nations at one's feet, revenues flowing in, the pride of royalty, all life's superfluities and necessities, in which I surpassed all the kings who were before me.[17] And after all this what is his judgment? 'All is vanity of vanities, all is vanity and vexation of spirit,'[18] that is, a kind of irrational impulse of soul and distraction of man who has been condemned to this perhaps because of the original fall. But, 'hear all the conclusion of my discourse,' he says: 'Fear God.'[19] Through this he ceases from perplexity. And this alone is your gain from life here, to be brought through the confusion of things which are seen and unstable to things which are firm and immovable.

(20) Let us not, then, bewail Caesarius, knowing from what evils he has his release, but ourselves, knowing to what evils we have been left and what we shall heap up for ourselves if we do not nobly devote ourselves to God, and, outrunning transitory things, press on to the life above, and though still living on earth, yet leave earth behind and nobly follow the spirit that bears us to heaven. These thoughts are grievous to the cowardly, but they do not daunt those of manly heart. Let us look at the matter thus. Caesarius will not rule? No, but neither will he be ruled by others. He will not strike terror into anyone? No, but neither will he fear a severe master who is often not even worthy to be a subject himself. He will not gather wealth? No, but neither will he be suspicious or envious or suffer loss to his soul by taking unjustly and always seeking to acquire as much again as he has acquired. For such is the

---
17 Cf. Eccle. 2.1-9.
18 Eccle. 1.14.
19 Eccle. 12.13.

disease of growing wealthy. It has no limit to further desires, but makes continued drinking the remedy of thirst. He will make no oratorical display? No, but he will be admired for his oratory. He will not study the works of Hippocrates and Galen and their adversaries? No, but neither will he be afflicted by diseases or experience personal grief at others' misfortunes. He will not expound the works of Euclid and Ptolemy and Hero? No, but neither will he be pained at the pompous boasts of uncultured men. He will make no display of the doctrines of Plato or Aristotle or Pyrrho or of a Democritus, an Heraclitus, an Anaxagoras, a Cleanthes, or an Epicurus, and I know not of what others of the venerable Stoa and Academy? No, but neither will he be concerned about solving their specious arguments.

What else need I mention? Well, there remain, of course, things that are precious and much sought after by all. He will not enjoy a wife or children? No, but neither will he mourn them or be mourned by them, nor will he leave them behind to others nor he himself be left behind as a monument of misfortune. He will not inherit property? No, but he will be succeeded by the most satisfactory of heirs, and such as he personally desired, so that he could leave this world bearing all his wealth with him. What a glorious ambition! What a novel consolation! What magnanimity in his executors! An announcement worthy of the attention of all was heard and a mother's sorrow is removed by a beautiful and holy promise to give entirely to her son his wealth as his personal funeral gift and to leave nothing to those who were expecting legacies![20]

(21) Is this not yet sufficient for consolation? I have still to offer the most efficacious remedy. I believe the words of wise men that, when every beautiful and divinely loved soul is

---

20 Caesarius had expressed this wish that his wealth be distributed to the poor and this wish was carried out by his parents.

loosed from the body to which it has been bound and is released from this world, it immediately enters on the perception and contemplation of the good awaiting it, inasmuch as the darkening element has been purged, or put off, or whatever the correct expression may be. It enjoys a certain marvelous pleasure, and exults, and goes joyfully to its Lord, having escaped from life here as if from some hard prison and having shaken off the fetters with which it was bound and with which the wing of the intellect was held down; it enters into the possession of the blessedness reserved for it such as it has already conceived in imagination. Shortly afterwards, it takes up its own related flesh, united with which it meditated on heavenly topics, from the earth which both gave it and was entrusted with it, and, in a way which God knows who bound them together and separated them, it is joint heir with it of supernal glory. And just as such a soul shared its sufferings because of its natural union with its flesh, so also it shares its own joys with it, having assumed it wholly into itself and having become with it one spirit and mind and good, life having absorbed the mortal and transitory element. Hear at least what holy Ezechiel teaches about the joining of bones and sinews,[21] and, after him, what St. Paul says about earthly habitation and a house not made with hands, the one to be dissolved, the other to be reserved in heaven. He asserts that absence from the body is presence with the Lord, and mourns his life with it as an exile,[22] and for this reason desires and seeks for his dissolution.[23] Why am I faint-hearted regarding my hopes? Why am I so earthly in my thoughts? I shall await the voice of the archangel,[24] the last trumpet,[25] the transformation of heaven, the change of earth, the freedom of the

---

21 Cf. Ezech. 37.3ff.
22 Cf. 2 Cor. 5.1.
23 Cf. Phil. 1.23.
24 Cf. 1 Thess. 4.15.
25 Cf. 1 Cor. 15.52.

elements, the renewal of the universe.²⁶ Then shall I see Caesarius himself, no longer in exile, no longer being buried, no longer mourned, no longer pitied, but splendid, glorious, sublime, such as you were often seen in a dream, dearest and most loving of brothers, whether my desire or truth itself represented you.

(22) But now, having put aside lamentations, I will look into myself, that I may not unconsciously be guilty of anything to be lamented, and I will consider my own state. 'O ye sons of men,' for the saying pertains to you, 'how long will you be slow of heart' and dull of mind? 'Why do you love vanity and seek after lying?'²⁷ Why do you consider our life here as something great and these few days as many, and turn from this separation, which is welcome and sweet, as if it were something grievous and horrible? Shall we not know ourselves? Shall we not cast off what is seen by the senses? Shall we not look upon what is perceived only with the mind? Are we not, on the contrary, even if there must be some grief, to be annoyed at our prolonged sojourn,²⁸ like the inspired David, who calls things here tents of darkness, and place of affliction, and mire of the deep, and shadow of death,²⁹ because we delay in the tombs we bear about with us, because we die like men the death of sin, although we have been made gods? This is my fear, and I live with it night and day. The thought of glory on the one side and of punishment on the other does not let me breathe. The first of these I desire until I can say: 'My soul faints for Thy salvation,'³⁰ but at the second I shudder and turn away. Yet I do not fear that this body of mine through dissolution and corruption will utterly perish, and that the glorious creature of God—for it is glorious if it is

---

26 Cf. 2 Peter 3.10-13.
27 Ps. 4.3.
28 Cf. Ps. 119.5.
29 Cf. Ps. 68.3; 43.20 (Septuagint).
30 Ps. 118.81.

upright, just as, if sinful, it is dishonorable—in which there is reason, law, and hope, may be condemned to the same dishonor as irrational things and be no more than they after its separation: a lot that is due the wicked, who are worthy even of the eternal fire.

(23) Would that I might mortify my members that are upon the earth![31] Would that I might spend all for the spirit, walking in the way that is narrow and trodden by few, not the way that is broad and easy![32] For what comes after this life is splendid and great, and our hope is greater than our worth. 'What is man that Thou art mindful of him?'[33] What is this new mystery concerning me? I am small and great, lowly and exalted, mortal and immortal, earthly and heavenly. I am connected with the world below, and likewise with God; I am connected with the flesh, and likewise with the spirit. I must be buried with Christ, rise with Christ, be joint heir with Christ,[34] become the Son of God, even God Himself.

See whither my speech has brought us in its progress. I am almost thankful to the calamity which has led me to make such reflections, and I have thereby become the more eager for my departure from this life. This is the meaning of the great mystery for us. This is the intent of God who for our sake was made man and became poor, in order to raise our flesh and restore His image and remake man, that we might all become one in Christ, who perfectly became in all of us all that He is Himself, that we might no longer be male and female, barbarian, Scythian, slave or freeman,[35] the distinctions of the flesh, but might bear in ourselves only the stamp of God by whom and for whom we were made, so far formed and modeled by Him as to be recognized by it alone.

---

31 Cf. Col. 3.5.
32 Cf. Matt. 7.13,14.
33 Ps. 8.5.
34 Cf. Rom. 8.17.
35 Cf. Gal. 3.28.

(24) And would that our hope might be realized according to the great kindness of the munificent God, who, asking little, makes great gifts both now and in the time to come to those who truly love Him! Bearing all things, enduring all things[36] for our love and hope regarding Him, let us give thanks for all things,[37] both favorable and unfavorable alike, I mean pleasant and painful, since reason often knows even these as arms of salvation, commending to Him our souls and those of men who, anticipating us as it were on the common way, have come to rest before us. Having done this ourselves, let us end our speech, and you your tears, hastening now to your own tomb which Caesarius has from you as a sad and abiding gift. It was seasonably prepared for the old age of his parents, but it has been bestowed on their son in his youth, unexpectedly, but not without reason to Him who disposes of our concerns.

O Lord and Maker of all, and especially of this body of ours! O God and Father and Pilot of mankind! O Master of life and death! O Guardian and Benefactor of our souls! O You who make and change all seasonably by Your creative Word, and as You Yourself know by the depth of Your wisdom and providence, receive Caesarius now, the first fruits of our pilgrimage! And if the last is first, we yield to Your Word, by which the universe is ruled. And receive us, ready and not troubled by fear of You, not turning away in our last days, nor forcibly drawn from things of earth, as is the misfortune of souls loving the world and the flesh, but eagerly drawn to the heavenly life, everlasting and blessed, which is in Christ Jesus our Lord, to whom be glory forever and ever. Amen.

---

36 Cf. 1 Cor. 13.7.
37 Cf. 1 Thess. 5.18.
38 Cf. Ps. 31.6.

ON ST. BASIL THE GREAT

IT WAS INEVITABLE that the great Basil, who constantly used to furnish me with subjects for my discourses—and he gloried in them as no man ever gloried in his own—should now present me in the person of himself with the loftiest theme ever given to those who have engaged in oratory. For I believe that if anyone, testing his oratorical power, wished to gauge it with reference to one discourse selected from all others as a standard, as painters do with model pictures, he would set this subject aside as beyond the power of eloquence, and choose what was first among the subjects that remained. So arduous a task is the eulogy of this man, not only for myself, who long ago put aside all love of glory, but even for those who have devoted their lives to eloquence and made their one and only object the gaining of distinction from subjects such as this. This is my judgment in the matter and it is, I am convinced, quite correct. Yet I do not know in what subject I could be eloquent if not in this, or in what better way I could gratify myself, or the admirers of virtue, or eloquence itself, than by honoring such a man. For myself, it will be a convenient way of paying a debt that is due. And, surely, a discourse is due above all else to those who have excelled especially in eloquence. To the admirers of virtue may this discourse of mine be at once a pleasure and an inspiration to virtue. I am well aware that whatever is praised is thereby magnified, and that there is not a single instance in which this does not hold true. As for eloquence itself, things should go well in either case. If it approaches his merit, it will demonstrate its own power. If it should fall far short, an altogether necessary consequence for those who praise Basil, the very failure will be an acknowledgment that the subject of the eulogy is beyond all the powers of eloquence.

(2) These, therefore, are the reasons which have moved me to speech and the undertaking of this task. And if I have come forward so long after the occasion, and after so many others have eulogized him in public and private, let no one wonder. But may his sacred spirit, ever revered by me, both now and in the past, grant me pardon. When he was among us, he used to correct me on many points according to the rights of friendship and a still higher law. I am not ashamed to say this, for he was a norm of virtue for all. So now, also, from his place on high, he will be indulgent to me. May I be pardoned, too, by those of you who have been more fervent in praising him, if, indeed, anyone can be more fervent than another, and all of us are not zealous for his good fame.

I have not failed through any negligence on my part to render what was due. Far be it from me to be so careless of the claims of virtue or friendship, or to think that the duty of praising him befitted anyone more than myself. First of all, to tell the truth, I shrank from speaking before I, like those who approach holy places, had cleansed my voice and my mind. Secondly, though you are not unaware of the fact, I will remind you that I was engaged in the defense of the true doctrine, then in peril. This occupation was a glorious coercion, which carried me away from home, according to the will of God, perhaps, and with the approval of that noble champion of the truth, whose very breath was pious doctrine and salvation for the whole world. Of my bodily health I should not venture, perhaps, to speak at all, when my subject is a man so high-minded and superior to the body even before he departed hence, and who claimed that the noble qualities of the soul should not be hindered by these bodily shackles.

Here let my apology rest. I do not think there is need of a longer one in addressing my speech to him and to those who are well acquainted with my affairs. I must now proceed to my eulogy, choosing his God as the guide of my discourse, that I may not dishonor him by my praises nor yet fall far short of the rest, even though we all fail in like measure, as those who gaze upon the heavens and the rays of the sun.

(3) If I saw that he gloried in his birth or in the advantages of his birth, or, in general, in any of those petty objects of pride to men who have their eyes fixed upon the ground, a new catalogue of heroes would have to be made. How many details could I have gathered from his ancestors to redound to his glory! Nor would I have had to yield any advantage to history in this respect, possessing this advantage above all, that my subject is embellished not by fictions and fable, but by facts themselves to which there are many witnesses. On his father's side, Pontus furnishes us with many narratives, not at all inferior to the ancient wonders attached to the place in which all history and poetry abound. Many, too, are furnished by this, my native land, noble Cappadocia, goodly nurse of youth no less than horses. Hence, we can match his mother's family with that of his father. As for military commands, high civil offices, and power in imperial courts, and again, as to wealth and lofty thrones and public honors, and splendors of eloquence, what family has been more often or more highly distinguished? If it were permitted me to speak of them freely, the Pelopidae, the Cecropidae, the Alcmaeonids, the Hera-

cleidae and all the other noblest families would be as nothing in comparison. For, having nothing of their own deserving of manifest praise, they have recourse to obscurity, boastfully connecting certain demigods and gods with their ancestors, in all of which what is illustrious is incredible and what is credible is a disgrace.

(4) My discourse is about a man who claimed that a man's nobility is to be gauged by individual worth. Just as forms and colors and the noblest and the meanest horses are rated on their own merits, so we ourselves, he thought, should not be painted in borrowed hues. Therefore, after speaking of one or two qualities which he inherited—qualities, too, which characterized his own life, and which he would be especially pleased to have mentioned—I shall turn to the man himself. Each family and each individual has a characteristic trait and history, great or small, which is like a patrimony that comes down to posterity by a shorter or a longer line. The distinguishing characteristic of both his mother's and his father's family was piety, as my discourse will now make clear.

(5) There was a persecution, and the most frightful and cruel of persecutions. You know that I refer to the persecution of Maximinus, who, coming after the many persecutors just before him, made all appear humane, raging as he did with extreme ferocity and striving earnestly to win the palm for impiety. Many of our athletes overcame him, enduring the contest even unto death or just short of death, spared to the extent that they survived their victory and did not succumb in their contests. But they remained as teachers of virtue for others—living martyrs, breathing monuments, mute proclamations. In their numerous company were also Basil's paternal ancestors, to whom, practicing every form of piety, that occasion brought a noble crown. For they were so prepared and disposed in mind to bear readily all the trials for

which Christ crowns those who have emulated His contest in our behalf.

(6) But, since their contest had also to be a lawful one—for this is the law of martyrdom, not to advance to the contest deliberately out of regard for the persecutors and the weaker brethren, and not to shrink from the contest when it is upon us, since the first act is a mark of rashness, and the second of cowardice—to show homage to the Lawmaker, in this respect, what should they devise? Or, rather, to what did Providence, who governed all their counsels, direct them? They betook themselves to one of the forests of the Pontic mountains—these forests are numerous and dense and very extensive—taking with them only a very small number to aid their flight and supply their needs. Let others admire the long duration of their exile, for in all it lasted, it is said, seven years or a little longer; and their manner of life, trying and strange for bodies nobly nurtured, as one may imagine; and the distress they endured beneath the open sky, in cold and heat and rain; and the solitude, without friends and social intercourse, which assuredly must have been a grievous burden to those accustomed to throngs to attend and honor them. But for myself, I intend to speak of something more significant and admirable than all this, and no one will doubt me save the man of perverse and perilous judgment, who sees nothing great in enduring persecutions and dangers for Christ's sake.

(7) Weary of their long exile and filled with distaste for their poor food, these noble men longed for something more palatable. Yet they did not use the language of the Israelites.[1] They did not murmur like the Israelites[2] when they were distressed in the desert after their flight from Egypt and thought that Egypt was better for them than the desert, be-

---
1 Cf. Exod. 16.2ff.
2 Cf. 1 Cor. 10.10.

cause it had furnished them with an abundance of fleshpots and all the other things they had left behind, for in their folly they counted the brick-making and the mortar as nothing. How different was their language and how suggestive of greater piety and faith!

Why, they said, should it be incredible that the God of miracles, who so generously nourished a wandering and fugitive people in the desert,[3] as to rain down bread and supply them with quail, nourishing them not only with necessities, but with superabundance, who divided the sea,[4] and made the sun stand still,[5] and held back the river[6]—and they added all the other things that He had done, for the soul tends in such circumstances to devote itself to such narratives and to glorify God for His many wonders—why should it be incredible, they went on, that the same God should also today nourish us, as athletes of the faith, with delicacies? Many wild beasts that have escaped the tables of the rich, such as we once had, lurk in these mountains. Many succulent birds fly above us who long for them. What one of them but could be captured, if only Thou will it? So they spoke, and game was at hand, food spontaneously offered, a banquet prepared without toil, deer suddenly appearing in herds from the hills! How magnificent they were! How sleek! How ready for the slaughter! It almost seemed that they were annoyed that they had not been summoned sooner. Some drew others after them by signs, and the rest followed. Who was pursuing or forcing them? No one. What horsemen, what dogs, what bark or shout, or what youths occupying the exits according to the laws of the chase? They were the captives of prayer and just petition. Who in our time or at any time has known of such hunting?

---

3 Cf. Exod. 16.13.
4 Cf. Exod. 14.21.
5 Cf. Josue 10.12.
6 Cf. Josue 3.16.

(8) Oh, the wonder of it all! They themselves were masters of the chase. The mere desire was enough to capture as much as they pleased. What was left was sent away to the thickets for a second meal. The cooks were improvised, the feast was excellent, and the banqueters were grateful, counting the present wonder as a prelude to future hopes. Hence they became more eager for the struggle in return for which these things had been lavished upon them. Such is my story. But do you tell me of your Dianas, and of your Orions and Actaeons, those ill-fated hunters, you, my persecutor, who marvel at fables and the hind substituted for the maiden,[7] if you wish to present any such tale in emulation and if we grant that this story is not mythical. As for what follows in the story, how extremely shameful it is! For what good is the substitution if it saves the maiden that she may be taught to murder her guests and to repay humanity with inhumanity?

My story, such as it is, is but one chosen out of many, and as I think, typical of the rest. I have not narrated it for the purpose of adding to his glory. For neither the sea has any need of the rivers flowing into it, however many and great they may be, nor has he whom we praise today any need of contributions to his glory. But I wanted to show what kind of ancestors he had, and, having such models before his eyes, how far he surpassed them. For, if it is a great thing for others to receive title to honor from their ancestors, it was a greater thing for him to add to his ancestors' glory from his own, like a stream flowing back to its source.

(9) The union of his parents in a common esteem of virtue no less than in body was evidenced in many ways, notably in their care of the poor, their hospitality toward strangers, their purity of soul, achieved through austerity, the dedication of a portion of their goods to God—a practice not yet pursued by many at that time, though today quite wide-

---

7 An allusion to the story of Iphigenia.

spread and honored, thanks to such previous examples, and in many other noble actions, shared alike by Pontus and Cappadocia, which have been a source of satisfaction to all who have heard of them. But their greatest and most distinguishing feature, in my opinion, is the excellence of their children. Legend does, perhaps, record men whose children were many and beautiful. But these parents are known to us through actual acquaintance, and their character was such as to suffice for their own glory, even if they never had such children. Yet they brought forth children of such a character that, even if they themselves had not been so zealous for virtue, they would have surpassed all by the excellence of their children. That one or two of their children should merit praise may be ascribed to nature, but when eminence is found in all, the honor is clearly due to those who reared them. This is evidenced by the enviable number of priests and virgins, and of those who in marriage did not in any way allow their union to be an obstacle to an equal repute for virtue, making the distinction between them consist in a choice of career rather than in conduct.

(10) Who has not known Basil, our Basil's father, a great name among all, who attained a father's prayer as very few have ever done? Though he surpassed all in virtue, he was prevented from gaining the first place only by his son. Who has not known Emmelia, whose name was a presage of what she became or whose life exemplified her name. She truly bore the name of Emmelia, which means harmony, for, to speak briefly, she was regarded among women as he was among men. And so, if he whose eulogy we are now undertaking was to be given to men to serve the bondage of nature, like any one of the men of old who were given by God for the public benefit, it was neither fitting that he be born of any other parents, nor that they be called the parents of any other than him. Accordingly, this was happily realized.

In obedience to the divine precept which ordains that all honors be rendered to parents, I have bestowed the first fruits of my praises on those whom I have commemorated. Let me now proceed to Basil himself, stating at the outset, and I believe that this will appear true to all who knew him, that his own voice itself would be required to eulogize him. For he is at once a magnificent subject for eulogy and the only one with powers of eloquence adequate to deal with it. Beauty and strength and size, in which I see most men delight, I shall leave to those who are interested in them. Not that he was inferior even in these points to those small-minded men who are continually busy with the things of the body, while he was still young and had not yet tamed his flesh by philosophy.[8] But I do not wish to suffer the experience of unskilled athletes, who waste their strength in vain and minor contests, and are defeated in the main events which decide victory and in which crowns are awarded. I therefore shall proceed to praise what no one will consider either superfluous or outside the scope of my discourse.

(11) I take it all intelligent men agree that among human advantages education holds first place. I refer not only to our nobler form of it which disdains all the ambitious ornaments of rhetoric and attaches itself only to salvation and the beauty of spiritual contemplation, but also to that external culture which many Christians by an error of judgment scorn as treacherous and dangerous and as turning us away from God. The heavens, the earth, the air, and all such things are not to be condemned because some have wrongly interpreted them and venerate the creatures of God in place of God. On the contrary, we select from them what is useful both for life and enjoyment and we avoid what is dangerous, not opposing creation to the Creator, as the foolish do, but acknowledging the Maker of the world from His works,[9] and as the holy

---
8 Cf. above, p. 6.
9 Cf. Wisd. 13.5.

Apostle says, bringing every mind into captivity to Christ.[10] Thus, we know that neither fire nor food nor iron nor any other element is in itself either very useful or very harmful, but that all depends on the will of the user. Even from certain reptiles we have at times compounded salutary medicines. So also from the pagans we have received principles of inquiry and speculation, while we have rejected whatever leads to demons, and error, and the abyss of perdition. And from such material we have drawn profit for piety, by learning to distinguish the better from the worse, and from its weakness we have made our own doctrine strong.

Therefore we must not dishonor education because certain men are pleased to do so. Rather, we should regard such men as ignorant and uncultured who would have all others be like themselves, that their own deficiencies might be hidden in the general mass, and their want of culture escape reproach. With this premise made and acknowledged, contemplate the life of Basil.

(12) His earliest years were spent under the direction of his illustrious father, whom Pontus put forward at that time as its common teacher of virtue. He was swathed and fashioned in that best and purest fashioning which holy David happily calls the daily formation[11] as opposed to that of the night. Under him, therefore, as his life and learning grew and developed together, the admirable youth was educated. He did not boast of any Thessalian mountain cave as his workshop of virtue, nor of any arrogant centaur,[12] the preceptor of the heroes of his day. Nor was he taught by this teacher to shoot hares, or run down fawns or hunt deer, or excel in warlike pursuits or in breaking young horses, having him at once as mount and master. He was not nourished on the marrow of

---
10 Cf. 2 Cor. 10.5.
11 Cf. Ps. 136.16.
12 The allusion is to Chiron, the teacher of Asclepius, Jason, and other heroes of Greek legend and mythology.

deer and lions, as in the fable, but he was trained in general education and exercised in piety and, in a word, he was led on from the beginning of his studies to his future perfection. For those who are successful in either life or learning only, but deficient in one or the other, do not differ at all, in my opinion, from one-eyed men, whose disadvantage is great indeed, but their deformity is even greater when they look at others or are regarded by them. But those who excel in both and are, as it were, ambidextrous, are in a state of perfection and live lives of heavenly happiness.

This was the happy destiny that befell him, having as he did in his own home a model of virtue, on which he had only to keep his eyes to be excellent from the beginning. Just as we see colts and calves from their birth skipping by the side of their mothers, so he, running close at the side of his father, with the ardor of a colt, was not left far behind in his lofty impulses toward virtue. Or, if you prefer it, in this very adumbration of virtue he gave an indication of the future beauty of his virtue and, before the time of perfection arrived, presented a sketch of perfection.

(13) When he was sufficiently instructed at home, as he was to neglect no form of excellence, nor to be surpassed in diligence by the bee which collects what is most useful from every flower, he hastened to the city of Caesarea to attend its schools. I mean this illustrious city of ours, since she was also the guide and mistress of my studies, and not less the metropolis of letters than of the cities which she rules and which have submitted to her power. To rob her of her supremacy in letters would be to despoil her of her fairest and most singular distinction. Other cities take pride in other embellishments, either old or new, depending, I think, on their annals or their monuments. This city's characteristic mark, like the identification marks on arms or on plays, is letters. What followed, let those tell the story who instructed him and profited by his

instruction. Let them tell of his standing in the eyes of his masters and his companions, as he equaled the former and surpassed the latter in every form of learning. Let them tell what glory he gained in a short time in the sight of all, both of the common people and the leaders of the city, exhibiting a learning beyond his years and a constancy of character beyond his learning. He was an orator among orators, even before the lecturer's chair, a philosopher among philosophers even before advancing doctrines. And, what constitutes the highest tribute in the eyes of Christians, he was a priest even before the priesthood. In such wise did all defer to him in everything. With him, eloquence was only an accessory, and he culled from it only what would be helpful for our philosophy, since its power is necessary for the exposition of thought. For a mind incapable of expression is like the movement of a paralytic. But philosophy was his pursuit, as he strove to break from the world, to unite with God, to gain the things above by means of the things below, and to acquire, through goods which are unstable and pass away, those that are stable and abide.

(14) Next, he went to Byzantium, the capital city of the East, for it was famed at the time for its accomplished rhetoricians and philosophers. From these in a short time he absorbed what was best through the quickness and the force of his genius. From there he was sent by God and by his noble craving for learning to Athens, the home of eloquence, Athens, a city to me, if to anyone, truly golden, patroness of all that is excellent. Athens brought me a more perfect knowledge of Basil, although he was not unknown to me before. And in my search for learning I found happiness. Yet, in a different manner, I had the same experience as Saul,[13] who, when seeking the asses of his father, found a kingdom, and gained as an accessory what was worth more than the principal.

Up to this point my discourse has proceeded smoothly,

---

13 Cf. 1 Kings 9.3ff.

bearing me along on an even, and very easy, and truly royal highway in my praises of this man. But now I am at a loss for words and know not which way to turn, for my speech has encountered an obstacle. At this point I should like to profit by the occasion to add some facts concerning myself to what has been said, and to delay a little in my narrative to tell you about the origin, the circumstance, and the beginning of our friendship, or, to speak more exactly, about our full accord of heart and nature. For the eye is not wont to turn away readily from attractive sights, and if it is forcefully drawn away, it is wont to return to them again. And the same is true of discourse when there is question of narrating what is very pleasing to us. Yet I fear the difficulty of the undertaking, and I will speak, therefore, with all possible reserve. If loving regret forces me beyond bounds, pardon this most just of all feelings, not to experience which would be a great loss, at least in the judgment of intelligent men.

(15) We were at Athens, after having been separated, like the current of a river upon leaving the same native source, to go abroad by different ways in our pursuit of culture, and again reunited, as though by agreement, God so willing it. I preceded him to Athens, but he came shortly afterwards, where he had been awaited with lively and manifest impatience. His name was on the tongues of many before his arrival, and everyone considered it important to be the first to obtain the object of their desire. Nor will it be out of place to add, as a sort of relish to my discourse, a little anecdote, which will be a reminder for those who know it and a source of instruction to those who do not.

At Athens, most of the young men, and the more foolish, are mad after Sophists, and not only the ignoble and obscure but even the noble and illustrious. They form a rather confused mass, at once young and difficult to restrain. Now, you may notice how those who delight in horses and spectacles conduct themselves at the horse races. They leap up, they shout, they raise clouds of dust, they drive in their seats, they beat the air as their horses, with fingers for whips, and they yoke and unyoke them. Although they have control of none, they readily exchange with one another drivers, horses, stables, and officials. And who are they that do this? They are often poor men, indigent and without means of support for a single day. It is exactly thus that the students conduct themselves in respect to their masters and their masters' rivals, eagerly striving to increase their own numbers and thereby enrich them. The whole thing is quite senseless and insane. They seize upon cities, roads, harbors, mountain peaks, plains, frontiers; in fact, every part of Attica and the rest of Greece, and even most of their inhabitants. For they have divided these into factions by their rivalries.

(16) Whenever a newcomer arrives and falls into the hands of those who seize him, willingly or unwillingly, they observe this Attic custom, which is a mixture of the gay and the serious. First of all he is guided to the house of one of those who first received him, either friends or kinsmen or compatriots, or of those expert in sophistry and purveyors of arguments, who for that reason are held in high esteem among them. They regard it as a recompense, also, to gain new adherents. The newcomer is then rallied by everyone who wishes. Their purpose, I think, is to humble the pretensions of the newcomers and to bring them under their power from the start. The rallying is coarse or reasonable, depending upon the boorishnness or the urbanity of the rallier. The practice, to those who are ignorant of it, seems fearful and brutal, but, to those who already know it, quite pleasant and charming, for there is more display than actuality in its threats. Next, he is led in procession through the market place to the bath. Those in charge of the procession in honor of the youth arrange themselves in two separate ranks, and precede him to the bath.

When they are close to it, they raise great shouts and leap up and down, as though in a frenzy, the shouting being a command not to advance any further but to stop, as though the bath were closed to them. At the same time they pound at the doors and frighten the youth with the uproar. Then they allow him to enter, and finally grant him his freedom, and on return from the bath receive him on equal terms with themselves. This is the most pleasing feature of the whole ceremony for the youths, as it brings instant and final relief from their persecutors.

At that time, not only was I myself unwilling to subject my friend, the great Basil, to shame, reverencing as I did his gravity of character and his maturity of judgment, but I also persuaded the other youths who did not know him to share my sentiments. For he was already respected by most of them, since his renown had preceded him. The result was that he was almost the only newcomer to escape the general rule, a distinction beyond that generally accorded to new students.

(17) This was the prelude to our friendship. This was the spark that enkindled our union. It was thus that we were struck with a mutual love. Then something of a similar kind occurred, which ought not to be passed over either.

I find the Armenians not an open people, but quite dissembling and crafty. At this time, some of them who had long been his intimates and friends, dating from early association under his father's instruction—for they had belonged to his school—approached him with the appearance of friendship, though prompted by envy, not benevolence. They plied him with questions of a contentious rather than a reasonable character, and strove to vanquish him at the first onset, both because they had long recognized the genius of Basil and because they could not endure the honor being shown him at this time. They bitterly resented the fact that they who had taken the philosophical mantle and had already received training in oratorical skill should have no advantage over him, a stranger and a newcomer. And I myself, vain lover of Athens, not suspecting the envy but crediting the pretense, when they were giving way and turning their backs, felt piqued that in their persons the glory of Athens should be destroyed and so quickly put to shame, and I came to the support of the young men and re-established the discussion. I graciously lent them the weight of my authority, and, as the least addition in such circumstances is all-powerful, I made 'equal their heads in the battle,' as the saying has it.[14] When I realized what was behind the discussion, for it could not be kept back, but eventually revealed itself clearly, I changed my position immediately and, putting my ship about and ranging myself on his side, I made his victory decisive. He was at once quite pleased with what had happened, for he was extraordinarily sagacious. And full of ardor, to describe him fully in the words of Homer, he drove in confusion[15] those proud youths by his reasoning, and did not cease smiting them with arguments until he had completely routed them and gained a crowning victory. This was the second step in our friendship, no longer a spark but a flame that burned bright and high.

(18) They withdrew, therefore, without effecting their purpose, severely reproaching themselves for their rashness and extremely annoyed at me because of the trap in which they had been caught. They even openly manifested their hatred and charged me with treason not only to them but to Athens itself, since in their first onset they had been vanquished and put to shame by a single man, and that, too, by one who had not yet had the opportunity to develop a confident attitude. It is a common human experience, when, after conceiving high hopes, we suddenly chance upon their realization, to look upon the result as falling short of our expectations. Basil

---
14 Homer, *Iliad* 11.72.
15 Cf. *Iliad* 11.496.

had this experience, and was sad and distressed, and could not praise himself for coming to Athens. He was seeking what he had hoped, and he called Athens an empty happiness. Such were his feelings.

As for myself, I strove to dispel his disappointment for the most part by entering into discussion with him and soothing him by my arguments. I told him, and this was true, that just as a man's character is not to be detected immediately, but only after a long time and an intimate association, so culture is not a thing to be judged from a few brief experiences. In this way I restored his good spirits, and by this mutual experience I bound him to myself all the more.

(19) Then, as time went on, we mutually avowed our affection for each other, and that philosophy was the object of our zeal. Thenceforth we were all in all to each other, sharing the same roof, the same table, the same sentiments, our eyes fixed on one goal, as our mutual affection grew ever warmer and stronger. Carnal loves, centered on that which passes away, also pass away, like the flowers of spring. The flame does not endure when the fuel is exhausted, but disappears along with what kindles it. Desire, likewise, does not abide when its source wastes away. But those loves which are pleasing to God, and chaste, since they have a stable object, are on that account more lasting, and, the more beauty is revealed to them, the more does it bind to itself and to one another those whose love is centered on the same object. This is the law of the higher love.

I feel that I am being carried beyond due and proper bounds. I do not know how I chance upon these topics, yet I have no way of checking my narrative. For, constantly, what I have omitted seems essential and superior to what I had chosen. And if anyone attempts to push me forward by force, I shall suffer the lot of the polyps, which, when they are pulled from their lairs, cling to the rocks with their suckers, and cannot be torn away until forceful pressure has been exerted on every one of these. If, therefore you grant me leave, I have what I ask; if not, I shall take it from myself.

(20) Thus mutually disposed to each other, and raising our fair-walled chamber on such pillars of gold, as Pindar says,[16] we went forward with God and our affection as our helpers. Oh, how can I evoke such memories without tears! We were impelled by equal hopes in the pursuit of learning, a thing especially open to envy. But envy was absent, and emulation intensified our zeal. There was a contest between us, not as to who should have first place for himself, but how he could yield it to the other, for each of us regarded the glory of the other as his own. We seemed to have a single soul animating two bodies. And while credence is not to be given to those who claim that all things are in all,[17] we at least must believe that we were in and with each other. The sole object of us both was virtue and living for future hopes, having detached ourselves from this world before departing from it. With this in view, we directed our life and all our actions, following the guidance of the divine precept, and at the same time spurring each other to virtue, and, if it is not too much to say so, being for each other a rule and a scales for the discernment of good and evil. For companions we consorted, not with the most dissolute but with the most modest, not with the most quarrelsome but with the most peaceable, and with those with whom association was most profitable. We knew that it is easier to be contaminated by vice than to communicate virtue, just as it is easier to contract a disease than to bestow health. As for our studies, we found pleasure not so much in the most agreeable as in the most excellent, since this also is a means for moulding to virtue or to vice.

---

16 *Olymp.* 6.1.
17 An allusion to a doctrine ascribed to Anaxagoras and other Greek philosophers.

(21) Two ways were familiar to us: the first and more precious leading us to our sacred buildings and the masters there; the second and the one of less account, to our secular teachers. All else—festivals, spectacles, assemblies, and banquets—we left to those with a taste for such things. For nothing is worthy of esteem, in my opinion, which does not lead to virtue and render better those who apply themselves to it. Different men have different names, derived from their ancestors or their own pursuits and deeds. Our great concern, our great name, was to be Christians and be called Christians. We were prouder of this than Gyges of the turning of his ring, if this is not a fable, by which he became King of the Lydians, or than Midas of his gold by which he perished, according to another Phrygian fable, after his prayer that all he had be turned to gold was fulfilled. Why should I mention the arrow of the Hyperborean Abaris or the Argive Pegasus, for whom it was less important to be borne through the air than for us to be lifted up to God together by our mutual efforts?

But, to be brief. Athens is harmful, in general, to the things of the soul, and the pious are not wrong in being of this opinion. It abounds in the evil riches of idols beyond the rest of Greece, and it is difficult not to be led astray by their admirers and advocates. But in our case no harm resulted, as our minds were protected by an impenetrable armor. On the contrary, to speak paradoxically, our own experience there confirmed us in the faith. For we recognized their deceit and fraudulence, and we despised those divinities in the very place they are admired. And if there is or is believed to be a stream flowing with fresh water through the sea, or an animal that can dance in fire that destroys all, such were we among our companions.

(22) Best of all, there was about us a company not without renown, which was instructed and directed under the guidance of Basil, and shared the same pleasures. Yet it was as foot

soldiers that we ran beside a Lydian chariot—his course and conduct. Hence, we became famous not only in the sight of our own masters and companions, but even throughout Greece and especially among the most illustrious men. Our fame went even beyond its borders, as was clear from numerous accounts. For our masters were known wherever Athens was known, and wherever they were the subject of report or conversation, so were we, also, since among them we were, and were spoken of as, a famous pair. Orestes and Pylades[18] and others like them were not to be compared with us, nor the Molionidae,[19] celebrated in Homer for their union in misfortune, and their skill in driving the chariot, as they shared the reins and the whip between them. But I have been drawn unawares into praising myself, a thing I have never tolerated in another. But it should not be a cause for wonder that in this instance, also, I have profit from his friendship. While he lived, he aided me in virtue, and now after his death he has added to my renown. But let my discourse return to its proper course.

(23) Who was so venerable for prudence, even before his hair was grey? For it is in this way that Solomon defines old age.[20] Who was so respected by both old and young, not only of our generation, but of generations long past? Who, because of his character, had less need of training? Who possessed more knowledge along with such character? What branch of learning is there in which he did not engage, or rather, what branch in which he did not excel as though it were the only one? He passed through them all as no one ever did through one, and through each most intensely, as though there were no others. In his case, application went hand in hand with natural ability, and it is through these that superiority in the arts and the sciences is achieved. Because of his powers of concentration

---

18 One of the most famous pairs of friends in Greek legend.
19 Cf. *Iliad* 2.621; 11.750.
20 Cf. Wisd. 4.8.

he had little need of natural quickness, just as he had little need of concentration because of his natural quickness. He possessed and united two qualities in such a way that it was not clear for which of the two he was the more distinguished.

Who was like him in rhetoric, 'breathing forth the might of fire,'[21] though his character differed from that of the rhetoricians? Who was like him in grammar, which makes us Greeks in language, which composes history, which presides over meters and makes laws for poems? Who was like him in philosophy, that truly sublime science which soars aloft, whether one consider the practical and speculative side, or that which deals with logical demonstrations and oppositions and with controversies, namely, dialectic? In this, he so excelled that it would have been easier for those who disputed with him to extricate themselves from labyrinths than to escape the meshes of arguments he wove whenever he had need. As for astronomy, geometry, and mathematics, he was content with a knowledge sufficient to avoid being confused by those who were clever in these sciences. Anything beyond that he scorned as useless for those who wished to lead a pious life. And so one can admire more what he chose than what he passed over, and, more than what he chose, what he passed over. His bodily weakness and his care of the sick made medicine, the fruit of philosophy and industry, a necessity for him. From such a beginning he advanced to mastery of this art, and not only of the branches that deal with the visible and what is immediately apparent, but also of those which deal with principles and theory. But what are these accomplishments, significant as they are, compared to his knowledge of moral science? In the eyes of those who have made trial of Basil, the famous Minos and Rhadamanthus[22] were mere humbugs, whom the Greeks judged worthy of the meadows of asphodel

---
21 *Iliad* 6.182.
22 Famous judges of the lower world in Greek mythology.

and the Elysian fields, for they had acquired the notion of our Paradise, in my opinion, from the books of Moses, which are also ours. Though their terminology is somewhat different, this is what they convey under other words and names.

(24) Such were our circumstances. We had a full cargo of knowledge, at least the measure attainable by man's nature. One cannot sail beyond Gades. There only remained our return home, our entrance upon a more perfect life, and the realization of common purpose. The day of our departure was at hand, and with it all that is involved in departure: speeches of farewell and escort, salutations, laments, embraces, and tears. For there is nothing so painful to anyone as for those who have been fellow students at Athens to be separated from the city and from one another. Then, indeed, occurred a pitiable spectacle and one worthy to be recalled. About us were gathered our companions and classmates, as well as some of our masters, all crying out, in the midst of their entreaties, threats of violence and attempts at persuasion that, come what may, they would not let us go. They said and did everything natural to men in grief.

Here I shall be presumptuous and bring an accusation against myself and also, it may seem, against that holy and irreproachable soul. He, after explaining the pressing reasons for his return, overcame their restraint, and they, although it was against their will, consented to his departure. I myself was left behind at Athens, partly because I weakened before the entreaties of friends, for the truth must be told, but partly because of his betrayal, for he had been persuaded to forsake one who had not forsaken him and to hand me over to those who were holding him there. It was a thing that, before it happened, was incredible. For it was like cutting a body in two parts, with the resulting death of both, or like the parting of two oxen that have shared the same manger and yoke, bellowing piteously for each other in distress at their separation. My loss, however, was not of long duration, for I could not bear for long being a pitiable spectacle and explaining to everyone the reasons for our separation. So, after staying at Athens a little while more, my longing made me like the horse in Homer; I burst the tie with those holding me back and, coursing over the plain, rushed to join my companion.[23]

(25) On our return, we paid a little homage to the world and the stage, and that only to satisfy the desire of the multitude; we ourselves had no love for theatrical display. We quickly became independent and were accounted men instead of beardless youths, advancing in more manlike fashion in philosophy. We were no longer together, for envy prevented this, but we were united in desire. The city of Caesarea took possession of Basil, as a second founder and protector. As time went on, since I could not be with him, he went abroad on voyages which were necessary and in full keeping with his philosophical resolution. Reverence for my parents, the care of their old age, and successive misfortunes separated me from him. This was not good, perhaps, nor fair, but at any rate they kept me from him. I ask myself whether this was not the cause of all the inconsistency and difficulty which has befallen me in my life, and which has made my progress in philosophy so uneven and unworthy of my desire and purpose. May my affairs follow the course that God wills, but may they follow a better course because of Basil's intercessions. As for him, the manifold kindness of God and His providence toward our family, after making him known by many manifest circumstances and showing him forth day by day as more illustrious, set him up as a brilliant and celebrated light of the Church, for he had been enrolled meanwhile in the sacred order of the priesthood to illumine, through the single city of Caesarea, the whole

---

23 Cf. *Iliad* 6.506ff.

world. And in what manner? It was not by suddenly advancing him, nor by cleansing and instructing him in wisdom at the same time, as is true of the majority of those today who aspire to the episcopate. He received the honor according to the law and order of spiritual advancement.

(26) I do not approve of the confusion and disorder that exist among us, sometimes even in those who preside in the sanctuary. I will not go so far as to accuse all, for that would not be just. I approve of the naval custom which first puts oars in the hands of the future pilot and later leads him to the prow and entrusts him with the duties forward, seating him at the helm only after long experience at sea and in observation of the winds. The same holds true in military affairs: one is soldier, captain, general. This order is the best and most advantageous for subordinates. If the same system were in force in our case, it would be of great value. As it is now, the most holy of all the orders among us is in danger of being the most ridiculous. For the episcopate depends not so much on virtue as on intrigue, and the sees belong not so much to the most worthy as to the most powerful. Samuel, who foresaw the future, is numbered among the Prophets, but so also is Saul, the outcast. Roboam, the son of Solomon, is among the kings, but so also is Jeroboam, the slave and apostate. And there is no physician or painter who has not first observed the nature of diseases or blended many colors and sketched various figures. But a bishop is easily found, without the experience furnished by toil, having but recent repute and being sown and springing up at once, as in the fable of the giants. We manufacture holy men in a day and we bid them to be wise, when they have had no training in wisdom, and no previous warrant to this dignity except desire. One man is content with his lowly position, and remains humble, though worthy of the highest place, having devoted himself to frequent meditation on the divine Scriptures and striven much to sub-

ject his flesh to the law of the spirit. Another arrogantly seats himself in first place, raises his brow at his betters, does not tremble on his throne, and does not shudder at the sight, as he looks down on the man of self-control. On the contrary, he supposes that, together with his power, he has acquired superior wisdom, betraying the false judgment of a man whom high office has robbed of his senses.

(27) It was not so with our great and noble Basil. As in all other things, so in this he appears as a model of order to others. First, he read the sacred Books to the people and was their interpreter, not deeming this function of the sanctuary beneath him. Similarly, in the chair of the priests and then in that of the bishops he praised the Lord, not having gained this authority by stealth or force, not having sought the honor but having been sought by it, not having received it as a human favor but as coming from God and divine. But let my account of his episcopate be deferred, and let us now dwell a little on his priesthood. How nearly this escaped me, although it should occupy a central place in my discourse!

(28) A disagreement arose between Basil and his predecessor in the government of this church. It is better to pass over in silence its origin and character, but the fact remains. Eusebius[24] was in many respects a man not without nobility, and remarkable for piety, as the persecution of that time and the opposition to him clearly indicated, yet he developed a natural antipathy for Basil. Momus[25] seizes not only upon the common crowd but on the best of men, since it belongs to God alone to be completely infallible and uninfluenced by the passions. All the more select and wiser members of the Church were roused against Eusebius; since they are wiser than the multitude, they have separated themselves from the world

---

24 Eusebius of Caesarea, predecessor of Basil in the see of Caesarea, is not mentioned by name in the Greek original.
25 Greek god of grumbling and fault-finding.

and consecrated themselves to God. I speak of the Nazarites[26] among us, who are especially zealous in such matters. They were indignant that their chief should be ignored, outraged, and set aside, and they ventured upon a most dangerous undertaking. They contemplated defection and revolt from the great and indivisible body of the Church, severing along with themselves a considerable portion of the people, including some of lowly station and others of high rank. This was quite easy for three weighty reasons. First of all, Basil was venerated, to my knowledge, as no other philosopher of our time and, if he wished, he could give encouragement to the faction. Second, his opponent was under suspicion by the city because of the tumult connected with his election, on the grounds that he had received the episcopal office not so much in a regular and canonical manner as by violence. Finally, some bishops had come from the West and drew to themselves the whole orthodox portion of the Church.[27]

(29) What action, then, was taken by that noble man and disciple of the peaceful One?[28] He could not resist his slanderers or his partisans, nor did it befit him to fight or to rend the body of the Church, already attacked and put in peril by the power of the heretics at the time. Following our sincere counsels and exhortations on this point, he retired in flight to Pontus and, assuming the direction of the monasteries there, established for them some memorable regulations. He embraced solitude as had Elias and John, those perfect philosophers, deeming this more advantageous for him than to make any plans in respect to the present difficulty that would be unworthy of his philosophy, or than to lose in the tempest the control which in time of calm he exercised over his reason. Although his departure was so philosophical and worthy of

---

26 I.e., the monks.
27 Allusion is made to the papal legates, Lucifer of Cagliari and Eusebius of Vercelli.
28 Cf. Matt. 11.29.

admiration, we shall find that his return was even more admirable. For so it was.

(30) While we were thus engaged, there suddenly arose a cloud full of hail and shrill with death, devastating every church on which it burst and fell: an emperor,[29] too fond of gold and most hostile to Christ. Afflicted with those two greatest of maladies, avarice and blasphemy, he was a persecutor following a persecutor, and following the Apostate. Although he was not an apostate himself, he was no better to Christians, or rather to that most pious and pure portion of the Christians who worship the Trinity, which I call the only true piety and saving doctrine. We do not weigh out the Godhead, nor do we divorce the one and inaccessible Nature from Itself by unnatural differences. Nor do we cure one evil by another, dissolving the impious contraction of Sabellius by a more impious separation and division. This was the disease of Arius, who gave his name to the madness, and who threw into confusion and brought to ruin a great part of the Church. Without honoring the Father, he dishonored what proceeded from Him by maintaining unequal degrees in the Godhead. But we recognize one glory of the Father, the equality of the Only-begotten, and one glory of the Son, the equality of the Holy Spirit. And we believe that to subordinate anything of the Three is to destroy the whole. We venerate and acknowledge Three with respect to attributes; One, with respect to Godhead. Having no understanding of this, and unable to look upwards, and debased by those who led him on,[30] he had the audacity to debase the nature of the Godhead along with himself. He became an evil creature, reducing majesty to servitude, and putting the uncreated and timeless Nature on the same level with created things.

---

29 Valens, champion of Arianism.
30 I.e., the emperor was following the lead of demons in promoting Arianism.

(31) Such, then, were his views, and it was with such impiety that he took the field against us. There is no other way of regarding it than as a barbarian invasion, having for its object, not the destruction of ramparts, or cities, or houses, or any of the little things that are made by hand and soon restored or replaced, but the ravaging of men's souls. He was joined in his attack by an army worthy of him, the wicked leaders of the churches, the cruel governors of his world empire. They were already masters of some churches and were attacking others, and they were hoping to gain others still through the influence and might of the emperor. One form of violence was being exercised and another threatened. They came to destroy our church, also, relying on nothing so much as the pusillanimity of all those of whom I have spoken, on the inexperience of the man who was then our bishop and on the infirmities that existed among us.

Great, then, was the struggle in prospect. The ardor of the multitude was not wanting, but their battle line was weak for lack of a champion and one trained to fight for them with the power of the Word and the Spirit. What was the reaction of that noble and sublime and truly Christ-loving soul? There was no need of long speeches to gain his presence and his assistance. He had no sooner seen me on my mission, for the struggle was common to us both as defenders of the faith, than he yielded at once to my plea. And, for his part, he made an excellent and very wise distinction, based on the precepts of the Holy Spirit, namely, that there is a time for captiousness—if one must indulge in such feelings at all—that of security, and another time for forbearance, that of necessity. At once he departed with me from Pontus and was filled with zeal in defense of truth in danger, offering himself as a willing ally in the fight and dedicating himself to his mother, the Church.

(32) But if he manifested such zeal beforehand, was his

ardor less in the combat? Or if he was valiant throughout the conflict, was he lacking in prudence? Or if he fought with skill, did he shrink from danger? Or if in all these respects he evidenced a perfection beyond description, did he cherish in his heart some trace of chagrin? By no means. But simultaneously he effected his reconciliation, took counsel, and prepared the defense. He removed all the obstacles and stumbling blocks in our way and all that had given encouragement to those attacking us. He gained in one quarter, held his ground in another, and drove back the attack in a third. He became to some a strong wall and a rampart,[31] to others an axe breaking the rock to pieces,[32] or a fire among the thorns,[33] as divine Scripture says, easily destroying the fagots which were insulting the Godhead. And if Barnabas, who speaks and records these things, had some share in the struggles of Paul, the thanks are due to Paul, who chose him and made him his partner in the conflict.

(33) They therefore departed without accomplishing their purpose, and, base men that they were, they were basely put to shame and worsted for the first time. And they learned that, of all men in the world, the Cappadocians were not to be lightly despised. There is nothing so characteristic of them as the firmness of their faith and the sincerity of their belief in the Trinity. And from the Trinity come their unity and strength, and for assistance rendered, assistance in return, only far greater and more powerful.

The next object of Basil's toil and zeal was to conciliate the bishop, to dissipate his suspicions, to persuade all men that the vexation that had been felt was a temptation and an attack of the evil one, envious of virtuous concord, and that he himself recognized the laws of obedience and the spiritual

---
31 Cf. Jer. 1.18.
32 Cf. Jer. 23.29.
33 Cf. Ps. 117.12.

order. Therefore, he was at his side, instructing him, giving ear to him, advising him. He was everything to him, a good counselor, an expert assistant, a spiritual director, a guide of conduct, a staff for his old age, a bulwark of the faith, the most worthy of trust within the household and most active outside—in a word, as much disposed to benevolence as he had once been thought to hostility. The result was that he was invested with the government of the church, though he was second in rank in the see, for, in return for the benevolence he displayed, he received authority. And their harmony and union in power was wonderful. One led the people; the other, the leader, like a lion keeper, as it were, skillfully taming the possessor of power. He had been newly installed in the see, while still breathing worldly air, and not yet adjusted to the things of the Spirit, when a violent storm was raging and the enemies of the Church were menacing. He was in need, therefore, of a directing and a sustaining hand. For this reason he cherished this alliance and considered himself the master of one who had mastered him.

(34) Of Basil's care and protection of the Church there are many other examples. There was his independence toward magistrates and the most powerful men in the city. There were his decisions of disputes, which were accepted with confidence, the mere seal of his word taking on the character of law. There was his support of the needy, more often in cases of spiritual want, but often, also, in those of physical distress. For this is frequently a means of touching the soul and reducing it to subjection by kindness. There were his support of the poor, his hospitality toward strangers, his solicitude for virgins, written and unwritten legislation for monks, formulation of prayers, regulations for good order in the sanctuary, and other ways in which one who was truly a man of God and ranged on God's side could benefit the people. But there was one example of special importance and fame.

There was a famine, the most severe within the memory of man. The city was in distress, but there was no help forthcoming from any quarter, nor any remedy for the calamity. The maritime cities support without difficulty occasions of want like these, since they can dispose of their own products and receive in exchange those which come to them by sea. But we in the inland can make no profit on our superfluous products, nor procure what we need, having no means of disposing of what we have or importing what we lack. In situations like this, nothing is so distressing as the cruelty and avarice of those who enjoy plenty. They watch for occasions of trafficking in want and they reap a harvest from misfortune. They do not heed: 'He that hath mercy on the poor, lendeth to the Lord'[34] and 'He that hideth up corn, shall be cursed among the people,'[35] or any other of the promises made to the merciful or the threats against the inhuman. Their insatiate desire runs beyond bounds in their false wisdom. While they close their bowels of mercy to others, they close those of God to themselves, not perceiving that they are in greater need of Him than others of them. Such are these buyers and sellers of gain, having no regard for their fellow men or thanks to God, by whose benefit they enjoy plenty when others are in distress.

(35) But Basil could not rain down bread from heaven[36] by prayer to feed a fugitive people in the desert, nor cause food to well up without cost from the depth of vessels[37] which are filled by emptying—a paradox, indeed, that she who fed the Prophet might be fed in turn for her hospitality. Nor could he feed many thousands of men with five loaves,[38] of which even the fragments sufficed for many tables. For these

---
34 Prov. 19.17.
35 Prov. 11.26.
36 Cf. Exod. 16.15; Ps. 77.24.
37 Cf. 3 Kings 17.14.
38 Cf. Matt. 14.19; Luke 9.16.

were the works of Moses and Elias and of my God who gave them this power, fitting also, perhaps, for those times and the conditions prevailing then, since signs are for unbelievers, not for believers.[39] But what was in accord with these works and tending to the same result, he devised and executed with the same faith. By his word and exhortations he opened up the storehouses of the rich and brought to realization the words of Scripture: he dealt bread to the hungry[40] and he satisfied the poor with bread,[41] and he fed them in famine[42] and 'he has filled the hungry with good things.'[43] And in what manner? For this contributed in no small way to his assistance. He assembled in one place those afflicted by the famine, including some who had recovered a little from it, men and women, children, old men, the distressed of every age. He collected through contributions all kinds of food helpful for relieving famine. He set before them caldrons of pea soup and our salted meats, the sustenance of the poor. Then, imitating the ministry of Christ, who, girded with a towel, did not disdain to wash the feet of His disciples, and employing his own servants or, rather, his fellow slaves and co-workers in this labor, he ministered to the bodies and the souls of the needy, combining marks of respect with the necessary refreshment, thus affording them relief in two ways.

(36) Such was our new provider of grain and second Joseph, save that on him we have something more to say. For Joseph trafficked in famine and gained Egypt by his humanity,[44] making use of the time of abundance with a view to the time of want, appointed for this purpose through the dreams of others, but Basil rendered service freely, relieving

---
39 Cf. 1 Cor. 14.22.
40 Cf. Isa. 58.7.
41 Cf. Ps. 131.15.
42 Cf. Ps. 32.19.
43 Luke 1.53.
44 Cf. Gen. 41.1ff.

the dearth of food without drawing any profit therefrom. He had in view only one object: to win mercy by being merciful, and to acquire heavenly blessings by his distribution of grain here below. He furnished also the nourishment of the Word, that more perfect charity and distribution of goods, truly celestial and sublime, since the Word is the bread of angels,[45] the food and drink of souls who are hungry for God and seek for food that does not pass away or fail, but abides forever. This was the bread that he furnished and in great abundance, that poorest and most needy man that I have known. And it was not to relieve a hunger for bread or a thirst for water, but a longing for the Word which is truly vivifying and nourishing and which leads to progress in the spiritual life whoever is well nourished thereon.

(37) After these and similar deeds, for there is no need to spend time in recounting them all, upon the death of Eusebius, whose name denotes piety, and who expired sweetly in the arms of Basil, he was soon exalted to the lofty throne of the episcopate. This was not effected without difficulty nor without the envious opposition of the bishops of the country and of the most vicious men of the city, who had ranged themselves with these. But it was inevitable that the Holy Spirit should be victorious, and the victory was truly a decisive one. For He roused up from distant parts to anoint him men celebrated and zealous for piety and among them, the new Abraham, our patriarch, I mean my father, in regard to whom a sort of prodigy occurred. For, though weakened by length of years, wasted by disease, and almost drawing his last breath, he braved the journey to bring the assistance of his vote, relying on the help of the Spirit. To speak briefly, he was placed on his litter like a corpse in the tomb; he returned in the vigor of youth, with head erect and eyes bright, strengthened by the imposition of hands and the anointing,

---

45 Cf. Ps. 77.25.

and, if it is not too much to say, by the head of him whom he anointed. Let this be added to those ancient narratives to the effect that toil brings health, zeal raises the dead, and old age leaps up when anointed by the Spirit.

(38) After Basil had been thus honored with the primacy, as it was fitting for a man who had lived such a life, attained such favor, and enjoyed such a reputation, he did nothing thereafter that could compromise his own philosophy or the hopes of those who trusted him. As he had previously shown himself to surpass others, he now appeared to surpass himself, conceiving the noblest and wisest ideas in this repect. For he thought that the virtue of a private individual consisted in avoiding vice and being good in a certain measure, but that in a ruler and chief it was a vice, especially in such an office as his, if he did not far surpass most men, manifest constant progress, and raise his virtue to the height demanded by his dignity and his throne. It was difficult, he felt, for one in high office to achieve his proper mean, and with surpassing virtue to lead the multitude to the common mean. Or, to be more philosophically precise here, I consider that the same thing happened in his case as I observe in that of our Saviour—and it holds true for every really wise man, I imagine—when He was among us in that form which was superior to us and yet was ours. As He advanced in age, it is said, so also did He in wisdom and grace.[46] Not that these qualities received any increase—for how could that which was perfect from the beginning become more perfect—but the meaning is that these qualities were gradually revealed and manifested themselves. In the same way, I think that Basil's virtue did not receive any increase but only wider exercise at the time, since his office supplied him with more abundant opportunity.

(39) He first made it clear to everyone that the office

---
46 Cf. Luke 2.52.

bestowed on him was not due to human favor, but was a gift of God. An instance that concerns myself will also make this evident. How his philosophy squared with my own at that time! Everyone thought that I would rush forward after his accesssion with great joy—as anyone else, perhaps, might have acted—and would share his power rather than rule beside him. Our friendship led men to surmise this. But fleeing the suspicion of arrogance, as I, if anyone, have always done, and at the same time avoiding jealousy together with its occasion, especially since Basil's position was still painful and troublesome, I remained at home, forcefully checking my desire. While Basil found fault with me, he nevertheless excused me. And afterwards, when I did approach him, and for the same reason would not accept the honor of this chair, nor even the first place of dignity among the priests, far from blaming me, he praised my action, and rightly. For he preferred to be charged with arrogance by a few men who were ignorant of these principles of conduct than to do anything contrary to reason or his own resolutions. And, truly, in what better way could he show that he was a man whose soul was superior to all adulation and flattery, and that he had only one object in view, the rule of good, than by the attitude he observed in regard to myself, whom he acknowledged as one of the first of his friends and intimates?

(40) Next, he sought to appease and heal the faction opposed to him by applying the principles of a magnanimous medicine. He acted without flattery or servility, but with great courage and nobility, as a man who not only envisaged the present but was bent upon securing future obedience. Observing that softness tends to laxity and weakness and severity to harshness and arrogance, he amended the one by the other. He tempered strictness with reasonableness and softness with firmness. He rarely had need of argument, but influenced men most effectively by his conduct. He did not enslave men by

artifice, but won them over by kindness. He did not avail himself of his authority, but drew men by his sparing use of authority. What is most important, all were conquered by his intelligence and recognized that his virtue was unapproachable. They believed that the one way to salvation was for themselves to be ranged on his side and under his command and that their one danger was to oppose him, for they considered that separation from him meant alienation from God. So they willingly gave way and surrendered and submitted as at a clap of thunder. They strove to anticipate each other with their excuses and to make the measure of their former hostility the measure of their good will and of their progress in virtue, which they found to be the only effective reparation. The only exceptions were those who because of their incurable perversity were neglected and set aside, to wear themselves out and be expended, as rust is consumed with the iron it feeds upon.

(41) When he had settled affairs at home to his satisfaction and as no one of the faithless who did not know him would have thought possible, he conceived a far greater and loftier design. While all other men had their eyes only on that which lay at their feet and considered how they might safeguard their own interests—if, indeed, this is to safeguard them—without going any further or being capable of conceiving or accomplishing any great or noble purpose, Basil, though he observed moderation in other respects, in this knew no measure. But lifting his head high and casting the eye of his soul in every direction, he obtained a mental vision of the whole world through which the word of salvation had been spread. He saw the great heritage of God, purchased by His own words and laws and sufferings, the holy nation,[47] the royal priesthood, in a miserable plight and torn asunder into an infinity of doctrines and errors. He saw the vine which had

---

47 Cf. 1 Peter 2.9.

been brought out of Egypt and transplanted from impious and
dark ignorance, and which had grown to a surpassing beauty
and grandeur, so as to cover the whole earth and extend above
the mountains and the cedars, now ravaged by that wicked
wild boar, the Devil. He did not think it enough to lament
misfortune in silence and merely lift up his hands to God to
implore deliverance from the pressing evils, but to be asleep
himself. But he thought he was bound to render aid and
make some personal contribution.

(42) For what could be more afflicting than this calamity
or what could excite more the zeal of one whose regard was
fixed on high to act in behalf of the common welfare? The
prosperity or adversity of an individual is of no significance
for the community, but when the community itself is in this
or that condition, the individual is of necessity affected in the
same way. Such were the thoughts and reflections of him
who was the guardian and protector of the community, for
an understanding heart is a moth to the bones, as is declared
by Solomon and Truth.[48] And while callousness is cheerful
compassion begets pain, and prolonged reflection wastes away
the heart. Therefore, he was troubled and grieved and
wounded. He experienced the feelings of Jonas[49] and David,
he renounced his soul, he gave no sleep to his eyes or slumber
to his eyelids.[50] What was left of his flesh he consumed in
anxieties until he should find a remedy for the evil. He
sought divine and human aid to stay the general conflagration
and disperse the darkness which was spreading over us.

(43) This device, and an exceedingly salutary one, came
to his mind. Withdrawing into himself as much as possible,
entering into close communion with the Spirit, and making
use of all human arguments as well as collecting all the pro-

---
48 Cf. Prov. 14.30 (Septuagint).
49 Cf. Jonas 4.8.
50 Cf. Ps. 131.4.

found truths of Scripture, he composed a treatise on the true religion, and by his opposition and counterattack he beat off the bold offensive of the heretics. Those who engaged in hand-to-hand conflicts he overthrew at close range by word of mouth. Those who engaged at a distance he struck with arrows of ink, no less significant than the characters on the tables of the Law, legislating not for one small Jewish nation, concerning meat and drink,[51] temporal sacrifices, and purifications of the flesh, but for every nation and every portion of the earth, concerning the true doctrine from which comes our salvation. Then, since unreasoning action and impractical reasoning are alike ineffectual, he added to reason the aid of action. He visited some, sent messages to others, and summoned still others; he admonished, reproved, censured, threatened, and upbraided; he assumed the defense of nations, cities, and individuals; he contrived every kind of deliverance and cured disease by medicines from every source. He was like Beseleel,[52] the builder of the holy tabernacle, employing for the work every kind of material and art, and fashioning all into the beauty and harmony of a single masterpiece.

(44) Why should I add anything further? That enemy of Christ and tyrant toward the faith, the emperor, with greater impiety and a fiercer assault, came against us again, persuaded that he had to deal with a stronger antagonist. He was like that unclean and evil spirit, who, having been driven from a man and having wandered about, returns accompanied by a greater number of spirits to take up the same abode, as we have heard in the Gospels.[53] This was the model he imitated and his purpose was to make good his former defeat by increasing his former efforts. He felt that it

---

51 Cf. Heb. 9.10.
52 Cf. Exod. 31.2.
53 Luke 11.24.

was strange and abominable that he, the ruler of so many nations, who enjoyed so much renown, who had subjected all those about him to his impious power and crushed every opposition that he encountered, should be worsted, in the sight of all, by a single man and a single city, and become a laughing-stock, not only to the champions of impiety, by whom he was led, but also, as he supposed, to all men.

(45) They say that the King of Persia, when he was making his expedition into Greece, and glowing with passion and pride as he led men of every race against the Greeks, was not content merely with exalting himself and making immoderate threats, but sought to make himself an object of terror all the more by the novel offenses which he committed against the elements. One heard of a strange land and sea produced by this new creator; of an army sailing on the mainland and traversing the sea on foot; of islands carried off and of the sea being scourged; and of all other phenomena which manifested the madness of that army and of its commander, a source of terror to the cowardly but an object of ridicule to men of braver and stouter hearts. The emperor, however, had no need of anything of this kind in his campaign against us. Yet he was reported to do and say what was worse and more harmful. He set his mouth against heaven, speaking blasphemy on high, and his tongue passed through the earth. Well did holy David, long before our time, stigmatize him who made heaven bend to earth, putting on the same level with creation that supramundane Nature which creation cannot contain, although for love of us It was associated in some measure with us, that It might draw to Itself us who were lying upon the ground.[54]

(46) And while those first wanton deeds of the emperor were notorious, his last conflicts against us were even more flagrant. What do I mean by the first?—exiles, banishments,

---

54 Cf. Ps. 72.9.

confiscations, open and secret plots, persuasion when it was opportune, violence when persuasion was impossible. Those who professed the orthodox faith, our faith, were thrust from their churches. Others were intruded who held the pernicious doctrine of the emperor, men who demanded certificates of impiety and were authors of still more detestable opinions. Priests were burned at sea.[55] Impious generals were occupied not in conquering the Persians or reducing the Scythians or driving out some barbaric nation, but in making war upon churches, dancing in triumph upon altars, defiling the unbloody sacrifices with the blood of men and victims, and violating the modesty of virgins. For what purpose? That the patriarch Jacob might be driven out, and Esau, who was hated even before his birth,[56] might be intruded in his place. Such is the history of those first wanton acts of his, the very recollection and mention of which brings tears to many eyes even now.

(47) But when, after having invaded all places, he launched his attack upon this unshaken and invulnerable mother of the churches, the only spark of truth still remaining unquenched, with the purpose of enslaving her, then for the first time he realized that he had planned badly. Just as a missile when it strikes a stronger body is repelled, and rope when broken snaps back, he encountered such a bulwark in the Church, and on such a rock was he shattered and broken. Other details one may learn from the mouth and narrative of the men who endured the trials of that time. And everyone without exception has something to tell. But all are in admiration who are acquainted with the struggles of that time: the assaults, the promises, the threats, the legal officials sent

---

55 At the order of the Emperor Valens, eighty ecclesiastics were sent to sea in a vessel off the coast of Bithynia in 370 and perished when it was destroyed by fire. It is reported that the fire was set at Valens' command.

56 Cf. Rom. 9.11ff. Gregory's Jacob here was Athanasius; his Esau, George of Cappadocia.

to attempt to win him over, the military and those from the women's apartments who are men among women and women among men, whose only manliness was their impiety, and who, incapable of natural licentiousness, prostitute themselves in the only way they can—with their tongues; the chief cook, Nabuzardan,[57] who threatened us with the knives of his art and was sent back to his own fire. But what to me was most admirable in the conduct of Basil and what I could not pass over, even if I wished, I will recount as succinctly as possible.

(48) Who does not know the prefect[58] of those days, who personally treated us with special arrogance? He was initiated —or rather finished—in baptism by the other party. He was excessively subservient to his chief and, by showing him compliance in every way, he strove to ensure and prolong his own possession of power. It was before this man, who was raging against the Church, having assumed the manner of a lion and roaring like a lion, so that most men did not dare to approach him, that our noble champion was brought. Rather, he entered his court as though summoned to a banquet and not a judgment. How can I give an adequate account either of the insolence of the prefect or of the wisdom with which Basil met his attack? 'What do you mean, you, sir,' he said, adding his name, for he did not yet deign to call him bishop, 'by daring to resist so great a power, and by being the only one to speak out with arrogance?' 'In what respect,' replied our champion, 'and what is this madness you speak of? I do not yet understand.' 'Because you do not honor the religion of your sovereign,' he said, 'when all others have given way and submitted.' 'I do not,' said Basil, 'for this is not the will of my

---

57 Better known by his Greek name Demosthenes, a creature of Valens, who in spite of his ignorance played a prominent role in the conflict between orthodoxy and Arianism.
58 Modestus, praetorian prefect of the East under Valens.

true Sovereign, and I cannot bring myself to worship a creature, as I am a creature of God and bidden to be a god.'[59] 'But we, what are we in your eyes? Or are we nothing,' said the prefect, 'who give you these commands? Besides, is it not a great thing for you to be ranged with us and have us as your associates?' 'You are indeed prefects,' said Basil, 'and illustrious, I will not deny it, but in no way more honorable than God. To be associated with you is a great thing, certainly. You also are creatures of God. But I would be associated with you as with any of my subjects. Faith, not the person, is the characteristic mark of Christianity'.

(49) Then the prefect became excited and seethed all the more with rage. He rose from his seat and addressed Basil in harsher tones. 'What,' he said, 'are you not afraid of my authority?' 'Afraid of what? What could I suffer?' 'Any one of the many punishments which lie within my power.' 'What are these? Make them known to me.' 'Confiscation, exile, torture, death.' 'If there is anything else,' said Basil, 'threaten me with that, too, for none of these you mentioned can affect me.' The prefect said to him: 'How can that be true?' 'Because,' said Basil, 'the man who possesses nothing is not liable to confiscation, unless you want, perhaps, these tattered rags, and a few books, which represent all my possessions. As for exile, I do not know what it is, since I am not circumscribed by any place, nor do I count as my own the land where I now dwell or any land into which I may be cast. Rather, all belongs to God, whose passing guest I am. And as for torture, how can they rack a body that exists no longer, unless you refer to the first stroke, for of this alone you are the master? Death will be a benefit, for it will send me to God sooner. For Him I live and order my life, and for the most part have died, and to Him I have long been hastening.'

---

59 Cf. John 10.34.

(50) These words astounded the prefect. 'No one,' he said, 'up to this day has ever spoken in such a manner and with such boldness to me,' and he added his own name. 'Perhaps you have never met a bishop,' said Basil, 'or he would have spoken in exactly the same way, having the same interests to defend. For in other respects, prefect, we are reasonable and more submissive than anyone else, for so our law prescribes. We do not show ourselves supercilious to such high authority or even to any ordinary person. But when God's interests are endangered or at stake, we count the rest as nothing, and look to these alone. Fire and sword and wild beasts and tongs that tear the flesh are a source of delight to us rather than of terror. Therefore, go on with your insults and your threats, do whatever you will, make the most of your authority. Let the emperor hear this, also, that you will never prevail on us or persuade us to make a covenant with impiety, even though you utter threats still more violent.'

(51) After this colloquy, the prefect realized that Basil's attitude was such that nothing could terrify or overcome him, so he sent him forth and dismissed him, no longer with the same threats but with a certain respect and deference. Then he himself hastened as quickly as he could to the emperor. 'My lord,' he said, 'we have been worsted by the head of this church. The man is superior to threats, deaf to arguments, incapable of persuasion. Some other more ignoble person must be tried. But on this man either open force must be used, or do not expect that he will yield to our threats.' At these words, the emperor, condemning his own conduct and overcome by the praises of Basil, for even an enemy can admire a man's courage, forbade the employment of force. And the same thing occurred in his case as happens to iron which, while it is softened in the fire, still remains iron. Although his threats had changed to admiration, he did not enter into communion with Basil, being ashamed to make the change,

but he sought the most expedient means to justify himself, as my discourse will now show.

(52) For the emperor entered the church with all his retinue. It was the day of Epiphany and the church was thronged. He took his place among the people and thus gave the appearance of professing unity. Once he was inside, the singing of the psalms struck his ears like thunder, and he observed the sea of people and the orderly behavior, more angelical than human, prevailing in the sanctuary and its precincts. He saw Basil posted, facing the people, standing erect, as the Scripture describes Samuel,[60] with body and eyes and mind undisturbed, as though nothing unusual had happened, but like a pillar, if I may say so, attached to God and the altar, while those about him stood in fear and reverence. At this spectacle, such as he had never seen before, the emperor experienced a feeling that was only human, and dimness and dizziness enveloped his eyes and his mind, because of his awe. This fact still escaped the notice of most of the people. But when the time came for him to present at the divine table the gifts which had to be offered with his own hands, and no one, as was the custom, assisted him, since it was not clear whether Basil would receive them, then his feelings were clearly manifested. For he began to stagger, and, if one of the ministers of the sanctuary had not lent his hand to support his wavering steps, he would have suffered a lamentable fall. But let this suffice.

(53) As to the words spoken by Basil to the emperor with such surpassing wisdom when once again he entered into communion with us in a sort of way, and passed within the veil to see and speak to Basil, as he had desired to do for a long time, what must I say but that in truth they were the utterances of God which were heard by those about the emperor and by us who had gone in with them at the same time.

---
60 Cf. 1 Kings 19.20.

This was the origin of the kindly feeling of the emperor toward us, and the beginning of our restoration. This reception dissipated like a stream most of the abusive treatment then besetting us.

(54) There was another incident no less important than those I have mentioned. The wicked were triumphant, exile was decreed for Basil, and nothing was lacking for the execution of this design. The night was at hand, the carriage was ready, our enemies were jubilant, the pious were disheartened, as we gathered about the eager traveler; in a word, all details pertaining to that honorable disgrace had been completed. What happened then? God rescinded the decree. He who struck the first-born of Egypt for its harshness against Israel[61] also afflicted the son of the emperor with a stroke of disease. And how great was the speed! There was the sentence of exile; here, the decree of sickness. The hand of the impious scribe was stayed, the saint was preserved, and the man of piety became the gift of a fever which curbed the arrogance of an emperor. What could be more just or more speedy? The sequel was this. The son of the emperor was sick and afflicted in body, and his father suffered with him. But what did the father do? He sought everywhere for a remedy for the malady, he called in the best physicians, he resorted to prayer as never before and prostrated himself on the ground. For suffering humbles even kings, and this is not to be wondered at, for Scripture records how David long ago suffered in the same way on account of his son.[62] Finding no remedy for the evil from any source, the emperor sought refuge in the faith of Basil. But he did not summon him in his own name, because of his shame at the recent outrage. He entrusted this mission to others of his closest and dearest friends. Basil presented himself without delay and without the

---

61 Cf. Exod. 12.29.
62 Cf. 2 Kings 12.16.

reluctance which, under the circumstances, anyone else would have shown. Immediately upon his arrival, the sickness became milder, and the father was in better hope. And if he had not mingled salt water with the fresh, since at the same time that he summoned Basil he still had faith in the heretics, the child would have recovered his health and been restored safely to his father's arms. This was the belief of those who were present at the time and shared in the distress.

(55) The same thing is said to have occurred also in the case of the prefect not long afterwards. An attack of sickness caused him likewise to humble himself beneath the hands of the saint. For men of sense a stroke of calamity really becomes a source of instruction, and affliction is often a greater blessing than prosperity. He fell sick, he wept, he was in distress, he sent for Basil, he entreated him: 'You have won your defense,' he cried out. 'Only grant me recovery.' And he truly obtained it, as he himself acknowledged and assured many who had not known of it, for he did not cease to recount with admiration the actions of Basil.

Such were his relations with these men, and such the results. But did he conduct himself differently toward others, or wrangle about petty things or in a petty manner, or exhibit philosophic conduct of the average sort, best passed over in silence, or at least not very praiseworthy? By no means. He who once roused the abominable Adad against Israel[63] roused against Basil the vicar[64] of the diocese of Pontus. This man pretended to be indignant concerning a poor woman, but in reality he fought on behalf of impiety and assailed the true religion. I pass over all his other insults, numerous and grave as they were, to Basil, or, I might equally say, to God, the end and object of the contest. But the principal incident which covered the author of the insult with shame and exalted

---
63 Cf. 3 Kings 11.14.
64 His name was Eusebius.

his antagonist, if there is really anything great and lofty in philosophy and in the manifest superiority over the multitude which it confers upon its possessor, I will describe in my discourse.

(56) A certain woman of distinguished birth, shortly after the death of her husband, was being violently importuned by the assessor of a judge, who sought to draw her into marriage against her will. Not knowing how to escape this oppression, she adopted a plan no less prudent than daring. She fled to the holy table and made God her protector against outrage. In the name of the Trinity Itself—to adopt somewhat the language of the courtroom in my panegyric—what should have been done, not only by the great Basil, who had established laws for all in such cases, but by any other who, although inferior to him, nevertheless was a priest? Was it not his duty to act in her defense, to receive her, to protect her, to raise his hand on behalf of the mercy of God and the law which commands respect for the altar? Was it not his duty to be willing to do and suffer all rather than take against her any inhuman measure, and outrage the holy table and the faith of her supplication? 'No,' said this strange judge; 'all must yield to my authority, and Christians must be traitors to their own laws.' The judge sought to seize the suppliant, but Basil protected her with all his power. The former became furious and finally sent magistrates to search the saint's bedchamber, not from any necessity, but rather to dishonor him. What are you saying? Search the house of that man who was above passion, whom the angels treat with respect, upon whom women shrink to look? But this was not enough. He ordered him to appear in court and justify himself, not in any mild or kindly manner, but as if he were a man condemned. And Basil obeyed the summons. The judge was in his seat, full of wrath and arrogance. Basil remained standing, like my Jesus before the judgment seat of Pilate. The thun-

derbolts did not strike; the sword of God still glittered, but remained suspended. The bow was stretched, but was being held back to furnish an occasion for repentance. Such is God's custom.

(57) Now watch another struggle between our champion and his persecutor. The judge ordered that the ragged pallium be torn from his neck. 'I will strip myself of my tunic as well, if you so desire,' said Basil. He threatened to lash that fleshless body. Basil bowed his back to have it torn with barbs. 'By such laceration,' he said, 'you will cure my liver. You see how it is wearing me away.' Such was the interplay between them. But the city, as soon as it was aware of the evil and the peril common to all, for each person considered this outrage a danger to himself, became completely distracted and fired with passion. And like a swarm of bees roused by smoke, one after another was stirred and arose, men of all classes and ages, but particularly the imperial armorers and weavers. For in such circumstances these men are rather impetuous and are daring because of the freedom they enjoy. Each man had for a weapon what his craft supplied him or anything else improvised for the occasion. With torches in their hands, with clubs ready, and hurling stones before them, they ran in a single mass and with one cry in an enthusiasm they all shared. Anger makes a formidable soldier or general. Even the women, provoked by the situation, were armed at this time. They no longer remained women, but, strengthened by zeal, they took on the courage of men. The rest of the account is short. Their hairpins were their spears. They thought they would be sharing in an act of piety if they tore him to pieces, and that he would be most pious in their eyes who should be the first to lay hands on him who had dared this outrage. What of that bold and haughty judge? He became a suppliant, pitiable, wretched, cringing in a

most abject manner until that unbloody martyr appeared, who had won his crown without blows, and who forcefully restrained the people. He overcame them through the reverence they had for him, and he saved his persecutor, now his suppliant. This was the work of the God of saints, who makes and transforms all things for the best, who resists the proud but gives grace to the humble.[65] And why should not He who divided the sea, and stayed the river, and subdued the elements, and by the stretching of hands set up a trophy to save a fugitive people, why should not He have also delivered this man from his dangers?

(58) This was the end of the war with the world, and with God's help, its issue was a happy one and worthy of Basil's faith. But at this point began the war with the bishops and their allies, which was a source of great scandal and still greater harm to their subjects. For, who could persuade others to be moderate when their religious leaders were not so disposed? Their ill will toward Basil was of long standing and based on three motives. They were not in agreement with him in the matter of the faith unless the pressure of the multitude absolutely forced them. They had not completely laid aside the resentment they felt at his election. And what vexed them most, though it would have been most shameful to admit it, was the fact that his prestige was far superior to their own. But still another dissension arose which revived these others.

When our country had been divided into two provinces and two metropolitan sees and a considerable portion of the older was being added to the new one, a renewal of party strife resulted. One bishop[66] maintained that the boundaries of our provinces should correspond with the civil division and for that reason he laid claim to the territory recently

---

65 Cf. James 4.6.
66 Anthimus, Bishop of Tyana.

added to the new province as belonging to him and as severed from its former metropolitan. The other[67] adhered to the ancient tradition and to the division coming down from our fathers. This contention resulted in many unfortunate incidents, some of which had already occurred, while others were impending. Congregations were withdrawn in underhanded fashion by the new metropolitan and their revenues appropriated to his use. The priests of the churches were either won over by persuasion or changed.

As a consequence, the affairs of the churches were reduced to a still worse state of dissension and division. For men take a certain delight in novelty and readily turn circumstances to their own unjust gain. And it is easier to overthrow the established order than to restore it when overthrown. But what enraged him most was that the revenues of the Taurus, which passed along before his eyes, were destined for Basil. He also set great store on gathering for himself the offerings at St. Orestes.[68] He went so far on one occasion, when Basil was journeying along his own road, as to seize his mules and, with the help of a gang of brigands, prevent him from proceeding. And what a specious pretext he gave! He pretended concern for his spiritual children, and souls, and the doctrine of the faith. These pleas merely masked his cupidity and were easy to invent, as was his assertion that revenues should not be paid to heretics. Anyone who irked him was labeled a heretic.

(59) Yet the holy man of God, truly the metropolitan of the Jerusalem above, was neither carried away with those who fell into error, nor did he suffer himself to overlook these events, nor did he contemplate a weak remedy for the evil. But let us consider how noble and admirable it was and, what else shall I say, how worthy of his soul. For he turned dis-

---
67 St. Basil.
68 A chapel at the foot of Mt. Taurus.

sension into a source of increase for the Church, and settled the trouble in the best possible way by the multiplication of bishops in the country. From this there followed three excellent results: a greater solicitude for souls, self-management for each city, and in this way a cessation of strife. In this project I fear that I myself was just an appendage, to use the most fitting term that occurs to me now. For, while in general I admire this man far more than I can say, of this one thing I cannot approve—I will acknowledge my chagrin, although from other sources it is not unknown to many of you—I mean his strangeness and distrust toward me, a cause of pain which not even time has effaced. This has been responsible for all the inconsistency and confusion in my life and for my inability to practice philosophy or to be esteemed for philosophy, although the last point is of little importance. Yet one should permit me to say in his defense that his thoughts were beyond those of men, and his detachment from this world before he departed from life caused him to refer all things to the Spirit. He recognized the respect due to friendship and he disregarded it only where the honor of God had prior claim and when he had to esteem the object of our hopes as more important than what he set aside.

(60) I am afraid that in trying to escape the reproach of negligence which may be made by those who are anxious to know every detail of Basil's life, I may be charged with prolixity by those who praise the golden mean, which he esteemed highly, approving especially the maxim, 'The mean in all things is best,'[69] and observing it throughout his life. However, I will disregard both those who are unduly concise and those who are too prolix, and will thus proceed with my discourse. Different men are successful along different lines, devoting themselves to one of the many forms of excellence. But no one, at least of those actually known to me, has ever

---
69 A saying ascribed to Cleobulus, one of the Seven Wisemen of Greece.

succeeded in attaining the highest degree in all. But he is best in my opinion who has attained eminence in most or pre-eminence in one. Basil reached such perfection in all things as to be a subject of pride for universal nature. Let us consider the matter further.

I take it that a man of simple and frugal life, without possessions of any kind, is a subject for praise. What did he ever possess except his body and the necessary coverings for his flesh? His wealth was to have nothing, possessing the cross, which alone was his life, and which he deemed more precious than great riches. No man, even if he has the desire, can gain possession of all things, but one can know how to despise all and thereby show himself superior to all. With such thoughts and leading such a life, Basil had no need of a pedestal, of empty glory, of a public proclamation: 'Crates sets Crates the Theban free.'[70] For he strove not to seem but to be excellent. He did not live in a tub in the middle of the market place[71] to gain publicity for himself and to turn his poverty into a novel means of enriching himself. He was poor and unkempt without any trace of pride. And being content to throw overboard all that he once possessed, he sailed lightly laden across the sea of life.

(61) An admirable thing is temperance and contentment with little and freedom from the tyranny of pleasures and from the servitude of that cruel and degrading master, the belly. Who was so independent of food, I could almost say even free from the flesh? Surfeit and satiety he renounced to the foolish whose life is servile and prone to baseness. He had little regard for those things which, when they passed below the gullet, are of equal value. He was content to live on mere necessities as long as he could, and the only luxury he knew was to prove himself free from luxury, and on that

---

70 A saying ascribed to the Cynic philosopher, Crates of Thebes.
71 The allusion is to Diogenes, the Cynic, and his tub.

account to have no need of more. But he looked to the lilies
and the birds,[72] whose beauty is natural and whose food is
found at random, in accordance with the great precept of
my Christ, who assumed the poverty of the flesh for our
sake, that we might be enriched with His divinity.[73] Hence,
he had only one tunic and one threadbare cloak, the ground
was his bed, he kept vigils, and he went unwashed. Such were
the forms of his luxury. For his favorite repast and relish he
had bread and salt, that new delicacy! And his sober and
plentiful drink was what fountains supply without toil. As a
consequence, or, rather, as an accompaniment of these things,
came the care of the sick and the practice of medicine, our
common intellectual avocation. For I must reckon myself his
equal in distress, though his inferior in other respects.

(62) A great thing is virginity and celibacy, and to be
ranked with the angels, and with the single nature. I shrink
from saying with Christ's, who, having willed to be born for
us who are born, was born of a virgin, giving the force of law
to virginity to detach us from this life and cut off the world,
or, rather, to put away one world for another, the present
for the future. Who, more than he, either esteemed virginity or
imposed laws on the flesh, not only by his own example but
by the objects of his zeal? Whose are the convents and the
written rules by which he subjected all the senses and regulated
all the members, and urged the practice of true virginity,
turning the eye of beauty inward, from the visible to the invisible, withering away the external, and withdrawing the
fuel from the flame, but showing what is hidden to God, who
alone is the pure bridegroom of souls, who takes in with
Him vigilant souls, if they meet Him with their lamps burning
and an abundant supply of oil?[74] The solitary life and the

---

72 Cf. Matt. 6.26-34.
73 Cf. 2 Cor. 8.9.
74 Cf. Matt. 25.1-13.

community life were then in conflict and dissension in many ways, and neither completely possessed advantages or disadvantages that were unmixed. The one is more tranquil and stable and leads to union with God, but it is not free from pride, because its virtue escapes testing and comparison. The other is more practical and useful, but does not escape turbulence. Basil reconciled and united the two in the most excellent way. He caused hermitages and monasteries[75] to be built, not far from his cenobites and his communities of ascetics. He did not divide and separate them from each other by any intervening wall, as it were. He brought them close together, yet kept them distinct, that the life of contemplation might not be divorced from community life or the active life from contemplation, but, like the land and the sea, they might interchange their blessings and be united in their sole object, the glory of God.

(63) What more? A noble thing is philanthropy and the support of the poor and the assistance of human weakness. Go forth a little from this city and behold the new city,[76] the storehouse of piety, the common treasury of the wealthy, where superfluous riches, sometimes even necessities, thanks to the exhortations of Basil, are laid up, unexposed to the moths[77] and no source of joy to the thief, escaping the assaults of envy and the corruption of time. There, sickness is endured with equanimity, calamity is a blessing, and sympathy is put to the test. Why should I compare with this work seven-gated Thebes or Egyptian Thebes, or the walls of Babylon, or the tomb of the Carian Mausolus, or the Pyramids, or the huge Colossus of bronze, or the grandeur and beauty of temples that are no more,[78] or any of the other things men admire and consign to history, things which

---
75 Used here in the literal sense of abodes for solitaries.
76 St. Basil's hospital or hospice for the sick.
77 Cf. Matt. 6.19.
78 Almost a complete list of the seven wonders of the ancient world.

brought no profit to their founders beyond a little glory? This to me is the most wonderful achievement of all, the short road to salvation and the easiest ascent to heaven. We no longer have before our eyes the terrible and pitiable spectacle of men who are living corpses, dead in most of their limbs, driven away from their cities and homes, public places, fountains, even from their dearest ones, and more easily recognized by their names than by their bodily features. They no longer appear at our public assemblies or social gatherings as objects, not of pity for their disease, but of loathing, expert in singing piteous songs, if any voice is still left in them.

But why should I deck out my description in tragic phrase, when no words are adequate to depict their suffering? It was he above all who urged us as men not to despise our fellows or to dishonor Christ, the one Head of all of us, by our inhumanity to these creatures, but in the misfortunes of others to consult well our own interests, and to lend to God the mercy of which we stand in need ourselves. Therefore, he did not disdain to honor disease with his lips, that noble man of noble family and dazzling renown, but he greeted the sick like brothers, but not, as one might think, from vainglory. For who was farther removed from that sentiment? But he set us an example by his own Christian spirit of approaching them and caring for their bodies, a mute but eloquent exhortation. Nor was the situation different in the city from that in the country and beyond. On the contrary, he proposed, as a common object of emulation for all leaders of the people, charity and generosity toward the sick. Others had their cooks and rich tables and enchanting refinements of cuisine, and elegant carriages, and soft flowing garments. Basil had his sick, and the dressing of their wounds, and the imitation of Christ, cleansing leprosy not by word but in deed.

(64) In the light of these things, what can they who charge him with pride and arrogance say to us—those

severe critics of such conduct, who to the standard apply standards which are not standards? Was it possible that he who embraced lepers and descended to such humiliation could yet treat with disdain those who were in health? And that he who consumed his flesh by austerity should puff up his soul with vainglory? Was it possible to condemn the Pharisee and dwell upon the debasing effect of his pride, to know Christ, who lowered Himself to the form of a slave, who ate with publicans and washed the feet of His disciples, who did not disdain the cross that He might nail my sin to it—although nothing is more wonderful than this, to contemplate God crucified, in the company of thieves and mocked by passersby, Him who was invincible and beyond all suffering—and yet for Basil to raise himself above the clouds and recognize no equal, as his slanderers believe? But the steadfastness and firmness and integrity of his character is, I imagine, what they have termed pride. These same men, in my opinion, would readily call courage temerity, and circumspection cowardice, and temperance misanthropy, and justice insociability. For that sage maxim was not badly stated, namely, that the vices are closely rooted beside the virtues and, in a certain sense, are next-door neighbors.[79] And it is very easy for a man to be mistaken for what he is not by those who are not well trained in such matters.

Who either cherished virtue or repressed vice more than he, or showed himself so benign to the upright or more severe to wrong-doers? His very smile was often a commendation and his silence a reproach, a touchstone of evil for the inner conscience. And if one has not been a chatterer and a jester and a man about town, or popular with the crowd, by becoming all to all and pleasing all, what of that? Does he not deserve praise rather than blame, at least in the eyes of men

---

79 The thought is found expressed in similar language in Aristotle and Menander.

of sense? Unless the lion is to be censured because he does not look like an ape, but is terrible and royal, and his leap a noble thing, admirable and pleasing, while actors are to be admired as charming and kindly, because they gratify the crowd and excite laughter by slapping one another in the face and raising a shout. Yet, if we may examine this point, who was so pleasant in social contact, as I myself know from long experience with him? Who was so delightful in his story-telling, so penetrating in his wit, so gentle in repartee? And never did he turn censure into arrogance or indulgence into weakness, but he avoided excess in either, making use of both fitly and in season, following the precepts of Solomon, who has assigned a season for all things.[80]

(65) But what are these things compared to his excellence in eloquence and the power of his teaching, by which he endeared to himself the ends of the earth? We are still engaged at the foot of the mountain, far from the summit. We are still crossing the narrows, having turned away from the deep and mighty ocean. For I think that if there ever has been, or will be, a trumpet penetrating the immensity of space, or a voice of God encompassing the world, or a universal earthquake resulting from some new wonder or miracle, his voice and mind were as all of these, leaving all men as far behind and below him as we surpass irrational creatures.

Who purified himself more for the Spirit and was better prepared to explain divine things? Who, more than he, was enlightened by the light of knowledge, and penetrated the depths of the Spirit and searched out the things of God with God's help? Whose language could better elucidate the thought of the mind, since he did not limp, as most men, through inability to express his ideas, or through the failure of his mind to keep pace with his eloquence. But he was remarkable on both counts alike and showed himself his own

---

80 Cf. Eccle. 3.1.

equal and truly perfect. To search out all things, even the deep things of God, is attested to be one of the attributes of the Spirit,[81] not because He is ignorant of them, but because He takes delight in their contemplation. Basil, accordingly, had searched out all the things of the Spirit, and from that Source came his power to instruct every character and deliver his sublime teaching and draw men's minds from present things to prepare for things to come.

(66) The sun is praised by David for its beauty, its grandeur, the rapidity of its course, and its power, splendid as a bridegroom, in magnitude as a giant;[82] so great is its power from its long circuit that it illumines the heavens with equal light from end to end, and distance does not diminish its heat. Basil's beauty was virtue, his greatness theology, his course the incessant movement that carried him up to God in its ascents, his power the sowing and the diffusion of the word. And so I will not hesitate to say that his sound has gone forth into all the earth and the power of his words unto the end of the world, as St. Paul has said of the Apostles, borrowing his words from David.[83] What other joy is there in any assembly today? What pleasure in banquets, in public places, in churches? What delight among those in office and their subordinates, among the hermits or the cenobites, among those who have leisure or those who are busy, among those who follow profane philosophy or ours? There is but one, running through all and the greatest: his writings and works. Nor do writers after him need any other source materials, beyond his writings. All the ancient work on which men toiled hard to elucidate the divine oracles are silent, while these new writings are bruited about, and he is considered most learned who happens to be best acquainted

---

81 Cf. 1 Cor. 2.10.
82 Cf. Ps. 18.6.
83 Cf. Ps. 18.5; Rom. 10.18.

with them, who has them on his tongue, and who expounds them to others. For he alone has sufficed to take the place of all in the minds of those who are eager for instruction.

(67) This only will I say of him. Whenever I take his *Hexaemeron* in my hands and savor its words, I am put in the presence of the Creator, and understand the account of creation, and I admire my Creator more than before, using my eyes only as my teacher. When I chance upon his controversial works, I see the fire of Sodom,[84] by which wicked and criminal tongues are reduced to ashes, or the tower of Chalane,[85] impiously constructed and justly destroyed. When I turn to his works treating of the Spirit, I find the God I possess, and I speak the truth boldly, thanks to the support of his theology and contemplation. When I peruse his other commentaries which he composed for the short-sighted, after inscribing them in three forms on the solid tablets of his heart, I am persuaded not to be content with the literal interpretation, or to fix my attention on things merely on the surface, but to advance further and to proceed from depth to depth, calling deep on deep,[86] and finding light after light, until I reach the topmost peak. When I peruse his panegyrics on the martyrs, I despise the body, I am in communion with those he is praising, and I am roused to the struggle. Whenever I peruse his moral and practical treatises, I am purified, soul and body, and become a temple ready to receive God, and an instrument struck by the Spirit, chanting hymns to the glory and power of God. By this means my mood is changed and I am put in harmony, and I become another man, undergoing a divine transformation.

(68) Since I have mentioned theology and the surpassing sublimity of Basil in treating of this subject, I will also add

---
84 Cf. Gen. 19.24.
85 Chalane is the Septuagint reading for Babel.
86 Cf. Ps. 41.8.

this to what has been said. For it will be most useful to the public and prevent it from harming itself by holding a somewhat low opinion concerning him. These words are directed against those perverse men who support their own vices by their calumnies against others. For he, in behalf of the true doctrine, and the union and co-equal divinity of the Holy Trinity, to use the most exact and the clearest terms, would have readily welcomed as a gain, not a peril, not only violent removal from the throne which not even from the very beginning had he been eager to assume, but also exile and death and tortures before death. This is clear from what he actually did and suffered. For when he had been sentenced to exile for the sake of truth, he concerned himself only to the extent of telling one of his attendants to take up his writing tablets and follow him. But he deemed it necessary to order his words with judgment,[87] according to the counsel of the divine David on this point, and tolerate for a little while the time of war and the domination of the heretics, until the time of liberty and peace should come and allow freedom of speech. For they sought to seize upon the bald statement concerning the Spirit, namely, 'the Spirit is God.' Though this is true, it was regarded as impious by them and by the wicked champion of their impiety. Their purpose was to banish Basil and his theological teaching from the city and, occupying the church themselves, to make it a base of operations for their wickedness, and from that point, as from a citadel, to overrun everything else. But he, by the use of other terms from Scripture, and by indisputable testimonies of identical meaning, and by conclusive arguments, so overpowered his adversaries that they could not withstand him, but found themselves trapped by their own statements—the best proof of the power and wisdom of his reasoning. This is clear also from the treatise he composed on the subject, in

---

87 Cf. Ps. 111.5.

which his pen was guided as though it belonged to the Spirit. He put off for the time the employment of the exact term,[88] asking it as a favor from the Spirit Himself and His loyal champions not to be annoyed at this procedure, nor, by clinging to a single expression, to ruin everything by an insatiable strictness at a time when the true religion was in process of being torn asunder. He urged that no injury would result to them from a slight change of expression, or by teaching the same truth in other terms, and that our salvation does not depend more on words than on actions. For not even the Jews should be rejected if they should consent to join our ranks, asking only that they be allowed for a time to use the word 'Anointed' for 'Christ,' whereas the greatest harm would come to the community if the Church were seized by the heretics.

(69) That he, as well as any one, acknowledged that the Spirit was God is quite clear from his frequent public preaching of this truth, whenever occasion offered, and from his forthright confession of it when he was questioned in private. But he indicated it more clearly in his conversations with me, as he concealed nothing when he took common counsel with me on this subject. He was not content with a simple declaration on this point, but, something he had rarely ever done before, he formulated against himself the most frightful imprecation, that he should be cast out by the Spirit Himself if he did not worship the Spirit as consubstantial and co-equal with the Father and the Son. If I am accepted as an associate of Basil even in such matters, I will disclose something hitherto unknown to most men. When circumstances had reduced us to such straits and he himself had adopted the procedure referred to, he yet granted freedom of speech to me, whom no one, because of my obscurity, was likely to hale into court or expel from the country, so that

---
88 I.e., the phrase, 'God, the Holy Spirit.'

through the efforts of both of us our Gospel might remain firm.

I have not mentioned these details to defend his reputation, for he is above his detractors, if there are any, but that men may not regard only the terms found in his writings as the standard definition of the truth, and feel their faith weakened, and consider the theology of Basil as an argument in favor of their own perversity, a theology which was shaped by the Spirit as well as by circumstances. Rather, they should ponder the sense of his writings and the purpose for which he composed them, and so be drawn to the truth and silence the impious. Would that his theology were mine and that of everyone dear to me! I am so confident of the integrity of this man as to make common cause with him in this as in all else. And may what is mine be ascribed to him, and what is his to me, before God and discerning men! For we would not assert that the Evangelists contradict one other because some have occupied themselves more with the humanity of Christ and others have emphasized more His divinity, some having begun with what is within our own comprehension and others with what is beyond it. They thus divided their preaching in the interest, I think, of those who receive it, and thus they were formed by the Spirit dwelling within them.

(70) There have been many men, we know, in the Old Testament and the New, remarkable for piety, as lawgivers, generals, prophets, teachers, men brave to the shedding of blood. Let us compare our Basil with them and thereby obtain a full appreciation of his worth. Adam was deemed worthy of the hand of God,[89] and the delights of paradise,[90] and the first legislation.[91] But unless I am saying something slanderous against the respect due our first parent, he did not keep the

---
89 Cf. Gen. 1.27.
90 Cf. Gen. 2.8.
91 Cf. Gen. 2.16.

command. But Basil received it and observed it and suffered no harm from the tree of knowledge, and I am certain that he has escaped the flaming sword and entered into the possession of paradise. Enos was the first who began to call upon the Lord.[92] Basil not only called upon Him, but, what is much more deserving of honor, he preached Him to others. Henoch was translated,[93] gaining his translation as the reward of a little piety—for the faith was still in shadow—and escaped the danger of a prolonged life. But Basil's whole life was a translation and he was completely tested in a complete life. Noe was entrusted with the ark[94] and the seeds of a new world were committed to a few bits of wood and preserved amid the waters. Basil escaped a deluge of impiety and made his city an ark of safety, sailing buoyantly over the waters of the heretics, and subsequently restored the whole world.

(71) Abraham was great and a patriarch and the offerer of a new sacrifice,[95] offering to Him who had given it the first fruit of His promise, a ready victim, hastening to the slaughter. But Basil's sacrifice was also great when he offered himself to God, without anything being offered in his place in equal compensation—for where could such be found? And so his auspicious sacrifice was consummated. Isaac was promised before his birth.[96] But Basil offered himself of his own free will, and he espoused his Rebecca, I mean the Church, not sought from afar through the mediation of a servant,[97] but granted and entrusted to him by God near his home. Nor was he outwitted in the preference of his children, but he apportioned to each what was deserved, without any deceit, with the judgment of the Spirit.

---

92 Cf. Gen. 4.26.
93 Cf. Gen. 5.24.
94 Cf. Gen. 6.13ff.
95 Cf. Gen. 22.1ff.
96 Cf. Gen. 18.10ff.
97 Cf. Gen. 24.3ff.

I praise the ladder of Jacob and the pillar which he anointed in honor of God, and his wrestling with Him— whatever was its nature. It was, I think, the contrast and opposition of man's lowly condition in relation to the sublimity of God, and from that struggle he bears also the marks of the defeat of his race. I praise also his skill and his success with his flocks and the twelve patriarchs born of him, and the distribution of his blessings, with their noble prophecy of the future. But I praise also the ladder of Basil, which he not only saw but mounted by his gradual ascents in virtue, and the pillar which he did not anoint but which he erected to God, branding with infamy the teachings of the impious. I praise the contest which he undertook, not against God, but in behalf of God, to overthrow the heretics. I praise his pastoral skill by which he enriched himself, gaining a greater number of the marked than the unmarked sheep. I praise his glorious fruitfulness in children begotten according to God and the benediction by which he supported many.

(72) Joseph was dispenser of grain,[98] but only in Egypt, and then not often, and for bodily sustenance only. Basil provided all men and at all times with spiritual food and, therefore, in my opinion, commands greater respect. Like Job of the land of Hus,[99] Basil was tried and prevailed, and he was gloriously proclaimed as victor at the end of his struggles. Unshaken by the attacks of his many assailants and winning a decisive victory over the tempter, he silenced the protests of his unreasoning friends, who did not understand the secret of his suffering.

'Moses and Aaron among His priests.'[100] Great indeed was Moses, who afflicted Egypt grievously and saved his people by many signs and prodigies,[101] who went within the

---
98 Cf. Gen. 41.40ff.
99 Cf. Job 1.1.
100 Ps. 98.6.
101 Cf. Exod. 7.8ff.

cloud and instituted the twofold law: the law of the letter without and the law of the spirit within. Aaron, also, the brother of Moses according to the flesh and the spirit, sacrificed and prayed in behalf of the people,[102] as consecrated minister of the great and holy tabernacle, 'which the Lord has erected and not man.'[103] Basil was a rival of both, afflicting not by bodily but by spiritual plagues the Egyptian race of heretics. He led an acceptable people, pursuing good works,[104] to the land of promise, inscribing on unbreakable and enduring tables laws no longer shadowy but completely spiritual. He entered into the Holy of Holies not once a year, but many times, even daily, I may say, and from this source he revealed to us the Trinity. Finally, he cleansed the people not by temporary sprinklings, but by eternal purifications.

For what was Josue most illustrious?[105] His generalship, and his distribution of the lots, and the taking possession of the Holy Land. But was not Basil a general, and a commander of those saved by the faith? Was he not a distributor of the various lots and abodes close to God, which he assigned to his followers, so that he also could say: 'The lines are fallen unto me in goodly places,'[106] and 'My lots are in Thy hands'?[107] These lots are far more precious than those which fall to us on earth and which can be snatched away.

(73) And if we wish to mention the judges in passing, or at least the most illustrious of the judges, there was 'Samuel among them that call upon His name,'[108] who was given to God before birth,[109] and was sanctified immediately after birth, and who anointed kings and priests with his

---

102 Cf. Exod. 29.4ff.
103 Heb. 8.2.
104 Cf. Titus 2.14.
105 Cf. Josue 1.2ff.
106 Ps. 15.6.
107 Ps. 30.16.
108 Ps. 98.6.
109 Cf. 1 Kings 1.20

horn.¹¹⁰ But was not Basil from infancy and from the very womb consecrated to God, and presented with a mantle at the altar?¹¹¹ Was he not a seer of heavenly things, and the anointed of the Lord, and the anointer of those who are perfected through the Spirit? David was celebrated among kings¹¹² and his many victories and triumphs have been recorded. Meekness was his distinguishing mark,¹¹³ and, before his kingship, his power with the harp, subduing by its enchantment even the evil spirit. Solomon asked and obtained from God largeness of heart,¹¹⁴ and advanced to the very highest degree of wisdom and contemplation, so that he became the most famous of all the men of his time. Basil, in my estimation, did not fall short, or but little, of the meekness of the one or the wisdom of the other. And so he calmed the arrogance of emperors who were under the spell of demons. The renown of his wisdom did not cause a queen of the south or any other such personage to come from the ends of the earth to meet him, but his wisdom was well known in all the ends of the earth themselves. The rest of the history of Solomon I shall pass over. It is known to all, even if we refrain from telling it.

(74) Do you praise the fearlessness of Elias in speaking to tyrants and his translation in fire¹¹⁵ and the noble heritage of Eliseus, the sheepskin mantle, accompanied by the spirit of Elias?¹¹⁶ Then praise also the life of Basil passed in the midst of the fire, I mean in the multitude of temptations, and his preservation through fire which burnt but did not consume, the miracle of the bush.¹¹⁷ Praise also the fair garment of

---

110 Cf. 1 Kings 16.13.
111 Cf. 1 Kings 2.19.
112 Cf. 2 Kings 5.1ff.
113 Cf. Ps. 131.1.
114 Cf. 3 Kings 4.29.
115 Cf. 4 Kings 1.1ff.
116 Cf. 4 Kings 2.9ff.
117 Cf. Exod. 3.2.

skin which came to him from on high, his fleshlessness. I shall omit other parallels, as the young men bedewed in the flames,[118] and the fugitive prophet praying in the belly of the fish[119] and coming forth from the monster as from a chamber. I shall pass over the just man in the den, restraining the ferocity of the lions,[120] and the struggle of the seven Machabees,[121] who with a priest and their mother were perfected by blood and all kinds of tortures. Basil emulated their endurance and achieved their glory.

(75) I shall pass now to the New Testament, and by comparing the life of Basil with its glorious heroes I shall honor the disciple through his teachers. Who was the precursor of Jesus? John,[122] the voice of the Word, the lamp of the Light, before whom he even leaped in the womb,[123] and whom he proceeded to limbo, sent there by the fury of Herod, that there also he might herald His coming. And if my language seems bold to anyone, let him assure himself at the outset that it is not my purpose in making this comparison to place Basil above or even on a par with him who was above all those born of women,[124] but to show that he emulated him and bore in his own person something of the character of John. For it is no little credit to the good that they are imitators of the greatest men, even in a small way. For was not Basil a visible image of the philosophy of John? He also dwelt in the desert and wore at night a garment of hair, concealing it from men and avoiding display. He was also content with the same kind of food, purifying himself for God by abstinence. He was also deemed worthy to be a herald, if not a precursor, of Christ. And there went out to

---

118 Cf. Dan. 3.5ff.
119 Cf. Jonas 2.1ff.
120 Cf. Dan. 14.28ff.
121 Cf. 2 Mach. 7.1ff.
122 Cf. Luke 3.4.
123 Cf. Luke 2.41.
124 Cf. Matt. 11.11.

him not only all the country round about but also that beyond its boundaries. He, also, standing between the two Testaments, abolished the letter of the one by publishing abroad the spirit of the other, and, by the dissolution of the visible law, bringing about the realization of the law which was hidden.

(76) He imitated the zeal of Peter,[125] the energy of Paul, the faith of both of these men famous in name and for their change of name, the sublime eloquence of the sons of Zebedee, and the frugality and the simplicity of all the disciples. Therefore, the keys of heaven were also entrusted to him.[126] And not only 'from Jerusalem round about as far as Illyricum,'[127] but he embraced a wider circle for the Gospel. He was a son of thunder,[128] not in name, but in fact. He reposed on the breast of Jesus and drew thence his power of speech and the depth of his thoughts. He was prevented from becoming a Stephen,[129] despite his eager desire, since he restrained by reverence those who would have stoned him.

To avoid going into details in each individual case, I shall have to speak more concisely as regards virtues; he discovered some, he emulated others, and others he surpassed. In his progress through all the virtues he was superior to all the men of our day. There is only one more point, and I shall cover it briefly.

(77) So great were the virtue and the surpassing reputation of this man that many of his minor traits and even his physical defects have been affected by others as means of gaining esteem. I mention, by way of example, his pallor, his beard, his manner of walking, his pensive and, in general,

---

125 Cf. Acts 4.8ff.
126 Cf. Matt. 16.19.
127 Rom. 15.19.
128 Cf. Mark 3.17.
129 Cf. Acts 7.58.

introspective, hesitation in speaking, which, in the badly conceived imitation of many, degenerated into melancholy. Then there were his style of dress, the shape of his bed, and his manner of eating, none of which were to him deserving of attention, being simple things and depending merely on circumstances. So you might see many Basils as far as external appearance goes, mere shadowy statues, for it would be too much to call them an echo, since an echo, while it only represents final sounds, does so quite clearly. But these men become further removed from him the more they desire to approach him. However, there is one thing which should not be regarded lightly but is a highly coveted honor, and that is to have had the opportunity to associate with him or serve him or to carry away as a souvenir some word or deed of his, gay or serious. I know that I myself have often taken pride in this. For the incidental things in Basil's life were far more precious and notable than the serious efforts of others.

(78) But when, after he had finished his course and kept the faith,[130] he had a desire to depart[131] and the time for the crown was imminent,[132] he did not hear the words: 'Go up into the mountain and die,'[133] but: 'Die and ascend to us.' At this very time he worked a wonder not inferior to those that have been mentioned. For when he was already all but dead and without breath, and life for the most part had ebbed away, he became more vigorous in his farewell words, that he might depart accompanied by pious utterances, and, by the imposition of his hands on the best of his servants, he gave them his hands and the Spirit, so that the sanctuary should not be defrauded of those who had been his disciples and assistants of his priesthood. I shrink from recounting

---

130 Cf. 2 Tim. 4.7.
131 Cf. Phil. 1.23.
132 Cf. 2 Tim. 4.8.
133 Cf. Deut. 32.49.

what followed, yet I will proceed, even though the recital would be more fitting to others than myself. For I cannot be philosophic in my sorrow, although I have tried earnestly to be so, when I think of the common loss and the calamity which has afflicted the whole world.

(79) He lay, drawing his last breath, and the choir above, upon which he long had fixed his gaze, was eagerly awaiting him. There poured about him the whole city, unable to endure his loss, crying out against his departure as against an act of tyranny, and seeking to lay hold of his soul, as though they could restrain and hold it with their hands and their prayers. Their grief rendered them distraught, and each one was eager to give him a part of his own life, if that were possible. But they were defeated, for he had to give proof that he was a mortal. When he had spoken his last words: 'Into Thy hands I commend my spirit,'[134] he joyfully gave up his soul to the angels who carried him away. Yet it was not before he had given some instruction in our holy doctrine to those who were present and rendered them better men by his final injunctions. Then occurred the most extraordinary wonder that has ever taken place.

(80) The saint was being carried out, borne aloft by the hands of holy men. All were consumed with eagerness, some to seize the hem of his garment,[135] others only to touch his shadow,[136] or the bier carrying its holy burden. For what was holier or purer than that holy body? Others sought to approach the bearers, others only to enjoy the sight, as though even this would bring them some blessing. Squares, porticoes, houses of two and three stories were filled with people escorting him, preceding, following, accompanying and treading upon one another, many thousands of every race and age, a

---

134 Ps. 30.6.
135 Cf. Luke 8.44.
136 Cf. Acts 5.15.

sight unknown before that day. The singing of psalms gave way to lamentations, and constancy of mind was destroyed by the calamity. A contest arose between our own people and outsiders, pagans, Jews, strangers, as to who should lament the more and thereby gain the greater benefit. In short, the calamity became a source of danger. Many souls departed along with him as a result of the violent pushing and tumult. And their consummation was regarded as a happy one in that they were the companions of his departure and that they were funeral victims, as one of the more emotional orators might say. When with difficulty his body had escaped the hands of those who would have seized it and had passed through those in procession before it, it was then committed to the tomb of his fathers, and the high priest was added to the priests; the mighty voice, which still rings in my ears, to the preachers; the martyr, to the martyrs.

Now he is in heaven, and there in our behalf, I am certain, he offers sacrifice and prays for the people. Though he has left us, he has not wholly left us. But I, Gregory, who am half dead and cut in two, now that our great union is sundered, drag out a painful and weary life, a natural result of my separation from him. I know not what my end shall be, now that I no longer have his guidance, although I am still being admonished and chided by him in nightly visions, whenever I fail in my duty. My purpose is not so much to mingle lamentations with my praises and sketch the manner of his life and propose a common model of virtue for all time, a salutary example for all the churches and all souls, upon which we may look as upon a living law and thus regulate our lives, but rather to counsel you who have been thoroughly imbued with his teaching, eyes fixed on him, as though he were seeing you, and you him, that you may be perfected by the Spirit.

(81) Come hither, now, and stand about me, all you

who made up his choir, both those of the sanctuary and those of lower rank, all you who are our own and all you who are ouside our fold—assist me in my eulogy, each giving or requiring an account of some virtue of his. Let those of you who have supreme authority consider the lawgiver; you public officials, the founder of the city; you of the people, his orderliness; you men of letters, the teacher; you virgins, the groom; you married people, the counselor; you hermits, him who gave you wings; you cenobites, the judge; you who are simple and sincere, your guide; you contemplatives, the theologian; you exuberant souls, the bridle; you unfortunate, your consolation; old age, its staff; youth, its preceptor; poverty, its relief; wealth, its dispenser. It seems to me also that widows should praise their protector, orphans their father, the poor the lover of the poor, strangers their host, brothers the lover of brothers, the sick their physician, whatever the disease or the treatment, the healthy the guardian of their health, and, finally, all men him who became all things to all men[137] that he might gain all, or at least as many as possible.

(82) This is my tribute to you, Basil, from a tongue that was once most sweet to you, and from him who was your peer in rank and age. If it approaches your worth, the thanks are due to you. For it was with reliance on you that I undertook this discourse concerning you. But if it is far below your worth and falls far short of your expectations, what must I feel, worn out with age and disease and longing for you? Yet, when a man does what he can it is pleasing to God. May you look down upon us from on high, O divine and sacred soul, and restrain by your intercession the thorn of the flesh,[138] given to us by God for our chastisement, or inspire us with courage to suffer it, and direct our whole life to

---

137 Cf. 1 Cor. 9.22.
138 Cf. 2 Cor. 12.7.

our greatest profit. And if we can be translated, may you receive us there also in your own tabernacle, that, living together and contemplating, with greater clarity and perfection, the holy and blessed Trinity, of which we have received now some faint image, we may put an end to our desire, and gain this recompense for all the struggles we have undertaken and endured. This, then, is my discourse in your honor. Who will there be to praise us, who leave this life after you, if indeed we should offer any matter worthy of a eulogy, in Christ Jesus our Lord, to whom be glory forever? Amen.

ON HIS SISTER, ST. GORGONIA

IN PRAISING MY SISTER, I shall be honoring my own family. Yet, while she is a member of my family, I shall not on that account praise her falsely, but because what is true is for that reason praiseworthy. Moreover, this truth is not only well founded but also well known. Nor would I be allowed to speak with partiality even if I wished to do so. The reason is that my listener stands like a skillful arbiter, between my discourse and the truth, and censures unmerited praise, yet also demands what is due, at least if he be just. And so I am not afraid of running beyond the bounds of truth, but, on the contrary, of falling short of the truth and thereby lessening her reputation by an inadequate eulogy. For it is a difficult task to find action and words to match her excellence. We should not, then, praise undeservedly the qualities of others nor should we disparage what is found in our own, if it be truly praiseworthy. Lack of relationship should not be an advantage and kinship prove to be a handicap. For in both cases, by the praise of the one and the disregard of the other, there would not be a fair and just evaluation of the truth. But if we make the truth our standard and rule, and fix our eyes on this alone, ignoring consideration of the vulgar and the mean, we shall both praise what merits praise and pass over what is deserving of silence.

(2) If we count it an unholy thing to defraud our kindred of anything, or to slander, accuse, or wrong them in any way, great or small, and regard injustice to those nearest to us as the greatest of crimes, it would be most absurd to think that we should be acting equitably in robbing them of such an oration—which is due the virtuous above all, and by which we can render their memory immortal—and be more concerned with the charges of partiality made by evil men than with the just demands of the good. Certainly, if lack of personal knowledge or evidence does not prevent us, although this would be far more just, from praising strangers, friendship and the envy of the multitude will not prevent us from praising those known to us, especially those who have departed this life, and with whom it is too late to curry favor, since they are beyond the reach, among other things, of praise or blame.

(3) Since I have sufficiently justified my position and shown that this discourse is altogether necessary on my part, let me now proceed to the eulogy proper, spurning all prettiness and elegance in style, for she whom we are praising was unadorned and regarded lack of adornment as beauty. And I shall be paying, as a most requisite debt, the last rites due the dead, and at the same time I shall be instructing all in the zealous imitation of the same virtue. My purpose in every word and action is to advance the perfection of those who are committed to my trust. Let another, with more regard for the laws of panegyric, praise the country and the family of the deceased. And he will not lack many excellent topics, if he wishes to deck her with external ornaments, as one decks a beautiful form with gold and precious stones and embellishments of art and hand. While these things betray ugliness by the very fact of their application, they cannot render more attractive the beauty which surpasses them. But having observed the rules in these matters to the extent of mentioning

our common parents, for it would be impious to pass over parents and teachers of such worth, I will turn my attention as quickly as possible to Gorgonia herself and not disappoint the wishes of those who are eager to hear about her.

(4) Who is there who does not know our new Abraham and the Sara of our time? I mean Gregory and his wife Nonna. For it is not right to omit the mention of names that are an exhortation to virtue. He was justified by faith, and she has dwelt together with the man of faith. He beyond hope has been the father of many nations and she has brought them forth spiritually. He fled the bondage of his father's gods, and she is the daughter and the mother of the free. He went forth from his kindred and his father's house[1] for the sake of the land of promise, and she was the occasion of his departure. In this one point, if I may speak a little boldly, she surpassed Sara herself. He nobly undertook this migration, and she was his zealous partner. He attached himself to the Lord, and she both called and considered her husband lord, and on that account she was in part justified. Theirs was the promise, theirs a son Isaac, as far as in them lay, and theirs the gift.

(5) This good shepherd was the product of his wife's prayers and guidance, and it was she who taught him the ideal of a good shepherd's conduct. He nobly fled from his idols, and later even put demons to flight, but she would never share salt with the worshipers of idols. They have been one in honor, one in mind, one in soul, and their bond no less a union of virtue and intimacy with God than of the flesh. They are equal in length of life and grey hairs, equal in prudence and splendor, vying with each other and excelling all the rest. Bound but a little by the flesh, even before their dissolution they have been translated hence in spirit. The world is not theirs, and the world is theirs, in that they have despised this

---

1 Cf. Gen. 12.1.

world and preferred in honor the world beyond. They have cast aside riches, yet they abound in riches through their noble traffic, since they scorn the goods of this world and deal rather in those of the next. Brief is the time remaining for them in this life, being only what is left over through their piety, but abundant and long-lasting is the life for which they have toiled. I will add still one more word about them. They have been fairly and justly apportioned to the two sexes. He is the ornament of men, she of women, and not only an ornament but also a pattern of virtue.

(6) From them Gorgonia received both her being and her good repute. They were the source of the seeds of her piety, of her noble life, and of her joyful departure with better hopes. These, indeed, are fair blessings and such as do not easily accrue to many of those who take pride in their noble birth and puff themselves up because of their lineage. But if I must discourse concerning her in a more spiritual and lofty vein, Gorgonia's native land was the heavenly Jerusalem, the city not seen by the eye but perceived by the mind, in which we are citizens and whither we are hastening. Christ is a citizen there and His fellow citizens are the 'company and the church of the firstborn who are enrolled in the heavens,'[2] and who feast about its great Founder, in contemplation of His glory, and who participate in a never-ending chorus. Her nobility lay in the preservation of the divine image, and in her assimilation to the Archetype, which is effected by reason and virtue and that pure desire, which forms ever more and more, in the things of God, those truly initiated in the heavenly mysteries, and, finally, in her knowledge of our origin, our nature, and our destiny.

(7) Such is my knowledge of these matters. Therefore, I know and proclaim that her soul was nobler than all the

---
2 Heb. 12.22,23.

people of the East,³ using a higher rule and standard for nobility and ignobility than the majority of men, and distinguishing these not by birth but by character, and judging those who are blamed or praised not according to family, but as individuals. Since, however, I speak of her virtues among those who know her, let each one contribute some particular and assist me in my discourse. It is impossible for one man, however gifted with observation and intelligence, to embrace all her qualities.

(8) She so excelled in modesty and so surpassed all the women of her own day, not to mention those of old who were greatly famed for modesty, that in the two universal divisions of life, I mean the married and the unmarried states, of which one is more sublime and divine but more difficult and perilous, while the other is lower but safer, she avoided the disadvantages of both and chose and united the sublimity of the one with the security of the other. And she was modest without being proud, blending the virtues of the married and the unmarried states, and showing that neither of these binds us completely to or separates us from God or the world. And so the one of its very nature is not to be altogether shunned nor the other exclusively praised. But it is the mind which nobly presides over both marriage and virginity, and these, like raw materials, are ordered and fashioned to virtue by the craftsman, reason. Though she was linked in carnal union, she was not on the account separated from the Spirit, nor because she had her husband as her head did she ignore her first Head. When she had served the world and nature a little, to the extent that the law of the flesh willed it, or, rather, He who imposed this law on the flesh, she consecrated herself wholly to God. And what is most excellent and honorable, she also won over her husband and gained, instead of an unreasonable

---

3 Cf. Job 1.3.

master, a good fellow servant. Not only that, she also made the fruit of her body, her children and her children's children, the fruit of her spirit, and dedicated to God, instead of her single soul, her whole family and household. And she rendered marriage itself laudable by her pleasing and acceptable life in wedlock and by the fair fruit of her union. And she exhibited herself, as long as she lived, as an exemplar of every excellence to her children. When she was summoned hence, she left her will behind her as a silent exhortation to her house.

(9) The divinely inspired Solomon in his instructive wisdom, I mean in his Proverbs,[4] praises the woman who keeps her house and loves her husband. And in contrast to the woman who wanders abroad, who is uncontrolled and dishonorable, who hunts precious souls with wanton ways and words, he praises her who is engaged honorably at home, who performs her womanly duties with manly courage, her hands constantly holding the spindle as she prepares double cloaks for her husband, who buys a field in season, and carefully provides food for her servants, and receives her friends at a bountiful table, and who exhibits all other qualities for which he extols in song the modest and industrious woman. If I were to praise my sister on such counts, it would be like praising a statue for its shadow, or a lion for his claws, to the neglect of greater perfections. Who was ever more worthy to be seen, yet was seen less and kept herself more inaccessible to the eyes of men? Who knew better than she the bounds of gravity and gaiety, so that neither her gravity might seem uncouth nor her tenderness wanton, but the one prudent and the other gentle? Her norm of propriety was kindliness combined with dignity. Listen, you women, you who are given overmuch to display and indolence, and who despise the veil of modesty. Who had such control over her eyes? Who so derided laughter that the very beginning of a smile seemed

---

4 Cf. Prov. 31.10ff.

almost too much to her? Who so barred the portals of her ears? And who opened them more to the divine words, or, rather, set her mind as guide over her tongue in narrating the judgments of God? Who so regulated her lips?

(10) I am sure that you wish me to mention also this special characteristic of hers. It regards something which to her, as to every woman truly modest and decorous in character, seemed of no account, but which is made to appear important by those who are overfond of ornament and elegance and do not suffer correction from those who try to instruct them on such matters. She was never adorned with gold fashioned by art into surpassing beauty, or with fair tresses fully or partly exposed, or with spiral curls, or with the ingenious arrangements of those who disgracefully turn the noble head into a show piece. Hers were no costly, flowing, diaphanous robes, hers no brilliant and beautiful gems, flashing color round about and causing the figure to glow with light. Hers were no devices and magic tricks of the painter, or that cheap beauty of the earthly creator who, by his rival craftsmanship, hides with deceitful pigments the image of God and disgraces it with adornment and exhibits to wanton eyes the divine form as a meretricious idol, that this counterfeit beauty may steal away that natural image which is to be preserved for God and the world to come. But while she was familiar with the many and various external ornaments of women, she recognized none as more precious than her own character and the splendor which lies within. The only red that pleased her was the blush of modesty, and the only pallor, that which comes from abstinence. But pigments and makeup, and living pictures, and flowing beauty of form she left to the women of the stage and the public squares, and to all for whom it is a disgrace and a reproach to feel ashamed.

(11) So much for this subject. But there is no one who could give an adequate account of her prudence and her

piety, or find many examples besides those of her natural and spiritual parents. On these alone she fixed her eyes, and to them she was not inferior in virtue, save that she readily gave way to them in this, that she acknowledged and confessed that she derived her goodness from them and that they were the root of her own illumination. Who could be keener in intellect than she who was known as a common counselor not only of her own family and those of the same people and the one fold, but also of all those about her, who regarded her suggestions and recommendations as an inviolable law? What was more sagacious than her words, more prudent than her silence? And since I have mentioned silence, I will add something especially characteristic of her, and most becoming to women, and most useful at the present time. Who knew better the things of God, both from the divine oracles and her own understanding? Further, who spoke less, confining herself within the womanly bounds of piety? And to mention the duty of a woman who has learned to be truly pious, that duty wherein alone insatiate desire is a noble thing, who has so adorned not only this temple, but other temples as well, with her offerings. I know not, now that she is gone, whether this one will ever be so adorned again. Who had such reverence for priests, and especially for him who was her fellow soldier and teacher, whose are the noble seeds, and the pair of sons consecrated to God?

(12) Who, more than she, threw open her house, with a courteous and generous welcome to those who live according to God? And, better still, who received them with such modesty, or advanced to meet them in a manner so pleasing to God? Further, who displayed a mind more tranquil in misfortune, or a heart more sympathetic to those in distress? Who was more liberal to those in want? I would not hesitate to praise her in the words of Job: 'Her door was open to

every traveler, the stranger did not stay without.'[5] 'She was an eye to the blind, and a foot to the lame, and a mother to orphans.'[6] Of her compassion toward widows, what more need I say than that she received as its fruit never to be called a widow herself? Her house was a common hospice for all her needy relatives, and her goods were as common to all the needy as their own personal belongings. 'She hath distributed, she hath given to the poor.'[7] Because of the infallible truth of the divine promise, she stored up many treasures in the heavenly coffers, and often received Christ Himself in the person of the many to whom she had shown kindness. Best of all, she was more truly what she was than she appeared to be, and in secret she cultivated piety for Him who sees secret things. She snatched everything from the prince of this world, and she transferred it to safe storehouses. She left nothing behind to earth except her body. She exchanged all things for the hopes above. The only riches she left to her children were imitation of her example and emulation of her virtues.

(13) While she possessed such incredible magnanimity, she did not deliver her body to delights and the unrestrained pleasures of the belly, that mad and ravenous dog, as though she relied on her beneficence, as most men do, trying to redeem their luxury by compassion toward the poor, and, instead of healing evil by good, receive evil in the place of good. Nor, while subjecting her dust[8] by fasting, did she leave to another the medicine of lying upon the ground, nor, while she adopted this means to benefit her soul, did she limit her sleep less than anyone else. Nor did she establish this law for herself as though independent of the body, and lie upon the ground while others passed sleepless nights standing erect,

---
5 Job 31.32, with a substitution of 'her' for 'my' to suit the context.
6 Job 29.15,16, with a shift from 'I' to 'she.'
7 Ps. 111.9, with a shift from 'he' to 'she.'
8 I.e., her body.

a specially favored ascetical practice of spiritual men. Indeed, in this respect she surpassed in her fortitude not only women but the most high-minded men, in her intelligent chanting of the psalms, in her reading, explanation, and timely recollection of the divine oracles, in her bending of knees which had grown callous and, as it were, attached to the ground, in her tears to cleanse her stains with contrite heart and humility of spirit, in prayer lifting her up, and in her mind fixed in contemplation and rapture. In all these things or in any one of them, what man or woman can boast of having surpassed her? And it is a great thing to say, but nevertheless true, that, while she emulated some virtues, she was an example for emulation in others, and, while she discovered some, she excelled in others. And if we grant that there were some who rivaled her in some particular virtue, she surpassed all to this extent, that she embraced all virtues. Thus, she reached a higher perfection in all than anyone else attained, even moderately, in one, and she attained such perfection in each that one alone would have abundantly sufficed in place of all.

(14) O body uncared for, and garments bright with virtue alone! O soul, holding fast to a body all but deprived of food, as though it were immaterial, or, rather, being forced to die even before dissolution, that the soul might receive its freedom and not be fettered by the senses! O nights of vigil, and psalmody, and standing from sun to sun! O David, whose songs were never overlong for faithful souls! O tender limbs, thrown prostrate on the earth, and being hardened, contrary to nature! O fountains of tears, sown in affliction that they might reap in joy![9] O cry of the night, piercing the clouds and reaching to Him who dwells in heaven! O fervor of spirit, braving out of love of prayer the dogs of the night, the cold, the rain, the thunder, the hail and the darkness! O

---

9 Cf. Ps. 125.5.

nature of woman which overcame that of man in the common struggle for salvation, and proved male and female a distinction of body but not of soul! O chastity preserved after baptism, and soul espoused to Christ in the pure chamber of the body! O bitter tasting, and Eve, mother of our race and our sin, and deceitful serpent, and death, overcome by her abstinence! O emptying of Christ, and nature of a slave,[10] and sufferings, honored by her mortification!

(15) Oh, how can I enumerate all her excellences, or, by passing over most of them, not do an injury to those who do not know them? But now it is proper to add an account of the rewards of her piety. I think that you who know her life are eagerly desirous of hearing in my discourse an account not only of present things and the rewards she enjoys in the world beyond which surpass the conception and hearing and sight of man, but also those which she received as requital from the just Rewarder in this life. For this serves to edify unbelievers, who attain to faith in great things from small, and in things unseen from those which are seen. I will mention some instances known to all, others which for the most part have been kept secret, because she scrupulously avoided priding herself on favors received.

You know the story of her mules getting out of control and running away with her carriage, and its dreadful overturn, how she was dragged along horribly and suffered serious injuries, and the scandal it became to unbelievers because the upright were allowed to suffer in this way, and the swift correction of their unbelief. Although crushed and mangled internally and externally in bone and limb, she would have no physician save Him who had permitted the accident, both because she shrank from the eyes and hands of men, guarding her modesty even in suffering, and also because she sought her vindication from Him who had allowed her to suffer thus.

---
10 Cf. Phil. 2.7.

Nor from anyone else but Him did she obtain her restoration. And so men were not more struck by her misfortune than they were amazed at her unexpected recovery, and they believed that the tragedy had happened for the very reason that she might be glorified by her sufferings. Although her suffering was human, her recovery was superhuman, and she gave to posterity a compelling argument for the display of faith in affliction and patient endurance in misfortune, but a far greater one for the loving kindness of God toward such as she. For to what is rightly said of the just man: 'When he shall fall, he shall not be bruised,'[11] there was added later: 'Although he shall be bruised, he shall be quickly raised up again and glorified.'[12] For if she was afflicted beyond what seemed possible, beyond what seemed possible also was she restored, so that returning health almost stole away her suffering, and the cure became more celebrated than the visitation.

(16) O renowned and admirable misfortune! O suffering more sublime than freedom from suffering! Oh, how those words, 'He will strike and He will bind us up, and He will heal us, and after three days He will raise us up,'[13] although bearing a greater and more mystical meaning, as indeed they did, are yet apposite to her sufferings! However, this event is known to all, even those far off, for the fame of the wonder reached all men and engaged the tongues and ears of all, along with the other wonderful works and powers of God. But a fact hitherto unknown and kept secret from most men, because of her spiritual attitude already referred to, and the absence of pride and ostentation in her piety, do you bid me tell it, O best and most perfect of pastors,[14] the pastor of this sheep, and do you finally give your assent? For this

---
11 Ps. 36.24.
12 Cf. Ps. 145.8.
13 Osee 6.1,2.
14 Faustinus, Bishop of Iconium, who was most probably present.

secret was entrusted to us alone and we were the mutual witnesses of the wonder. Or shall we continue to keep our faith to her who has departed? Yet it seems to me that, while there was then a time for silence, now is the time to reveal it, not only for the glory of God, but also for the consolation of those in affliction.

(17) She was sick in body and grievously afflicted with a malady of a strange and unusual character. All at once her whole body became fevered, with a heightening of the temperature and a racing of the blood, followed by a sluggishness inducing coma, incredible pallor, and a paralysis of mind and limbs. And this occurred not at long intervals, but sometimes quite frequently. The terrible disease did not seem human. Neither the skill of physicians who carefully examined the case, both singly and in consultation, proved of any avail, nor her parents' tears, which were often very efficacious, nor public prayers and supplications, which, as though for their individual preservation, all the people offered on her behalf. For they regarded her safety as their own, and, on the contrary, her sickness and affliction as a common disaster.

(18) What, then, was done by this great soul, worthy of the greatest favors, and what medicine was found for her malady? Herein lies the great secret. Despairing of all other help, she betook herself to the Physician of all, and, waiting till the dead of night, when the disease was somewhat abated, she prostrated herself with faith at the altar, and calling upon Him who is honored thereon, with a loud voice, and under every title, recalling all His miraculous works, for she was familiar with those of old as well as the new, she finally committed an act of pious and noble impudence. She imitated the woman whose hemorrhage was dried up by the hem of Christ's garment.[15] And what did she do? Placing her head, with a similar cry, on the altar, and pouring abundant tears

---

15 Cf. Matt. 9.20.

upon it, as she who had once watered the feet of Christ,[16] she vowed that she would not loose her hold until she obtained her recovery. Then she anointed her whole body with her own medicine, even a portion of the consecrated precious Body and Blood which she treasured in her hand, and with which she mingled her tears. O the wonder! At once she felt herself cured and went away relieved in body and soul and mind, having received what she hoped for as a reward of her hopes. By her strength of soul she gained that of body. These things are great indeed, yet they are not untrue. Believe them, all you who are sick and you who are well, that you may keep your health or recover it. That this account is not mere boastfulness is clear from the fact that as long as she was alive she kept silence concerning what I have now revealed. Nor would I have divulged it even now, I assure you, were I not afraid to keep so great a wonder hidden from believers and unbelievers of the present and of future generations.

(19) Such was her life. I have passed over most of its details that my discourse might not exceed due bounds and lest I seem to have an insatiate desire of praising her. But perhaps I would be wronging her holy and celebrated death if I did not also commemorate some of its excellences, especially since she so eagerly desired it. I will do this as briefly as possible. She longed to be dissolved,[17] for she had great confidence in Him who called her, and to be with Christ she valued above all the things of earth. And no one of the amorous and unlicensed so loves the body as she, having flung away these fetters and surmounted this slime with which we live, desired to be purely joined with her fair One and embrace her Beloved completely, and I will even add, her Lover. His faint rays now illumine only to the extent that we can know from whom we are separated. Nor did she fail of this

---

16 Cf. Luke 7.38.
17 Cf. Phil. 1.23.

inspired and sublime desire, and, what is even more significant, she enjoyed His beauty beforehand by her foreknowledge and her long vigils. One sleep gave her the sweetest of rewards, and one vision embracing her departure at the foreappointed time, and even indicating the very day, that, by the ordination of God, she might be prepared and not be troubled.

(20) The blessing of purification and perfection, the common gift which we have all received from God as a foundation of our second life, had recently been conferred upon her. Rather, her whole life was a purification and a process of perfection. She did, indeed, receive her regeneration from the Holy Spirit, but its security was hers because of her previous life. And almost in her case alone, to speak somewhat boldly, the sacrament was not a grace, but a seal. She was eager that one blessing be added to all she had received, the perfection of her husband. If you wish me to describe him briefly, let me say that he was her husband, for I know not what further need be added. She wished to be consecrated to God in her whole body, and not depart this life only half-perfected, nor leave behind any part of her imperfect. She did not fail to obtain an answer even to this petition from Him who does the will of them that fear Him,[18] and brings their pleas to fulfillment.

(21) All things had been accomplished according to her heart's desire, and no wish of hers lacked fulfillment, and the appointed day was near at hand. And so she prepared for death and departure, and, carrying out the usual law in this matter, she took to her bed. She enjoined on her husband, her children, and her friends such precepts as befitted one so full of love for her husband, her children, and her brothers, and she discoursed beautifully on the future life, making her last day a day of solemn festival. She then fell asleep, full, not

---

18 Cf. Ps. 114.19.

of the days of man for which she had never prayed, knowing them to be evil for her and so closely associated with our dust and wandering, but exceedingly full of the days of God, so that her like could not easily be found among those who have died at a ripe old age and have counted many cycles of years. Thus she was dissolved, or, better, taken to God, or she took wing, or changed her habitation, or departed a little before the body.

(22) Yet what a praiseworthy incident regarding her all but escaped me! But perhaps you, her spiritual father, would not have allowed its omission, since you carefully observed the wonder and made it known to me. It is a detail greatly enhancing her renown, and important for us, too, as a memorial of virtue and an inspiration to desire the same dissolution. But a shudder comes over me and tears arise when I recall the marvel. She was just passing away and was breathing her last, and about her was a group of relatives and friends, showing the customary solicitude for the dying. Her aged mother, whose soul was in agony with envy at the departure, was bent over her, while the love of all present was mingled with anguish. Some were eager to hear some word that might enkindle recollection within them; others desired to speak, but no one ventured to do so. There were silent tears and inconsolable pangs of grief, since it seemed an impious thing to honor with lamentation one dying in this way. There was profound silence and her death took on the semblance of a sacred ceremony. To all appearance she neither breathed nor stirred nor uttered any sound. Her silence seemed to indicate her dissolution, as though the organs of speech had ceased to function because of the withdrawal of the soul that moved them. But her pastor, who was carefully observing everything about her, because of the manifest wonder of the circumstances, perceived that her lips were moving slightly. He put his ear close to them, for his character

and sympathy gave him confidence—but do you yourself explain the mystery of this stillness! No one will disbelieve your word! She was faintly murmuring a psalm, the closing words of a psalm, and truly they are a testimony of her confidence in her parting. Blessed indeed is he who can close his life with the words: 'In peace in the selfsame I will sleep and I will rest.'[19] These were the words, fairest of women, which came to your lips, and they were appropriate to you. And your psalmody was given realization, a eulogy coincident with your departure. And you have attained to glorious peace after your sufferings, and have received, beyond the rest common to all, that sleep due to the beloved of God,[20] fitting indeed for one who lived and died amid the words of piety.

(23) I am sure that in comparison with those things which are seen by the eye, greater and far more precious are the blessings which you now enjoy, the sound of those feasting,[21] the choirs of angels, the heavenly host, the spectacle of glory, and the effulgence, more pure and more perfect than any other, of the Most High Trinity, no longer evading the mind fettered and dissipated by the senses, but beheld and comprehended wholly with the whole mind, and illuminating our souls with the whole light of the Godhead. May you enjoy to the full those things, the emanations of which you received while still upon the earth, because of the sincere inclination of your mind toward them. If you have any interest in our affairs, and the perception of such things is a privilege granted saintly souls by God, please accept in place of and above many funeral gifts this discourse of mine, a tribute rendered to Caesarius before you and to you after him, since I have been preserved to deliver funeral orations upon my brother and sister. Whether anyone, now that you have gone, will pay me like honor, I cannot say. But may I receive only that

---

19 Ps. 4.10.
20 Cf. Ps. 126.2.
21 Cf. Ps. 41.5.

honor which is pleasing to God, both during my pilgrimage and in my home, in Christ Jesus, our Lord, to whom with the Father and the Holy Spirit be glory forever. Amen.

ON HIS FATHER

MAN OF GOD,[1] AND FAITHFUL SERVANT,[2] and dispenser of the Mysteries of God,[3] and man of desires of the Spirit:[4] for these are the appellations Scripture gives to those who have attained sublimity and are superior to visible things. I will also call you the God of Pharao,[5] of all the Egyptian and hostile powers; I will call you a pillar and mainstay of the Church,[6] and the pleasure of the Lord,[7] and a star in the world holding fast the word of life,[8] a support of the faith and a resting place of the Spirit. Why should I enumerate all the titles which your virtue has gained for you, drawing them to you one by one and making them your own?

(2) But tell me whence you have come, and what is your purpose, and what favor have you come to confer upon us? For I know that in all things you act with God and through

---

1 Cf. Jos. 14.6.
2 Cf. Num. 12.7.
3 Cf. 1 Cor. 4.1.
4 Cf. Dan. 9.23.
5 Cf. Exod. 7.1.
6 Cf. 1 Tim. 3.15.
7 Cf. Isa. 62.4.
8 Cf. Phil. 2.16.

God for the benefit of those who receive you. Have you come to watch over us, or to seek the pastor, or to inspect the flock? We no longer exist, but for the most part have departed with him, unable to endure this place of affliction, especially now when we have lost our skilled pilot, the beacon of our life, to which we turned our eyes and directed our course, as it flashed the light of salvation above us. He has gone, with all this excellence and all the pastoral skill and practice acquired in his whole life, full of days of wisdom and crowned, to use the words of Solomon, with old age as a crown of dignity.[9] The flock is left without guidance, it is downcast, as you see, and filled with sorrow and dejection. It no longer finds rest in the place of pleasure or sustenance in the water of refreshment.[10] It seeks out the cliffs and desert places and abysses where it will be dispersed and perish. It despairs of ever obtaining another wise shepherd, although, while fully convinced that it will never find one like him, it would be content with one not too far below him.

(3) Three things, then, as I have said, and all in equal measure, render your presence necessary: ourselves, the shepherd, and the flock. Come, then, and according to the spirit of healing which is in you apply the suitable remedy to each. Order your words with discernment, that we may admire you all the more for your wisdom. And how will you order them? As for the shepherd, if you praise him in seemly fashion for his virtue, not only will you confer the tribute of a pure funeral oration on one who was pure, but you will also present the chosen pattern of his life to others as a moving example of true piety. In respect to us, you may discourse briefly on life and death, on the union and separation of body and soul, on the two worlds, both on that which is physically present but not permanent and on that which is

---

9 Cf. Prov. 2.16.
10 Cf. Ps. 22.2.

perceived by the mind and is eternal. Persuade us to despise the deceitfulness, the disorder, and the instability of the one, rising and falling like the waves of the sea, but to attach ourselves to the other, which is firm and stable, divine and unchanging, free from all disorder and confusion. In this way, those who have departed before us would cause us less sorrow, and would even bring us joy, if your discourse would draw us forth and raise us on high, and hide our present distress in future hope, and convince us that we, also, are hastening to a good Master, that our true home is better than our place of sojourn, and that, just as there is a calm haven for those at sea, so for those who are tossed on the storms of this life there is a migration and transfer to the other life. Or, just as those who have finished a long journey enjoy more ease and greater freedom from care than travelers still toiling on the way, so those who have reached the hospice beyond have a better and more tolerable life than those who are still advancing along the steep and crooked road of this life below.

(4) Thus, then, would you comfort us. But how will you comfort the flock? First of all, by pledging your care and guidance, for under your wings all would gladly take their rest, and we thirst more for your voice than those racked by thirst long for the purest fountain. Next, by convincing us that even now the good shepherd who lays down his life for his sheep[11] has not forsaken us, but is present to tend and guide, and knows his own, and is known by them. He is not actually seen by bodily eye, but is with us in spirit, defending the flock against the wolves, and suffering no one, in the manner of a robber or a traitor, to leap into the fold and ravage and steal by an alien voice souls rightly formed in the truth. I am persuaded that his intercession avails more now than his teaching did in the past, since he is closer to God. He has

---
11 Cf. John 10.11.

shaken off his bodily bonds and freed his mind from obscuring clay, and, divested of all obscuring elements, he holds direct and intimate converse with the prime and purest Mind, being deemed worthy—if it is not to bold to say so—of the privileged rank and freedom of the angels. But you, with the power of speech and the spirit that is yours, will treat and discuss these matters better than I can present them. Yet, in order that, through lack of acquaintance with his noble qualities, your discourse may not fall far short of his merit, I, from my personal knowledge of the departed, will give a brief outline or sketch of a eulogy to you, the skilled painter of such subjects, that you may depict more perfectly the splendor of his virtue and present it to the ears and minds of all men.

(5) The treatment of his country, race, bodily qualities, external splendor, and other things on which men pride themselves I shall leave to the laws of panegyric, and begin with what with us comes first and is most relevant. He was the son of undistinguished stock, and one not naturally disposed toward piety. I am not ashamed of his beginnings, because of my confidence in the final issue of his life. It was a stock not planted in the house of God,[12] but a most strange and unusual one, compounded of two extremes—pagan error and legal absurdity—and while it escaped some elements of each it combined features of both. For with regard to the first, its members reject pagan idols and sacrifices, but hold fire and lights in reverence; with regard to the second, they observe the Sabbath and petty regulations concerning certain foods, but they scorn circumcision. These lowly men call themselves Hypsistarii[13] and the Almighty alone is the object of their worship. What was to be expected of a man with this twofold

---
12 Cf. Ps. 91.14.
13 St. Gregory of Nyssa also refers to this obscure sect (*Or. 2 Contra Eunom.*), calling them Hypsistians. He says that they acknowledged a God whom they called the Highest (hence their name from the Greek) or the Omnipotent, but did not admit that he was Father.

tendency to impiety? Indeed, I do not know which to praise more: the grace which called him or his own good will and purpose. At any rate, he so cleaned the eye of his mind of the infection that clung to it, and ran with such speed to the truth, that for some time he endured the loss of his mother and his sustenance for the sake of his heavenly Father and his true inheritance, and bore this disgrace more readily than others carry the highest honors. Wonderful as this really is, I do not wonder at it so much, and for the following reason. He shared this glory with many others, and all must be gathered into the great net of God and be caught by the words of the fishermen, although some are netted sooner and some later by the Gospel. But I must now relate what especially in his life moves me to wonder.

(6) Even before he entered our fold he was one of us. Just as many of our own are not with us because their lives alienate them from the common body of the faithful, in like manner many of those outside are with us, in so far as by their way of life they anticipate the faith and only lack in name what they possess in attitude. My father was one of these, an alien branch, but inclined toward us by his way of living. He was so pre-eminent in self-control that he was at once most beloved and most modest, a combination rarely achieved. What better or more striking proof of his uprightness can be advanced than the fact that he held the highest offices in the state, yet did not enrich himself by a single penny, although he saw others reaching with the hands of a Briareus into the public funds and swollen with their ill-gotten gains? For thus do I label wealth unjustly acquired. While these facts are no small testimony to his prudence, many more examples will be presented in the course of my speech. As a reward for his conduct, I think, he received the faith. Let us show how this came about, for so important a matter should not be passed over in silence.

(7) I have heard sacred Scripture saying: 'Who shall find a valiant woman?'[14] and also that she is a gift of God, and that a good marriage is arranged by the Lord. Those outside, too, have the same thought—if indeed the saying is theirs: 'There is no greater boon for a man than a good wife, no worse, than the opposite.'[15] It is impossible to mention anyone who was more fortunate than my father in this respect. For I believe that, if anyone, from the ends of the earth and from all human stocks, had endeavored to arrange the best possible marriage, a better or more harmonius union than this could not be found. For the best in men and women was so united that their marriage was more a union of virtue than of bodies. Although they surpassed all others, they themselves were so evenly matched in virtue that they could not surpass each other.

(8) She who was given to Adam as a helper like himself, for it was not good for man to be alone,[16] proved to be an enemy rather than a helpmate and an opponent rather than a consort, beguiling her husband by pleasure and alienating him through the tree of knowledge from the tree of life. But she who was given by God to my father became not only a helper—for this would be less wonderful—but also a leader, personally guiding him by deed and word to what was most excellent. Although she deemed it best, in accordance with the law of marriage, to be overruled by her husband in other respects, she was not ashamed to show herself his master in piety. While she is deserving of admiration for this, he is to be admired all the more for willingly yielding to her.

While beauty, natural as well as artificial, is wont to be a source of pride and glory to other women, she is one who has ever recognized only one beauty, that of the soul, and the

---

14 Prov. 31.10.
15 Hesiod, *Works and Days* 1.700 (freely quoted).
16 Cf. Gen. 2.18.

preservation and, to the best of her power, the purification of the divine image in her soul. She rejected paint and other artificial means of adornment befitting women of the stage. She recognized only one true nobility, that of piety, and the knowledge of our origin and final destiny. The only wealth she considered secure and inviolate was to strip one's self of wealth for God and the poor, and especially for kinsfolk whose fortunes had declined. Assistance merely to the extent of their need she regarded as a reminder of misfortune rather than as a release from it, but more generous benefaction as a means of giving honor and lasting consolation.

While some women excel in the management of their households and others in piety—for it is difficult to achieve both—she nevertheless surpassed all in both, because she was pre-eminent in each and because she alone combined the two. She increased the resources of her household by her care and practical foresight according to the standards and norms laid down by Solomon for the valiant woman, as though she knew nothing of piety. She devoted herself to God and divine things as though she were completely removed from household cares. In nowise, however, did she neglect one duty in fulfilling the other; rather, she performed both more effectively by making one support the other.

(9) What time or place for prayer escaped her? This was the first thought of her day. Rather, who had more confidence in gaining a petition as soon as it was made? Who had such reverence for the hands and countenance of priests? Who showed such honor for every form of philosophy?[17] Who subdued her flesh more by fastings and watchings, or stood like a pillar during the night-long or daily singing of the psalms? Who had greater admiration for virginity, although she herself was under the bond of matrimony? Who

---

17 Used here in the sense of the life of Christian perfection and ascetical practices.

was a better champion of widows and orphans? Who relieved to a like degree the misfortunes of the distressed? These things, small perhaps, and, it may be, even despised by some because they do not lie within the reach of the majority—for the unattainable, out of envy, is generally considered as not even credible—I esteem highly, for they were the inventions of her faith and undertakings of her spiritual fervor. So, too, her voice was never heard in the sacred assemblies or places, except when necessary and required by the liturgy.

(10) It was once counted a glory for the altar that no axe had been lifted upon it, no stone-cutter's tool seen or heard,[18] with the higher meaning that whatever was consecrated to God should be natural and free from artifice. Why should it not redound to her great praise that she honored the sanctuary by her silence, that she never turned her back upon the holy table, nor spat upon the hallowed pavement, that she never grasped the hand or kissed the lips of any pagan woman, however honorable in other respects and however closely related? She would not even share salt, either willingly or perforce, with those coming from a profane and unhallowed table, nor suffer herself, contrary to the law of conscience, to pass by or look upon a polluted house. She would not let her ears or her tongue, which had received and uttered holy things, be defiled by pagan tales or theatrical songs, because nothing unholy is becoming to the holy. What is deserving of greater admiration is the fact that she restrained external manifestation of grief to such a degree, although she was deeply affected by the sufferings even of strangers, as never to let a cry of affliction burst forth before the Eucharist, or to let a tear drop from eyes mystically sealed, or let any sign of mourning remain when a festival day came, although many sorrows befell her. For she felt that the soul that loves God should subject all human things to the divine.

---

18 Cf. Deut. 27.5.

(11) I pass over in silence things more ineffable, of which God is witness, and the faithful handmaids to whom she confided such matters. What concerns myself is not even worthy of mention, perhaps, as I have not proved worthy of the hopes held out for me. Still, it was a great undertaking on her part to promise me to God even before birth, with no timidity for the future, and to dedicate me immediately after I was born. By the grace of God, her prayer did not completely fail of attainment, nor was her auspicious sacrifice rejected. Some of these things were already accomplished facts, some were to come into being, increasing by gradual additions. Just as the sun strikes the earth most pleasantly with its morning rays and becomes hotter and more brilliant at midday, so she, who from the beginning showed marked indications of piety, shone later with a brighter light.

He, therefore, had at home a strong stimulus to piety, who had established in his house her who was endowed by origin and descent with the love of God and Christ, and who had received virtue as her patrimony. She had not been engrafted as he from the wild olive upon the garden olive, nor, on account of the perfection of her faith, could she endure to be unequally yoked. Although in other respects she surpassed all women in patience and fortitude, this alone she could not bear, namely, to be but half-united to God, because of the estrangement of him who was part of her, and not possess spiritual union in addition to physical union. Therefore, she prostrated herself before God day and night and besought Him with many fastings and tears for the salvation of her head, and zealously devoted herself to her husband, and strove to win him in various ways, by reproaches, admonitions, attentions, estrangements, and most of all by her own character and fervent piety, by means of which the soul is especially swayed and softened and willingly constrained to virtue. It was inevitable that the drop of water, constantly striking the rock, should hollow it out and in time accomplish its purpose, as the sequel shows.

(12) These, then, were the things for which she prayed and hoped, in the fervor of faith rather than of youth. And no one ever had such confidence in the present as she had in her hopes, for she had learned from experience the bountifulness of God. My father's salvation was aided jointly by his reason, which gradually accepted the healing remedy, and jointly by the vision of dreams, a benefit which God often bestows on a soul worthy of salvation. What was the vision? This is for me the most pleasing part of the story. He thought that he was singing, what he had never done before, although his wife often prayed and made supplication, these words from the psalms of David: 'I rejoiced at the things that were said to me, we shall go into the house of the Lord.'[19] The psalm was strange and with its singing came desire. When his wife heard it, having now gained her prayer, she seized the opportunity, interpreting the vision most happily and truthfully, and showing by her joy the magnitude of the benefit, and urging forward his salvation, lest anything might occur to hinder the call and undo what she had zealously sought.

It happened at that very time that many bishops were hastening to Nicaea to oppose the madness of Arius, for the evil doctrine dividing the Godhead had just arisen. My father gave himself to God and the heralds of the truth and confessed his desire and begged of them common salvation. One of them was the famous Leontius, who governed our metropolis at the time. A marvelous thing then took place by God's grace, and I would certainly do an injury to grace itself if I passed it over in silence. There were not a few witnessses of the marvel.[20] The teachers of the ritual for catechumens com-

---

19 Ps. 121.1.
20 To be admitted into the ranks of the catechumens, Gregory the Elder should have remained standing. He fell on his knees and the bishop inadvertently pronounced over him the formula for ordination to the priesthood.

mitted a spiritual error, grace foreshadowed the future, and the formula for the priesthood was mingled with that for admission of the catechumen. O involuntary initiation! For bending his knee he was enrolled into the catechumenate in such a way that many of those present, not only those of superior but also those of duller intellect, relying on such clear signs, prophesied the future.

(13) A short time later, this wonder was followed by another. I will commend this account to the ears of the faithful, for among the profane nothing good is deemed worthy of belief. He was drawing near to that regeneration through water and the Spirit by which we confess to God the formation and perfecting of man according to Christ, and the transformation and reformation of the earthy to the spirit. He was advancing to the water of baptism with ardent desire and bright hope, after he had first cleansed himself as far as possible and purified himself in body and soul far more than those who were to receive the tablets from Moses.[21] For their purification was confined to dress, a slight repression of the belly, and a brief period of continence. In my father's case, his whole past life was a preparation for the divine illumination, and before his purification there was already a purification that assured the safety of the gift, that perfection might be entrusted to purity and that the gift might not be endangered in a state of soul which was confident with the help of grace. As he came forth from the water a light shone round him and a glory worthy of the disposition with which he had approached the grace of faith. It was seen clearly by some others, also, who at the time kept silence concerning the wonder. They did not venture to speak of it, for each thought that the vision had been granted to himself alone, but a little later they communicated it to one another. But it was so clear and evident to him who baptized and initiated

---

21 Cf. Exod. 19.10-15.

my father that he could not keep the mystery to himself but cried out publicly that he had anointed with the Spirit his own successor.

(14) No one will disbelieve this who has heard and knows that Moses, when he was still insignificant in the eyes of men and not yet deemed of any account, was called from the bush, which was on fire but was not burnt—rather, by Him who appeared in the bush[22]—and he was confirmed by that first miracle. I mean that Moses for whom the sea parted,[23] and bread rained down,[24] and the rock gushed forth water,[25] and the pillar of fire and cloud led the way in turn,[26] and the stretching forth of whose hands to represent the figure of a cross brought victory and overcame many thousands.[27] Then there was Isaias, who saw the glory of the Seraphim,[28] and after him Jeremias, who was entrusted with great power over nations and kings.[29] The former heard the divine voice and was cleansed by a coal of fire before prophesying;[30] the latter was known before his formation and sanctified before birth.[31] Paul, also, the great herald of the truth and the teacher of the Gentiles in the faith, while still a persecutor, was encompassed with a light and acknowledged Him whom he was persecuting, and he was entrusted with his great ministry and filled every ear and mind with the Gospel.[32]

(15) But why should I enumerate all those who were called and adopted by God by wonders such as those which confirmed my father in piety? Although the beginnings were

---

22 Cf. Exod. 3.4.
23 Cf. Exod. 14.22.
24 Cf. Exod. 16.4.
25 Cf. Exod. 17.6.
26 Cf. Exod. 13.22.
27 Cf. Exod. 17.11.
28 Cf. Isa. 6.1ff.
29 Cf. Jer. 1.10.
30 Cf. Isa. 6.6.
31 Cf. Jer. 1.5.
32 Cf. Acts 9.3ff.

such as these, so incredible and so marvelous, nevertheless his later actions put to shame nothing that had gone before, unlike those who quickly get their fill of what is good and then are disdainful of progress or even relapse completely into vice. This cannot be said of him. He was remarkably consistent with himself and his previous life. And so there was a harmony between his life before the priesthood and his excellences as a priest, and between his life after the priesthood and what had gone before. Nor would it have been becoming to begin one way and end another, nor to advance to an end different from that intended in the beginning. He received the priesthood, not with the ease and confusion now current, but after a brief interval, so that he might add to his own cleansing the skill and power of cleansing others, for that is the law of spiritual sequence. After he had received it, its grace was glorified all the more, since it was in reality a grace of God, and not, as Ecclesiastes says, an independent impulse or presumption of spirit.[33]

(16) He received a woodland and rural church, which had not been governed with pastoral care from long ago, but had been administered by only a single predecessor, a man of admirable and angelic character but simpler in heart than the present rulers of the people. After he had been quickly taken up to heaven, the church was neglected for a considerable period and grew wild for lack of a leader. At first, he sought to soften the dispositions of the people, not by severe measures, but by words of pastoral knowledge and by setting himself before them as a model, like a spiritual statue, exhibiting the polished beauty of all excellent conduct. Next, he gave himself earnestly to meditation on the divine words, and although he was late in learning such matters, he gathered such wisdom within a short time that he was in no way inferior to those who had spent the longest time upon

---

33 Cf. Eccle. 1.17 (Septuagint).

them. And he received this singular grace from God, of becoming the father and teacher of orthodoxy. He was not like the wise men of our day, yielding to the times, defending our faith in equivocal and ornate language, like those who lack firmness of faith or adulterate the truth. But he surpassed in piety those outstanding in rhetorical skill, and in his knowledge and learning he was superior to believers, or, rather, while he bore off second prize in oratory, he took the first in piety. He acknowledged one God worshiped in Trinity, and three[34] united in one Godhead. He did not Sabellianize as to the One, or Arianize as to the Three, either by impiously contracting and resolving the Godhead or by dividing it by unequal distinctions of greatness or nature. For, since every quality of the Godhead is incomprehensible and beyond our power of intellect, how can the transcendence therein be either conceived or defined? How can the infinite be measured and the Godhead experience what is proper to finite things and be measured by distinctions of greater and less?

(17) These were the reflections of that great man of God and true theologian, and he was inspired by the Holy Spirit concerning them. What else must be said but that, like the great Noe, the father of this second world, he caused this church to be called a second Jerusalem and a second ark borne above the waters? Clearly it rose, above the deluge of souls and the insults of the heretics, and in the measure it yielded to others in numbers it surpassed them in reputation. It has fared even as holy Bethlehem, which was hindered in no way from being at once a small city and the metropolis of the whole earth, since it was the nurse and mother of Christ, who made and conquered the world.

(18) Here is proof of what I have been saying. When we had been bitterly attacked by the more zealous element[35]

---

34 Without paraphrasing, it would be impossible to indicate in English that 'three' here is neuter plural in Greek. Reference is made, accordingly, to the doctrine of the three divine Persons in one God.

35 I.e., the monks.

in the Church on the ground that we had been led astray by a document and artful phrases[36] into association with evil, he alone was believed to have an unwounded mind and not to have stained his soul with ink, although he had been carried away by his simplicity and in his guilelessness had not been on guard against guile. But he alone, or, rather, he first, by his zeal for piety reconciled to himself and the rest the opposing faction, which was the last to desert us and the first to return, because of their reverence for him and the purity of his doctrine. And so a terrible storm in the churches was calmed, and a hurricane reduced to a gentle breeze, broken by his prayers and admonitions. At the time, I—if I may speak with the presumptuousness of youth—was his partner in piety as well as in action. Co-operating with him in every good work, accompanying him and running along beside him, as it were, I was deemed worthy to contribute a very large share of the labor. But here let my account of these matters, which has run a little ahead of itself, come to an end.

(19) Who could recount his many excellences or, while desiring to pass over most of them, find easily what to set aside? For whatever comes to mind always seems superior to what has gone before, I become absorbed in this, and I am more at a loss as to what I should omit than other panegyrists are as to what they should say. And so the abundance of material is in a way a disadvantage to me, and my mind is put to the test when it strives to test his qualities, and cannot find what is outstanding, when all are equal. There is a phenomenon which we observe in still waters. Whenever a pebble falls therein it becomes the center whence circle after circle develops, and each, constantly rippling, breaks up that which is beyond it. This is precisely what has happened to me. One thought comes into my mind, but another follows

---

[36] Perhaps the Creed formulated by the Council of Antioch in 363. Since the language of the formula and its explanation was somewhat ambiguous, it was open to interpretation in an heretical sense.

and displaces it, and I grow weary in making a choice, since what I have first grasped continually yields place to that which follows after.

(20) Who was more zealous for the common weal? Who was wiser in domestic affairs, since God, who orders all things well and in sundry ways, allotted him a house and adequate means? Who was more sympathetic of heart or more generous of hand to the poor, that most dishonored part of our nature which ought to be held in equal honor. For in reality his attitude toward his own property was that of a steward of another's. He alleviated poverty to the extent of his power, expending not only his superabundance but even his necessities for this end—the clearest proof, surely, of charity toward the poor. He gave a portion not to seven only, according to the precept of Solomon,[37] but even if an eighth also came forward he did not deal meanly, but disposed of his wealth more cheerfully than others who we know acquire it. He took away the chain[38] and the extension of the hand—I understand by this, meanness and testing the worthiness or unworthiness of the recipient, and the word of murmuring in the giving.[39] It happens with most men that they give indeed, but they do not do so freely and readily, which is a greater and more perfect thing than the mere act of offering itself. For it is far better to be generous to the unworthy for the sake of the worthy than to deprive the worthy out of fear of the unworthy. This seems to have a bearing on our duty of casting bread upon the waters,[40] not that it may be swept away, or perish, in the eyes of the just examiner, but that it may come to that place where all our goods will be stored up, and be there to meet us in due time, even though we may think otherwise.

(21) But the best and greatest feature is that with his

---
37 Cf. Eccle. 11.2.
38 Cf. Isa. 58.9 (Septuagint).
39 Cf. *ibid.*
40 Cf. Eccle. 11.1.

magnanimity went a contempt for ambition. Its extent and character I shall proceed to show. Although their wealth and the readiness to bestow it were shared equally by himself and his spouse, since they rivaled each other in contending for excellence, for the most part he left the function of dispensing it in her hands, for he believed her to be the best and most faithful steward of such matters. What woman and what sort of woman do I mean? She is one whose demands not even the Atlantic Ocean or any other still greater could satisfy, so great and so boundless is her love of liberality. She rivaled—but in a contrary sense—the horse leech of Solomon,[41] overcoming by her insatiable desire for good any leaning toward evil, and unable to satisfy her zeal for beneficence. Not only did she consider all the wealth they had from the beginning, as well as what they later acquired, as insufficient for her desires, but she would have readily sold herself and her children, if possible, as I have often heard her say, that the proceeds might be expended on the poor. Thus did she give full rein to her generosity, a fact which I consider a stronger argument than any example. For one also may easily find magnanimity in money matters among others, whether the money is spent on public or political ambitions or is lent to God through the poor—the only money which can be treasured up for those who spend it. But we do not easily find anyone who has forsaken the reputation connected with liberality. Indeed, the readiness to spend freely is prompted in many by their love of reputation. But where the benefaction is to pass unnoticed, there also the impulse to give is less keen.

(22) Such, then, was his generous hand. Further details I shall leave to those who knew him, so that if anything of the kind is ascribed to me, also, it is from that fountain and part of that stream. Who acted more closely with God in admitting men to the sanctuary, or, in resenting outrages

---
41 Cf. Prov. 30.15.

against it, or in cleansing, with reverent fear, the holy table from the unholy? Who with such unwavering judgment and balance of justice decided a case, or so hated wickedness, or so honored virtue, or preferred the most upright? Who was so disposed to pardon the sinner, or so encouraging to those running well? Who knew better the right time for employing the rod and the staff,[42] though he wielded the staff the more? Whose eyes were more on the faithful of the earth,[43] especially on those who, despising the earth and the things of the earth, live a solitary and celibate life for God?

(23) Who reproved vanity more or had a greater love for humility? This was no feigned or superficial attitude, like that of most of those who now make a pretense of practicing asceticism and appear as elegant as the silliest women, who, lacking natural beauty, have recourse to pigments, and, although showing themselves off prettily, are, if I may say so, uncomely in their comeliness and uglier through their ugliness. His humility was not a matter of dress, but a disposition of soul. He did not affect it by a bending of the neck or a lowering of the voice, by a downcast look, or length of beard, or close-shaven head, or manner of walking, things which may for a while give the impression of humility, but are quickly discredited, for all pretense is lacking in stability. While he led a most sublime life, he was most humble of heart, and although no one could approach his virtue, he was most approachable for consultation. His dress was ordinary, avoiding pride and meanness alike, but he surpassed all by the spendor within. No one better overcame the disorder and insatiable appetite of the belly, but he was not ostentatious about it, desiring, on the one hand, to purify himself, and on the other, not be puffed up by seeking a reputation for doing the unusual. He believed it to be the mark of a politician, for

---

42 Cf. Ps. 22.4.
43 Cf. Ps. 100.6.

whom there is no greater happiness than the present life, to do and say everything through which he may be held in esteem by those outside, but of a spiritual man and a Christian to look to one thing only, his salvation, and to regard as important what may lead to this and to despise what does not as worthless. Therefore, the Christian must condemn the visible and consider this only: how he may become interiorly perfect. He must esteem most highly whatever may increase his own merit and draw others by his example to the highest and best.

(24) But his noblest and most characteristic quality, recognized even by the multitude, was his simplicity, and his guileless and forgiving disposition. Of the men of ancient and modern times, different individuals are believed to have been conspicuous for different virtues according to the grace each happened to receive from God. Job was conspicuous for invincible patience in misfortune,[44] Moses and David for meekness,[45] Samuel for prophesying the future,[46] Phineas for the zeal for which he was reputed,[47] Peter and Paul for their eagerness in preaching the Gospel,[48] the sons of Zebedee for their lofty eloquence, whence they were also called the sons of thunder.[49] Why should I enumerate all of them, speaking as I am among those who know? But the distinguishing characteristic of Stephen and my father was freedom from malice. Not even when he was in danger did Stephen hate his persecutors, but while he was being stoned he prayed for those who were stoning him,[50] as a disciple of Christ, for whose sake he had to suffer, bearing for God in his long-suffering fruit greater than death. With my father

---

44 Cf. Job 1.21.
45 Cf. Num. 12.3; Ps. 131.1.
46 Cf. 1 Kings 9.9.
47 Cf. Num. 25.7; Ps. 105.30,31.
48 Cf. Gal. 2.7.
49 Cf. Mark 3.17.
50 Cf. Acts 7.59.

there was no interval between rebuke and pardon, so that grief itself was almost beguiled by the speed of forgiveness.

(25) We believe and hear that there are dregs, as it were, of the anger of God,[51] the residue of His action against those who deserve it, since the Lord is a God of vengeance.[52] Although He is inclined through His benignity toward mildness rather than severity, He does not completely pardon sinners, lest by His goodness they become worse. My father cherished no ill will against those who provoked him, although he was not entirely invulnerable to wrath, and in spiritual things especially he was wont to be carried away by zeal, unless he chanced to be prepared and armed and set in battle array to meet as an enemy from afar what was advancing to injure him. So not even by tens of thousands, as the saying goes, would this sweet disposition of his have been altered. For his wrath was not like that of the serpent,[53] causing him to smolder within, and to be ready to defend himself, nor quick to anger from the first excitement or exhibiting a desire of retaliation, but like the sting of the bee, that strikes but does not bring death. His benevolence was superhuman. The wheel and the lash were often threatened, and men were at hand to apply them, but the danger ended in the pinching of the ear or the slapping of the cheek or the cuffing of the temple. In this fashion was the threat carried out. When clothing and shoes were pulled off and the culprit stretched upon the ground, his anger was directed, not against the evil-doer, but against his eager assistant, as a minister of evils. How could anyone have appeared kindlier or worthier to offer gifts to God? Often, he had scarcely begun to be stirred to anger when he immediately made excuses for the one who had provoked him, blushing for the faults of others as though they were his own.

---

51 Cf. Ps. 74.9.
52 Cf. Ps. 93.1.
53 Cf. Ps. 57.5.

(26) The dew would more easily endure the morning rays of the sun than any trace of anger be left in his heart. As soon as he spoke, his indignation departed with his words, leaving behind only his love for the good and never lasting longer than the sun. He did not cherish the anger that brings ruin even to the prudent or show any mark on his body of any passion within, preserving his calmness even when he was roused. The most surprising result of all this was that while he was not the only one to deliver censure, he was the only one to be both loved and admired by those he reproved, since his goodness overcame his warmth of feeling. And surely it is more profitable to be chastised by a just man than to be anointed by a bad one, for the asperity of the one is pleasant because of its usefulness while the goodness of the other is suspect because of his wickedness.

Although he was so simple and godlike of soul and character, he was yet an object of fear to the insolent because of his piety, or, rather, nothing made such an impression on them as the simplicity they despised. It was impossible for him to utter a prayer or an imprecation without the immediate bestowal of some lasting benefit or temporary pain. For the prayer proceeded from his inmost heart, while the imprecation was only on his lips, as a fatherly rebuke. Indeed, to many of those who offended him requital was not slow in coming, nor was the judgment upon them of lagging foot, to use the words of the poet.[54] But they were struck down at the very moment of passion, were brought to their senses, turned to him, fell on their knees before him, obtained pardon, and withdrew, gloriously vanquished, and became better men, both for the chastisement and the pardon. Forgiveness also is often of great avail for salvation, as it curbs the evil-doer through shame and leads him from fear to love, a safer frame of mind. Some who were chastised were tossed by oxen,

---

54 The source of the allusion is unknown.

galled by the loops of the yoke, who suddenly rushed upon them, since the beasts had never suffered this treatment before. Others were thrown down and trampled upon by even the tamest and most obedient horses. Others were seized by intolerable fevers and troubled by visions of their daring deeds. Still others were disciplined in different ways and learned obedience from the things they suffered.

(27) Such, therefore, being the outstanding character and renown of his mildness, did he yield the palm to others in industry and excellence in practical affairs? By no means. While he himself was gentle, if any one ever was, his energy was in proportion to his gentleness. Although the two qualities, simplicity and severity, are generally repugnant and opposed to each other, the one naturally implying gentleness without enterprise, the other energy without kindliness, in him they were blended in a marvelous unity. On the one hand, he acted like a severe man, yet he displayed gentleness. On the other, he readily gave way as though a stranger to practical affairs, yet he displayed energy in patronage, in fearlessness of speech, and in every kind of ministry. He combined the wisdom of the serpent in regard to evil with the simplicity of the dove in regard to good, nor did he suffer his wisdom to degenerate into evil action, nor his simplicity into stupidity, but he fashioned and perfected from both, so far as it was possible, one form of virtue. Since he became so outstanding in character and in the exercise of his priesthood, what wonder is it that he was deemed worthy of the manifestations by which God confirms piety?

(28) One of the wonders concerning him was that he suffered sickness and bodily infirmity. But why should it be surprising that holy men suffer ills, either for the purification of some small stain, or for proving their virtue or testing their philosophy, or for the instruction of the weaker, who learn from their example to be brave instead of faint-hearted

in misfortune? He was sick, then, and the time of his sickness was the holy and glorious Easter, the queen of days, that splendid night that dissipates the darkness of sin, in which we celebrate with abundant light the feast of our salvation, and in which, dying with the Light who died on our behalf, we rise again with Him who rose. This was the time of his affliction. Its nature, to describe it briefly, was as follows. A violent, burning fever consumed all his vitals, his strength had failed, he was unable to take food, his sleep had departed, he was in great distress, suffering from palpitation of the heart. The whole interior of his mouth, including the palate and the whole upper surface, had broken out into so many and such virulent and incessant ulcers that the swallowing even of water was not easy or without danger. Neither the skill of doctors, nor the prayers of his friends, however assiduous, nor any healing application was of avail. He was, then, in this condition, breathing shortly and with difficulty, not even perceiving those present, but wholly intent upon his departure and the things he had long desired and now made ready for him.

We were in God's temple, and occupied both with the sacred rites and with our supplications, for we had despaired of all else and betaken ourselves to the great Physician and the power of that night as the last source of succor. With what intention, shall I say? To celebrate the feast or to mourn? To keep the festival or honor with funeral services one no longer here? Oh, those tears then shed by the whole people! Oh, the voices, and cries, and hymns mingled with the singing of psalms! They sought the priest from the temple, the minister from the sacred rites, their worthy protector from God. My Mary[55] led them and struck the timbrel,[56] not of triumph but of supplication, learning then for the first time

---

55 St. Nonna, his mother.
56 Cf. Exod. 15.20.

to put aside shame in the face of sorrow, and calling both upon the people and upon God: upon the people, to sympathize with her in her distress and to vie in pouring out their tears; upon God, that He might hear her petitions, reminding Him, with the inventive power of grief, of all His miracles in former times.

(29) What, then, was the response of the God of that night and of the sick man? Trembling comes upon me as I continue the story. And you, too, may tremble as you listen to me, but do not disbelieve—for that would be impious, since I myself am the relater and it concerns him. The time of the mystery was at hand. All were reverently in their places, in order and in silence for the sacred rites. My father was then revived by Him who raises the dead to life, and by the holy night. At first he moved a little, then with more vigor. Then he called by name, very weakly and in an indistinct voice, one of the servants who were attending him, and bade him come forward and bring his clothes and lend his hand to support him. He came in consternation, and eagerly ministered to him. My father, making use of the guiding hand as a staff, imitated Moses on the mount, and forming his enfeebled hands in an attitude of prayer, and in union with or in behalf of the people, eagerly celebrated the Mysteries.[57] He employed few words, such as his weakened condition allowed, but his intention, as it seems to me, was most perfect. What a most unusual and miraculous situation! In the sanctuary without a sanctuary, a sacrificer without an altar, a priest far from the sacred rites—yet all these things were at hand for him by the power of the Holy Spirit, and recognized by him, but completely invisible to those present. Then, after the customary words of thanksgiving and the blessing of the

---

57 St. Gregory does not mean that his father actually said Mass in his room, but that he was able to stand and say a few liturgical prayers while the Eucharistic Sacrifice was being offered in his church.

in misfortune? He was sick, then, and the time of his sickness was the holy and glorious Easter, the queen of days, that splendid night that dissipates the darkness of sin, in which we celebrate with abundant light the feast of our salvation, and in which, dying with the Light who died on our behalf, we rise again with Him who rose. This was the time of his affliction. Its nature, to describe it briefly, was as follows. A violent, burning fever consumed all his vitals, his strength had failed, he was unable to take food, his sleep had departed, he was in great distress, suffering from palpitation of the heart. The whole interior of his mouth, including the palate and the whole upper surface, had broken out into so many and such virulent and incessant ulcers that the swallowing even of water was not easy or without danger. Neither the skill of doctors, nor the prayers of his friends, however assiduous, nor any healing application was of avail. He was, then, in this condition, breathing shortly and with difficulty, not even perceiving those present, but wholly intent upon his departure and the things he had long desired and now made ready for him.

We were in God's temple, and occupied both with the sacred rites and with our supplications, for we had despaired of all else and betaken ourselves to the great Physician and the power of that night as the last source of succor. With what intention, shall I say? To celebrate the feast or to mourn? To keep the festival or honor with funeral services one no longer here? Oh, those tears then shed by the whole people! Oh, the voices, and cries, and hymns mingled with the singing of psalms! They sought the priest from the temple, the minister from the sacred rites, their worthy protector from God. My Mary[55] led them and struck the timbrel,[56] not of triumph but of supplication, learning then for the first time

---

55 St. Nonna, his mother.
56 Cf. Exod. 15.20.

to put aside shame in the face of sorrow, and calling both upon the people and upon God: upon the people, to sympathize with her in her distress and to vie in pouring out their tears; upon God, that He might hear her petitions, reminding Him, with the inventive power of grief, of all His miracles in former times.

(29) What, then, was the response of the God of that night and of the sick man? Trembling comes upon me as I continue the story. And you, too, may tremble as you listen to me, but do not disbelieve—for that would be impious, since I myself am the relater and it concerns him. The time of the mystery was at hand. All were reverently in their places, in order and in silence for the sacred rites. My father was then revived by Him who raises the dead to life, and by the holy night. At first he moved a little, then with more vigor. Then he called by name, very weakly and in an indistinct voice, one of the servants who were attending him, and bade him come forward and bring his clothes and lend his hand to support him. He came in consternation, and eagerly ministered to him. My father, making use of the guiding hand as a staff, imitated Moses on the mount, and forming his enfeebled hands in an attitude of prayer, and in union with or in behalf of the people, eagerly celebrated the Mysteries.[57] He employed few words, such as his weakened condition allowed, but his intention, as it seems to me, was most perfect. What a most unusual and miraculous situation! In the sanctuary without a sanctuary, a sacrificer without an altar, a priest far from the sacred rites—yet all these things were at hand for him by the power of the Holy Spirit, and recognized by him, but completely invisible to those present. Then, after the customary words of thanksgiving and the blessing of the

---

57 St. Gregory does not mean that his father actually said Mass in his room, but that he was able to stand and say a few liturgical prayers while the Eucharistic Sacrifice was being offered in his church.

people, he reclined again on his bed. After he took a little food and enjoyed some sleep, his spirit was revived and his health was gradually restored. When the new day of the feast came, for that is what we call the first Sunday after the Resurrection, he repaired to the temple of God, and with the whole congregation of his church present, he celebrated the renewal of his health and offered the sacrifice of thanksgiving. To me this event seems to be worthy of being regarded in the same category as the miracle of Ezechias,[58] who, when he was sick and prayed, was glorified by God with an extension of life. And this was signified by the bringing back of the shadow of the lines,[59] according to the petition of him who was restored. And God honored him at once both by the favor and the sign, confirming the extension of his days by the extension of the day.

(30) The same miracle occurred not long afterwards in the case of my mother, and it, too, ought not to be passed over. For I shall both pay her the honor which no one deserves more than she, and gratify him by associating her with him in my narrative. Hardy and vigorous and free from disease all her life, she herself was seized with sickness. Of the many ills she suffered, not to prolong my story, nothing affected her so grievously as the inability to eat. Her life was in danger for many days, and no remedy for the disease could be found. How did God sustain her? Not by raining down manna, as of old for Israel,[60] nor by striking the rock that gushed forth water for the thirsting people,[61] nor by feeding her with the help of ravens, as the great Elias,[62] nor by satisfying her need by a prophet carried through the air, as was done for Daniel of old when he suffered hunger in the lions' den.[63] In what

---
58 Cf. 4 Kings 20.1ff.
59 Cf. Isa. 38.8.
60 Cf. Exod. 16.14.
61 Cf. Exod. 17.6.
62 Cf. 3 Kings 17.6.
63 Cf. Dan.14.33.

manner, then? She thought that she saw me, her darling—for not even in dreams did she prefer any other of us—come up to her suddenly in the night with a basket of purest white bread, and after blessing and signing it with the cross according to my custom, feed and comfort her, and that she then recovered her strength. And this vision of the night was a thing of reality. For from that time she returned to herself and was of better hope. This is evidenced by a clear and manifest token. For on the day after, when I visited her early in the morning, I noticed at once that she was more cheerful. Then I asked her as usual how she had passed the night and whether she required anything. 'You fed me very readily and kindly, my son,' she said, 'and now you ask how I am! I feel splendid, and quite comfortable.' And at the same time her attendants made signs to me not to gainsay her and to accept her answer at once, lest she might be struck by despondency if the truth were revealed. I will add one more instance, common to both.

(31) I was voyaging from Alexandria to Greece over the Parthenian Sea. I sailed at a very unseasonable time, on an Aeginetan ship, impelled as I was by eager desire. What especially influenced me was that I had fallen in with a crew whom I knew well. We had proceeded but a little way when a violent storm arose, and one such as my shipmates said they had seldom experienced before. While all were afraid of a common death, I was in greater fear of spiritual death. Unfortunately, I was in danger of departing from life unbaptized, and I yearned for the spiritual water amid the waters of death. Therefore, I cried aloud and begged and implored a brief space of time. And my shipmates, in spite of their common danger, joined in my cries as not even many relatives would have done, being kindly strangers who had learned sympathy from their perils. Thus did I suffer, and my parents suffered with me, sharing my danger which became known to them in

a dream. And they brought help from the land, calming the waves by prayer, as afterwards we learned upon reckoning the time when I returned home. This was also revealed to me in a salutary sleep which I at length experienced when the storm abated a little. I seemed to be holding fast to a Fury of fearful aspect, threatening danger, for the night represented her clearly to me. Another of my fellow voyagers, a boy very well disposed and dear to me and deeply concerned for me, under the circumstances, thought he saw my mother walk upon the sea and seize the ship and with no great effort draw it to land. And this vision was believed, for the sea began to grow calm, and we quickly arrived at Rhodes, without experiencing any great distress in the meantime. As a result of that peril, we ourselves became an offering. We promised ourselves to God if we were saved, and, on being saved, we gave ourselves to Him.

(32) Such were the experiences common to both. But I think that some of those who know his life well have long been wondering why we have delayed on these points, as though we regarded them as his only claim to renown, and postponed mention of the difficulties of his times, against which he manifestly arrayed himself, as though he were unaware of them or did not consider them important. Come, then, let us add these also to our narrative. Our age brought forth its first and I think its last evil in the emperor[64] who was an apostate from God and reason. He deemed it a small matter to conquer the Persians, but one of the greatest importance to subject the Christians to his power. Together with the demons who led him and influenced him, he refrained from no form of wickedness, persuading, threatening, cajoling, and trying to draw them to himself not only by trickery but also by force. He could not indeed escape detection in striving to cloak persecution under sophistical artifices, nor in his

---
64 Julian the Apostate.

manifest use of authority, as he endeavored, in one way or another, by guile or force, to get us completely in his power.

Who can be found who more utterly despised or defeated him than my father? Among many other proofs of his contempt may be mentioned the incident of the bowmen and their commander whom he dispatched against our churches with the object of receiving their surrender or reducing them by force. For when, after attacking many others, he came here with like purpose and demanded the surrender of God's temple on the orders of the emperor, he failed to accomplish his objective to such a degree that, unless he had quickly given way to my father, either by his own decision or upon the advice of some one else, he would have departed with his feet mangled, so on fire was the priest with wrath and zeal against him in behalf of his shrine. And how could anyone appear to have effected the emperor's downfall more than he? In public, and with no fear of the times, he assailed the accursed one with the united prayers and petitions of the whole people; in private, he set his nocturnal array against him, wearing away those aged and tender limbs by lying on the ground and by watering the earth with his tears for almost a whole year. These practices he pursued for love of Him who alone knows secret things, striving to conceal them from us because of a piety removed from display, as I have said. And certainly he would have completely escaped notice had not I myself come suddenly into his room, and, having seen the signs of his lying on the ground, questioned his attendants what they meant, and so learned the mystery of the night.

(33) But there is a further story of the same period and of the same courage. The city of Caesarea was in turmoil over the election of a bishop. One had just departed and another was being sought, and there arose a violent dissension that could not be easily resolved. The city was naturally inclined

to be especially factious in this matter because of the fervor of its faith, and the splendor of the see only increased the rivalry. Such were the circumstances, and several bishops were at hand to consecrate the candidate chosen. The multitude was split up into many factions, all proposing different candidates, and, as usually happens in such cases, according as one chanced to be influenced by friendship for an individual or by piety toward God. Finally, the whole people, with one assent, selected by force one of their leading citizens,[65] a man of the highest character, but one who had not yet been sealed with holy baptism. Seizing him against his will, and with the help of the military detachment then in the city, they brought him into in the sanctuary and, leading him to the bishops, begged them to consecrate him and proclaim him bishop, mingling persuasion with force. They did not act in very orderly fashion, to be sure, but with great piety and ardor. And here it is not possible to mention anyone whom time showed more illustrious or more religious than he.

What happened then, and what course did the disorder take? The bishops were constrained, they purified him, proclaimed him, enthroned him, but by physical action rather than by spiritual judgment and disposition. This is manifest from what followed. For when they gladly withdrew and regained their freedom of judgment, they entered into council among themselves—that they were moved by the Spirit I am dubious. They resolved, at any rate, to consider nothing that had been done as valid, nor the appointment legitimate, pleading violence against him who had suffered no less violence, and seizing upon certain words uttered at the time more rashly than wisely.

But the great bishop and just appraiser of affairs was not carried away by those who adopted this course of action, nor did he approve their decision. He remained unbending and

---

65 Eusebius.

indomitable, as if no pressure at all had been put on him. For, since the violence was common, it followed necessarily that, if they brought a charge against him, they were open to a countercharge; or, if they acquitted him, they could likewise be acquitted; or, more justly still, not even if they acquitted him could they thereby be acquitted. If they were deserving of pardon, he certainly was, also; and if he was not to be excused, much less should they. For it would have been far better to have run the risk at the time and to have resisted to the very end than later to form designs against him, and in this crisis especially, when it would be better to dissolve existing enmities than to devise new ones. For matters stood as follows.

(34) The emperor was at hand, raging against the Christians. He was incensed at the consecration and threatened the new bishop, and the city was in the most imminent peril,[66] as to whether it would cease to exist after that day, or survive and receive some merciful treatment. The unusual character of the election had added to the exasperation he felt at the destruction of the temple of Fortune in a time of prosperity, and he concluded that he had been robbed of his authority. The governor of the province was anxious to turn the occasion to his own account, and was somewhat ill disposed to the new bishop, inasmuch as he had never been on friendly terms with him, because of disagreement on political grounds. He summoned the consecrators by letter, requesting them to bring charges against the new bishop, and in no gentle terms, but adding threats, as though this was commanded by the emperor. When the letter reached my father also, he replied without fear or delay. Let us consider the remarkable courage and spirit of his answer: 'Most excellent governor, we have one examiner and one Emperor of all our

---

66 The Greek reads literally 'on a razor's edge,' an expression going back to Homer, *Iliad* 10.173.

actions, and He is now under attack. He will scrutinize the present election, which we have carried out in a manner that was lawful and pleasing to Him. In any other matter you may very easily employ force if you wish to do so, but no one shall take from us the right to defend what has been done as rightly and justly done. Unless you pass a law to that effect, you have no right to meddle in our affairs.'

The recipient himself admired this letter, although for a while he was annoyed, according to the reports of many of those familiar with the case. It also stayed the onset of the emperor, and delivered the city from danger, and ourselves—and it is not inappropriate for me to add—from disgrace. This was the work of a bishop of a small city and a suffragan see. Is it not far better to hold such a primacy than to speak forth from a superior see, to be strong in action rather than in name?

(35) Who is so far removed from our world as not to know what is last in order of his deeds but the first and greatest in significance? The same city was again in turmoil over the same matter when the bishop who had suffered honorable violence had been suddenly carried off and had departed to God, for whom he had contended so nobly and courageously in the persecutions. The agitation was as heated as it was unreasonable. Who was pre-eminent, as not even the sun among the stars, was not unknown; it was perfectly clear, not only to all others, but to the select and purest portion of the people, those concerned with the sanctuary, and the Nazarites[67] among us. To them alone, or to them above all, should the right of making such appointments belong—for thus there would be no evil in the churches—instead of to the most wealthy and powerful, or to the impulse and rashness of the people, and especially to the most corrupt. But now I am almost ready to consider that civil government

---

67 I.e., the monks.

is more orderly than ours, to which divine grace is attributed, and that such matters are better controlled by fear than by reason. For who of sound mind could ever have approached another, ignoring your sacred and divine person,[68] molded by the hands of the Lord, the unwedded, without possessions, all but lacking flesh and blood, who in your words come next to the Word Himself, wise among philosophers, superior to the world among the worldly, my companion and my associate, and, to speak more daringly, the sharer of my soul, the partner of my life and education? I wish I were free to speak and describe you before others and not, because of your presence, be forced to consider each point carefully and pass over most of your praises, lest I be suspected of flattery. To return to what I began to say, the Spirit knew His own, for how could it be otherwise? But envy stood in the way, and on the part of those whom I am ashamed to mention. And would that it were not possible to hear it from others, who make it a point to ridicule our affairs. But passing this by, as rivers pass by rocks in the middle of their courses, let us honor with silence what deserves to be forgotten and proceed to what comes next in our discourse.

(36) The man of the Spirit had a clear insight into the things of the Spirit, and therefore he felt that he ought not to adopt a submissive attitude, nor contend with the aid of factions and prejudices, which depend more on favor than on God, but to look to one thing only, the good of the Church and the common salvation of all. Accordingly, he wrote letters, gave advice, united the people, the priests, and all others connected with the sanctuary. He gave testimony, he voted and ordained, even while he was absent, and he assumed the prerogative of age in exercising authority over strangers as if they were his own people. Finally, since it was necessary that

---

68 St. Basil is being addressed in these terms.

his consecration be canonical and one bishop of the number[69] required for the proclamation was lacking, dragging himself from his couch, although broken by age and disease, he hastened courageously to the city, or rather he was borne along, with body dead or scarcely breathing, persuaded that, if anything happened to him, this zeal of his would be a noble burial. Thereupon occurred a prodigy not unworthy of belief. He grew strong from the great exertion and, vigorous from his zeal, he took charge of affairs, he participated in the conflict, enthroned the bishop, and was escorted home, no longer on a funeral bier but as if in a divine ark. His forbearance, which I have but lately ceased praising, was in this case even more fully shown. For when his colleagues could not brook the shame of defeat and the influence of the old man in affairs, and for that reason began to be annoyed at him and abuse him, he had the strength of endurance to overcome them also, finding in moderation his most effective ally, and in declining to meet abuse with abuse. For what a terrible thing it would be, he felt, if, when he had actually won the victory, he should suffer himself to be vanquished by his tongue. Consequently, he so won them over by his forbearance, gaining time also as an aid for his judgment, that with their irritation changing to admiration they fell at his feet and excused themselves. They were ashamed of their previous conduct and, casting aside their hatred, submitted to him as their patriarch, their lawgiver, and their judge.

(37) The same zeal was shown in his opposition to the heretics, when, inspired by the emperor's[70] impiety, they marched against us with the purpose of vanquishing us also and of adding us to the others who were nearly all enslaved. For here, too, he was of no little assistance, both in his own

---

69 Three bishops were required to be present.
70 Valens.

person, and through ourselves perhaps, whom he urged on, like well-bred dogs, against these most savage beasts, striving to train us in piety. One thing I have to blame in both of you, and I beg you not to be vexed at my frankness in speaking, for I will disclose the cause of my pain, even though you find this somewhat annoying. When I was disgusted with the evils of this life, and filled with a passionate desire for solitude, such, to my knowledge, as no one of our age possessed, when I strove eagerly to avoid the surge and dust of public life and escape to a place of safety, somehow or other you seized me and, by the glorious title of the priesthood, handed me over to this mean and treacherous mart of souls. As a result, some evils have befallen me and others are yet to be expected. For the man who has suffered in the past is somewhat diffident of the future, even though reason in its optimism may urge the contrary.

(38) There is another excellence of his which I must not leave unmentioned. He was capable of great endurance in all respects and was superior to the garment of the flesh. During his last sickness, a long and dangerous one, adding its assault to the affliction of old age, he had the weakness common to all men, but there was a circumstance that was not common, but was quite characteristic of him, and in keeping with the other marvels. Although there was never a time when he was not troubled by suffering but was in pain often every day, sometimes hourly, his only relief was the liturgy, to which his suffering gave way, as though banished by decree. When he had lived almost a hundred years, exceeding David's limits of man's age,[71] and had spent forty-five years, the average span of human life, in the priesthood, he closed his life in a good old age. And in what manner? With the words and habit of prayer, leaving behind no trace of vice, but many memorials of virtue. In consequence, there was for him, on

---

71 Cf. Ps. 89.10.

the lips and in the hearts of all, a reverence greater than the lot of man. And it is not easy to find anyone who recollects him and does not lay his hand upon his mouth, as Scripture says,[72] and honor his memory. Such was his life and such its completion and perfection.

(39) Since it was fitting that a memorial of his magnanimity be left for posterity, what was more appropriate than this temple, which he erected for God and for us, helped a little, certainly, by the people, but defraying the greater portion of the cost from his own means? It is a work not to be passed over in silence, for in size it surpasses most and in beauty nearly all. Graced with eight regular equilaterals, it rises aloft in the beauty of its two stories of pillars and porticoes, adorned with lifelike statues. Its vault above is brilliant, dazzling the eyes with its abundant sources of light, truly the dwelling place of light. It is surrounded by jutting equiangular ambulatories of the most brilliant material, which encompass a wide area within them. It is splendid in the loveliness of its doors and vestibules and welcomes those approaching from afar. I have not yet spoken of its external adornment, the beauty and size of its square and perfectly fitted stonework, both the marble in the bases and capitals which cover the corners, and the native stone, inferior in no way to that from abroad. Nor have I mentioned the various and multicolored friezes, projecting or inlaid, from the foundation to the roof, which taxes the spectator by limiting his view. How could a brief account do justice to a work requiring so much time and so much toil? Or will it be enough to say that while many works, both private and public, adorn other cities, this by itself alone has been able to render us celebrated among men everywhere? Such is his temple. But since there was also need of a priest, he provided one at his own expense. Whether he was worthy of the temple, I cannot say, but at any rate he provided him.

---

72 Cf. Job 39.34.

And when sacrifices were required, he supplied them also in the misfortunes of his son and his patience in adversity, that God might receive from him a rational holocaust, a spiritual victim, to be consumed instead of the sacrifice of the Law.

(40) What do you say, my father? It this enough, and do you accept this eulogy accompanying you to the tomb as recompense for those labors you undertook for my education? And according to your old custom, do you grant peace to my discourse, and set a limit upon it, shunning excess, that it may be of right measure? Or do you require some addition? You bid me cease, I know, for I have spoken long enough. But let me add one thing more. Reveal to us what glory you enjoy, what light encompasses you, and receive in the same abode your consort, soon to follow you, and the children you laid to rest before you, and me, also, when I have suffered no further or little more at least of the ills of this life. And before coming to that abode, receive me in this sweet stone, which you erected for both of us, honoring even here your priest and namesake. Excuse me both for the people whom I left and for the people whom for your sake I accepted.[73] And guide safe from danger the whole flock and all the bishops, whose father you were called, and especially me, who was overpowered by you and coerced in fatherly and spiritual guise, so that I may not entirely blame you for that tyranny.

(41) But what think you,[74] O judge of our words and actions? If my discourse has been adequate and meets with your desire, indicate this by your decision and we shall accept it. For your decision is really the decision of God. But if it falls far short of his glory and your expectations, I have an ally near at hand. Let your voice be heard, awaited by his merits as a shower in season. Surely, he had bound you to himself by the closest ties, as pastor to pastor and as a father to his

---
73 He resigned the see of Sasima to become Bishop of Nazianzus.
74 St. Basil is being addressed here.

son in grace. What wonder, if he[75] who through you has thundered to the whole world should himself also reap some benefit from your voice. It remains only to join in spiritual reflection on the last rites with our spiritual Sara, the lifelong partner of our father Abraham.

(42) The nature of God and men, my dear mother, or, to speak more generally, the nature of divine things and earthly things is not the same. The divine both in its essence and in its properties is unchangeable and immortal, for the attributes of things constant remain constant. But how is it with us? Our nature is in a state of flux and corruption and suffers change upon change. Life and death as they are called, although they seem to differ very much, somehow succeed and replace each other. The one, beginning from the corruption which is our mother, passes through the corruption which is the uninterrupted change of the present, and ends in the corruption which is the dissolution of this life. The other, which gives us release from present ills and often translates us to the life above, cannot, to my way of thinking, properly be called death, as it is fearful more in name than in reality. We are even likely to be somewhat unreasonably afraid of what is not fearful and to pursue as preferable what ought to be feared. There is one life: to look to life. There is one death, sin, for it is the destruction of the soul. But all else, in which some take pride, is but a dreamful vision mocking realities, and deceitful phantasms of the soul. If such is our nature, mother, we shall neither pride ourselves on life, nor be overtroubled by death. What dread fate do we suffer in being transferred hence to the true life, if, on being released from the vicissitudes, the insolence, the turmoil, and the base tribute exacted by this life, we shall be amid stable and unvarying things, as little lights which dance about the great Light?

---

75 St. Gregory the Elder was largely responsible for St. Basil's elevation to the episcopacy.

(43) Does the thought of separation grieve you? Then let hope cheer you. Is widowhood a grievous burden? Yet it is not grievous to him. And where is love's goodness if it gives the easier role to itself and the more arduous one to its neighbor? Why should it even be grievous at all to one who is soon to be dissolved? The appointed day is near at hand; the pain will not last long. Let us not by ignoble thinking give weight to the merest trifles. Great is the loss we have suffered, for great was the blessing we enjoyed. Loss is common to all, but the enjoyment of blessings belongs to but few. Without being depressed by the first thought, let us be consoled by the second. For it is more reasonable that the better should prevail. You have endured most bravely and sensibly the loss of children still in their prime and qualified for longer life. Endure also the laying away of an aged frame, already weary of life, although the vigor of his mind preserved his senses unimpaired. But you need someone to care for you? Where, then, is this Isaac of yours, whom he has left behind for you in place of all? Ask him for small favors, such as lending you his hand and serving you, and repay him with the greater benefits of a mother's benediction, and prayers, and the freedom of heaven. Are you vexed at being admonished? I praise you for it. For you yourself have admonished many who in the course of your long life have availed themselves of your sagacity. In no way do my words apply to you who are supremely wise. But let them be a common balm of consolation to those who mourn that they may realize that they are mortals escorting mortals to the grave.

SAINT AMBROSE

ON THE DEATH OF HIS BROTHER SATYRUS

Translated by
JOHN J. SULLIVAN, C. S. Sp., Ph.D.
Duquesne University

and

MARTIN R. P. McGUIRE, Ph.D.
The Catholic University of America

INTRODUCTION

URANIUS SATYRUS, brother of St. Ambrose, died early in the year 378 (not in 375, as is still stated in most books of reference). The two brothers had been closely associated from boyhood and were unusually devoted to each other through similarity of temperament and their common pursuit of the highest Christian ideals. Both had entered upon careers in the imperial service and had risen to high posts. When Ambrose was unexpectedly elected Bishop of Milan, Satyrus resigned his position in the imperial government and returned to Milan, where he devoted himself to the administration of the family property and also relieved Ambrose to a large degree from the temporal cares of his episcopal household and diocese. Satyrus was excessively shy and simple in manner, but was a most efficient and successful administrator. He also revealed great tact in composing occasional differences which arose between St. Ambrose himself and their strong-willed sister, Marcellina, the eldest of the three. From an early age, she had become a consecrated virgin, and lived in her mother's house at Rome. Satyrus, whose health was not too robust, fell seriously ill after shipwreck and exposure on a return voyage from Africa in 377 and died shortly after reaching home. The grief of Ambrose and his sister for such a devoted brother was very great and it was shared by the public at large, for Satyrus was universally admired and loved for his amiability and fairness.

The body of Satyrus lay in state for a week, and was then carried by the nearest relatives accompanied by a vast throng of people, in funeral procession, to the cemetery church at Milan, where Mass was celebrated. Marcellina was present at the funeral. Following the reading of the Gospel, St. Ambrose mastered his deep grief sufficiently to deliver a very touching and personal funeral oration, *On the Death of His Brother Satyrus*. This oration, which was undoubtedly recorded by notaries, was subsequently revised and expanded and given the final form in which we now read it.

It was also customary to commemorate the dead on the third and the thirtieth, or on the seventh and fortieth day, after the funeral. Mass was offered, and a commemorative address was frequently delivered. Accordingly, St. Ambrose gave a second funeral oration on his brother on the seventh day after the funeral. This address was carefully prepared and written out before delivery. It is less personal and more definitely related to the pagan literary genre known as the consolation. While drawing freely from pagan models, and especially from the lost *De consolatione* of Cicero, St. Ambrose naturally lays greater emphasis on the consolation to be derived from basic Christian ideas on death and resurrection. The idea of resurrection, in fact, is stressed so much that this second oration is frequently called *On Faith in the Resurrection* (*De fide resurrectionis*) or *On the Resurrection of the Dead* (*De resurrectione mortuorum*) in many manuscripts. St. Ambrose himself, moreover, in a later work (*Enarr. in ps.* 1.51) refers to his two orations on Satyrus as his 'books on consolation and resurrection.' The first oration in its elaborated written form was thus combined with the second and regarded as a work in two books dealing with the theme indicated.

FIRST ORATION

WE HAVE BROUGHT HERE, beloved brethren, my sacrifice in the person of my lord and brother Satyrus, an untainted victim and one pleasing to God. I was mindful that he was subject to death and the thought was not false, but grace has abounded beyond measure.[1] Consequently, far from complaining, I even have reason to thank God. For my desire has ever been that, in any troubles awaiting either the Church or me, they should fall rather upon me and my household. Thanks be to God, therefore, that in the present state of universal apprehension, when barbarian invasions make for every sort of misgiving,[2] my personal sorrow has put an end to public grieving, and there has been visited upon me the kind of calamity that we were fearing for all. I only wish that this has been fully accomplished here, namely, that my sorrow is the price paid for ransoming the people from their sorrow.

(2) I have considered nothing, dear brethren, in human relationships more priceless than such a brother, nothing worthier of my affection, nothing more dear. But public

---
[1] Cf. 1 Tim. 1.14.
[2] The barbarian peril referred to would seem to be the threatened invasion of the Goths in 377 ff. Cf. Faller, *op. cit.* 85*-88*.

concerns come before personal matters. Were someone also to sound my brother's sentiments, it would be discovered that he would prefer to be slain for others than to live for himself, since for that reason Christ according to the flesh died for all, so that we might learn to live not for ourselves alone.[3]

(3) Furthermore, I cannot be ungrateful to God. For it should be a cause for joy that I had such a brother rather than a source of sorrow for having lost him. For to have had him was a gift; to have lost him was the price to be paid. Hence, so long as it was permitted, I enjoyed the loan entrusted to me. Now, He who deposited the loan has withdrawn it. There is no difference between swearing that no loan has been made and grieving because it has been returned. In either case, faith wavers and salvation is in peril. If refusal to repay a debt is a fault, is refusal to make a sacrifice an act of virtue? Granted a lender of money can be tricked out of his wealth, the Author of nature, who lends us our kinsmen, cannot be cheated. The greater the amount of the sum loaned, the more handsome must be the interest to be paid on the capital.

(4) Hence, I cannot be ungrateful over my brother. He has given back only what is common to nature and he has merited the reward which belongs to grace alone. For who can raise objection to a condition universal in application? Who can grieve because a security especially dear to him has been taken away, when for our comfort the Father delivered His only Son unto death for us?[4] Who should fancy that he ought to be exempted from dying, if he has not been exempted from being born? It is a great mystery of divine love that not even Christ was exempted from bodily death and that, even though Lord of nature, He did not object to the law of the flesh which He had taken upon Himself. I must die. For

---
3 Cf. 2 Cor. 5.15.
4 Cf. Rom. 8.32.

Him there was no such necessity. Could not He who said of a servant: 'If I wish him to remain until I come, what is it to thee?'[5] have Himself remained alive if He had so wished? But by his continuance in this life, he would have lost his reward and nullified my sacrifice. What greater comfort have we, therefore, than the fact that even Christ died according to the flesh? Or why should I weep excessively over my brother, so long as I know that the divine love of Christ could not die?

(5) Why should I be the one to show more grief for my brother than all you other mourners? I have dissolved my personal grief in the public sorrow, especially since mine is of no avail, while yours builds up faith and provides comfort. You who are wealthy mourn, and by your mourning you show that accumulated riches are no aid to salvation. For death cannot be put off with a payment of money, and the last day carries off rich and poor alike. You who are old mourn, because in this situation you fear for the lot of your children. Since, then, you cannot prolong human life, train your children not for the enjoyment of the body but for the service of virtue. Even you who are in the bloom of youth grieve, because the end of life is not ripe old age. The poor, too, have mourned, and, what is much more valuable and fruitful, they have washed away his transgressions by their tears. These are ransoming tears, these are groans that conceal the sorrow of death, this is the grief which hides the feeling of former grief by the fullness of an unending joy. Therefore, while the funeral is that of a private individual, there is general mourning. Hence, that mourning cannot last long which is hallowed by the affection of all.

(6) Why, indeed, should I weep for you, my dearest brother, when you were thus taken away from me that all might have you in common? I have not lost you; I have simply altered my manner of enjoying you. Before, we were

---

5 John 21.22.

inseparable in a corporeal sense; now, we are undivided in our affection. For you abide with me, and you will abide with me forever. When you were living among us, our country never took you away from me. You yourself never preferred our country to me, and now you have given me our other country. For I have begun to be no longer a stranger in the land where the better portion of myself now is. I really never lived for myself alone, since the better part of both of us was in each other. Yet we were both in Christ, in whom is the sum of all things and the portion of every individual. This grave, within which is the fruit not of nature but of grace, is more precious to me than our native soil. In your body, which now lies lifeless, is the better effort of my life, and in this body also, which I carry about, the richer portion belongs to you.

(7) As I recall you with gratitude, so I wish that I could breathe into your life whatever of vital spirit I possess, and that half of my days might be cut off and be available for your enjoyment! For it would seem proper that we who always kept our paternal inheritance undivided should not have our span of years divided, or, at least, that we who have lived inseparable lives should not have separate appointments with death.

(8) But now, brother, what progress can I make, in what direction shall I turn! If ever an ox has sought the stricken mate with which it was accustomed to be yoked to the plow, and has felt that a part of itself is missing, and has given proof of its tender affection by frequent bellowing, why, brother, should I not long for you? How can I ever forget the one with whom I always drew the plow of this life? In labor I was inferior to you, but in love no less united. I was not suitable so much because of my own strength as endurable through your patience. With anxious and devoted affection you always protected my side with yours as a brother in

love, as a father in your care, as an elder in solicitude, and as a younger person in respect. Hence, in one relationship you so exercised the offices of several toward me that in you I seek, not one, but many lost dear ones. In you, flattery was unknown, and dutiful affection was manifest. Your love was so all-embracing that you had nothing to add by resorting to guile. Thus, you could not receive an increase and you did not look forward to reciprocation.

(9) But where is such unrestrained sorrow carrying me in my recollection of kindness and forgetfulness of duty? The Apostle recalls me and puts a curb on my grief, saying, as you recently heard: 'We would not, brethren, have you ignorant concerning those who are asleep, lest you should grieve, even as others who have no hope.'[6] Forgive me, dear brethren. For not all of us can say: 'Be ye imitators of me, as I am of Christ.'[7] But if you seek a model to imitate, you have one whom you can imitate. Though we are not all suited to teach, would that we were all apt to learn!

(10) But we have not committed a serious fault by our weeping. Not every display of sorrow is a sign either of a lack of trust in God or of weakness in ourselves. Natural grief is one thing, sorrow which comes from lack of hope is another, and there is a great difference between longing for what you had and grieving because you have lost it. Not only does sorrow beget tears, but joy does, also. Piety excites tears, prayer waters the couch, and supplication, as the Prophet has said, washes the bed.[8] Whenever a patriarch was buried, his people wept profusely. Tears are, therefore, indicators of devotedness, not inciters of grief. Hence, I frankly allow that I, too, have wept, but the Lord also wept. He wept for a stranger;

---

6 1 Thess. 4.13.
7 1 Cor. 4.16.
8 Cf. Ps. 6.7.

I weep for my brother.⁹ In one He wept for all; I will weep for you, my brother, through all.

(11) He wept not through His feeling of emotion but through ours, for the Godhead knows no tears. He wept in the human nature in which He was sad.¹⁰ He wept in the human nature in which He was crucified, in which He died, in which He was buried. He wept in that nature of which today the Prophet spoke, saying: 'Shall not Mother Sion say: Man and man is born in her and the Highest Himself hath founded her?'¹¹ He wept in the nature in which He called Sion Mother, being conceived of the Virgin and born in Judaea. He could not, however, have a mother according to His divine nature, because He is his mother's Creator. He was made, not by divine, but by human generation. Because He was made man, God was born.

(12) So we have in another place: 'A child is born to us, and a son is given to us.'¹² In the term 'child' there is an indication of age; in the term 'son' a reference to the fullness of Godhead. He was made of His mother, and born of the Father, but, as the same Person, He was both born and given. Do not think of two but of one. For the Son of God is one Person, both born of the Father and sprung from the Virgin. The names differ in order but unite in one, just as the Scriptural lesson just read teaches: 'Man was made in her and the Highest Himself hath founded her.'¹³ He was man indeed in body, but the Highest in power. And while He is both God and man through diversity of nature, He is the same person, not two persons, though being both God and man. He has, therefore, something peculiar to His own nature

---

9 Cf. John 11.35.
10 Cf. Matt. 26.38.
11 Ps. 86.5 (Septuagint).
12 Isa. 9.6.
13 Ps. 86.5.

and something in common with us, but in both cases He is one and in both He is perfect.

(13) It should not, therefore, be a cause for wonder that God made Him both Lord and Christ. He, therefore, made Him Jesus, Him indeed who received the name in His human nature. God made Him of whom also the patriarch David writes: 'Shall not Mother Sion say: Man and man is born in her and the Highest Himself hath founded her?'[14] He is unlike the Father, not, of course, in divinity, but in His body. He is not distinct from the Father except in function. He remains His associate in power, though separated from Him in the mystery of the Passion.

(14) A discussion of this topic calls for further exposition to show the authority of the Father, the attributes of the Son, and the unity of the whole Trinity.[15] But today I have assumed the task, not of theological discussion, but of giving consolation, even though it is customary in consoling to distract the soul from sorrow by fixing the attention on discussion. Yet I wish to temper my grief rather than to destroy my feeling of affection, to assuage my longing rather than to remove it from my mind. For I do not want to digress too far from my brother and be distracted with other matters, since I have undertaken this address for the sake of being, as it were, his traveling companion, that in spirit I may attend him longer on his journey, and embrace with my mind him whom my eyes behold. I like to fix my whole gaze upon him, to linger with him, and show him all the offices of the heart, to address him with all endearing terms. Meanwhile, my mind is numbed into believing that I have not lost him whom I am still able to see present. I cannot realize that he is dead, and I am

---
14 Ps. 86.5.
15 It should be recalled that St. Ambrose was speaking when Arianism was at its height. Hence his preoccupation with the attributes and position of Christ in the Trinity.

still not seeking in vain for those services of his to which I attributed my life and every breath.

(15) How, then, can I make a return for such kindness and such labors? I, brother, had made you my heir, and you left me yours. I wanted you to survive me, and I am your survivor. That I might make some return for your kindnesses, I used to extend my best wishes. Though I am now deprived of the opportunity even of wishing you well, I have not lost your benefits to me. As successor to my own heir, what shall I do? As one who has outlived his own life, what shall I do? As one with no right to this light which I still enjoy, what shall I do? What gratitude and what favors can I show you in return? From me you receive nothing save tears. Or, perhaps, the tears, which are all I have left, you do not seek, because you are secure in your reward. For even when you were still alive, you used to forbid tears and to state that our grief was a greater cause of pain to you than the thought of your own death. Tears prevent my going further, and weeping restrains me. But for your sake they forbid also lest, while we shed tears for our own loss, we seem to be despairing of your deserts.

(16) Certainly, for me at least, you have lessened the pangs even of this grief. I, who once feared for you, have now no cause for fear, and I no longer have anything for the world to take from me. Though your holy sister is still living, reverenced for her purity, your equal in character and no less your rival in kindness and duty, we both used to fear more for your sake, because we thought that our joy in this life was centered in you. For your sake it was a pleasure to live, and for your sake the thought of death caused us no pain. We both prayed that you would survive us, and the thought of our surviving you was a forbidding one. Did not our hearts shrink when a fear of this kind scarcely touched

us? Were our minds not completely stunned at the news of your sickness?

(17) What a sorry notion of things we had! We thought that you, whom we see taken away, were restored to us. Now we realize that it was your vows to the holy martyr Lawrence that obtained for you a return home.[16] And would that you had obtained not only a safe passage, but also greater length of days! Since you were able to obtain the privilege of coming hither, you certainly could have obtained many more years of life. But truly I thank Thee, almighty and everlasting God, that Thou didst not refuse us at least these last consolations, and that Thou didst grant us the longed-for return of our most beloved brother from Sicily and Africa. He was snatched away so quickly after he came back that his death would almost seem to have been delayed to enable him to return to his brother and sister.

(18) I now have my precious treasure, and no journeying can again tear him from me. I possess his relics to embrace, his grave to cover with my body, and his sepulchre to lie upon. And I believe that I shall become more pleasing to God for resting above the bones of this holy body. Would that I had been able in similar fashion to employ my body to prevent his death! Had you been attacked with swords, I would rather have offered myself to be pierced in your stead. Had I been able to recall your departing soul, I would rather have offered my own.

(19) It availed me nothing to have caught your last breath and to have breathed into your mouth as you were dying.[17] For my thought was that I could either receive your death or transfuse my life into you. Oh, how sad, and yet

---

16 Satyrus had recently made a successful trip to Africa to recover family property which had been taken over illegally by a certain Prosper. On falling ill after shipwreck and exposure, he petitioned St. Lawrence that he might be granted the favor of being able to reach home.
17 Cf. Vergil, *Aeneid* 4.684,685.

how sweet, were the pledges of our last kisses! How sorrowful those embraces, in the midst of which your dying body grew tense and your last breath vanished! I tightened my arms about you, but, as I took the last breath from your mouth that I might share in your death, I had already lost you as I held you. In a manner which I cannot explain, that breath became a source of life to me, and diffused, even in death, a richer odor of affection. Even if I could not prolong your life by my breath, I wish, at least, that the vigor of your own last breath might have been transfused into my mind, and that our attitude would now be reflecting the noble innocence and purity of your heart. Then, dearest brother, you would have left me an inheritance which would confer noteworthy honor and favor on your heir.

(20) What, therefore, shall I do, now that I have lost all the sweetness, all the consolations, in fine, all the charm of this life? For you alone were my comfort at home, my glory abroad. You, I repeat, advised me in counsels, shared my cares, relieved my anxiety, dispelled my sadness, supported my acts, and defended my thoughts. Upon you alone, finally, rested domestic responsibilities and public cares. I call your holy soul to witness that in my work of church-building I was often afraid of displeasing you. Thus, upon your last return, you reproved me for delay. At home and abroad you thus assumed the role of teacher and adviser to the bishop, that you would not allow him to think about domestic matters and would advise him to devote himself to public concerns. Hence, I have no fear of seeming to speak boastfully— for this is your just meed of praise—when I say that you managed the home of your brother without offense to anyone, and that you won honor and favor for his episcopate.

(21) I perceive, indeed, that my heart is filled with emotion as I recount your services and enumerate your virtues. But I find respite in my very emotion itself, and, al-

though these recollections renew my grief, they also afford me pleasure. Is it possible for me either not to think of you, or ever to think of you without tears? And shall I ever be able either not to remember such a brother, or to remember him without a kind of tearful joy? For what delight was ever mine that did not proceed from you? What enjoyment, I repeat, was mine without you, or yours without me? What experience did we not have in common, including almost our very sight and sleep? Were our wills ever in disagreement? Were even our steps not common? Truly, when I raised my foot, did you not seem to be moving my body or I, yours?

(22) But if ever one of us had to journey forth without the other, you would fancy that his side was unprotected, you would see his troubled countenance, and you would judge that his soul was sad. That accustomed affability, that usual vigor, was no longer conspicuous. The appearance of one of us alone aroused the suspicion and fear of some illness—so strange it seemed to everyone when we were apart! As for myself, in fact, forgetting my brother's absence, I would often turn my head to speak to him as if he were present, and I seemed to be seeing him and talking with him. But whenever I was disappointed in my hopes I used to imagine that I was carrying, as it were, a heavy yoke upon my neck. I found it difficult to proceed, I was self-conscious at being seen, and I would hurry back home, because I did not like to go farther without you.

(23) But when both of us had to journey forth together there was a word for every step we took, our speech was as unbroken as our pace, and we had no thought of our walking but only of the pleasure of conversation, for each of us hung on the lips of the other. We gave no attention to our surroundings as we passed along, but listened to each other with mutual interest, drinking in the love in each other's eyes and reflecting our radiant pleasure in each other's sight and

presence. How I used secretly within myself to admire your virtues! How I used to congratulate myself that the Lord had given me such a brother, so modest, so capable, so innocent, so simple of heart! When I would think of your innocence I would begin to have doubts of your capability, and when I would see your ability for getting things done I could hardly think of innocence as being one of your traits. Yet you combined both qualities through your unusual strength and perfection of character.

(24) Hence, whatever business we had not been able to settle together you carried through successfully alone. Prosper, as I hear, was congratulating himself because, since I had become a bishop, he did not imagine that he would have to restore what he had stolen. But he found your ability alone more formidable than that of both of us combined. And so he paid all, fully appreciative of your moderation and without adopting a mocking attitude toward your native shyness. He was even grateful that you were so retiring, nor, in the face of your competence, was he arrogant. But for whom, brother, did you strive to get what you did? We intended that the reward for your efforts should be in full keeping with their demonstration. You finished everything to the last detail and, when your work was done, you came home. Now you alone, who are dearer to me than all, are snatched away, just as if you had postponed death to give full realization to your love for me and to carry off the palm for effective action.

(25) What little pleasure, dearest brother, did we take in the honors of this world, since they kept us separated! Consequently, we accepted them, not because we wanted to do so, but because we feared that a lack of interest on our part might seem reprehensible. Or perhaps they were given to us in order that, since your sudden death was to destroy our pleasure, we might already learn how to live without each other.

(26) When I reread again and again my letters to you, I realize what deep forebodings occupied my mind. I tried to dissuade you, brother, from going to Africa and urged, rather, that you send someone else. I was afraid to have you begin this journey and to entrust you to the deep. Even a greater apprehension than usual oppressed my mind. But you made the trip, settled the business at hand, and once more entrusted yourself to the sea in a vessel, as I hear, which was old and full of leaks. Since you had set your mind on a speedy return, you neglected all caution, eagerly desiring our company again and ignoring your own danger.

(27) How deceitful is joy, and how uncertain the course of human life! I thought that because you got back from Africa, were restored from the sea, and saved from shipwreck, you could no longer be taken from us. But we, though we are on land, are experiencing a more grievous shipwreck. For the death of my brother, who saved himself from perishing in shipwreck through his strong swimming, has become a shipwreck for us. What enjoyment is left to us, now that we have lost such a dear and glorious ornament, now that our light in the darkness of this world has been extinguished? In him not only the glory of our family but also that of our whole country has perished.

(28) Naturally, I am most grateful to you, beloved brethren, my holy people, that you consider my sorrow as your own sorrow, that you think that our bereavement has fallen upon yourselves, and that with this new and wonderful exhibition of affection you are offering the tears of the whole city, of every age, and of all orders. This is not the sorrow proper to private sympathy, but a public offering and service inspired by general good will. Yet, if you feel any sympathy for me personally because I have lost such a brother, I derive a rich recompense from this, since I have the pledge of your love. I wish my brother were alive. But I must grant that,

while proof of public kindness is pleasant in prosperity, it is especially welcome in adversity.

(29) Indeed, it strikes me that such a wealth of kindness deserves more than the usual form of gratitude. For it is not without point that, in the Acts of the Apostles, widows are described as weeping when Tabitha died,[18] or that, in the Gospel, a crowd is represented as moved by a widow's tears and as joining the funeral procession of the young man who was soon to be raised from the dead.[19] Widows alone wept for Tabitha; the whole city weeps for Satyrus. It is certain, therefore, that the protection of the Apostles is obtained. It is certain, I repeat, that Christ was moved to pity when He saw you weeping. Though He has not now touched the coffin, He has received the spirit commended to Him. Though He has not summoned the dead with a human voice, by virtue of His divine power He has liberated his soul from the pains of death and the assaults of evil spirits. Though the deceased has not sat up in the coffin, he has found rest in Christ. Though he has not spoken to us, he sees the things which are above us and he already rejoices in his superior knowledge. For by the words which we read in the Gospel we understand what is in store for us, and what we behold in this life is an indication of what shall be.

(30) He for whom is reserved a restoration of life for eternity has no need of being restored for a little while in time. Why should he fall back into this miserable and wretched corruption? Why should he return to this life of tears? Should we not be more than happy that he has been rescued from such impending evils and threatening perils? For, if no one mourned for Henoch after he was taken up bodily to heaven[20] in an age of peace and cessation of war,

---

18 Cf. Acts 9.36-39.
19 Cf. Luke 7.14,15.
20 Cf. Gen. 5.24.

and if, on the contrary, the Prophet gave praise, as Scripture says of him: 'He was taken away lest wickedness should alter his understanding,'[21] how much more justly must this be said now, when to the alluring dangers of the world there is added the uncertainty of life! He was taken away so that he might not fall into the hands of the barbarians; he was taken away so that he might not witness the destruction of the whole earth, the end of the world, the burials of his relatives, the death of his fellow citizens, and, last but not least, something more painful than any death, the pollution of virgins and widows.

(31) Therefore, brother, I count you fortunate, both in the glory of your life and in the opportuneness of your death. Not from us were you taken away, but from perils. You did not lose your life; you escaped the fear of impending afflictions. What holy compassion you would feel for your family if you knew that Italy was now threatened by an enemy who is so near! How you would groan and lament that our greatest safety lay in the barrier of the Alps and that purity's last defence consisted of barricades of wood! With what anguish would you grieve at the sight of your friends being so poorly protected from a lustful and cruel enemy, who spares neither chastity nor life!

(32) How, I repeat, could you bear what we shall be compelled to endure and perhaps, what is worse, to witness: virgins ravaged, infants dragged from their mothers' arms and tossed upon spears, the violation of bodies consecrated to God, and even aged widows made to serve the purposes of lust? How, I ask, could you endure these things? Even with your last breath, unmindful of self but much concerned for us, you repeatedly warned us of the danger of barbarian invasion and said that you had good reason for urging that we should flee. You did this, perhaps, because you saw that we

---

21 Wisd. 4.11.

would be left destitute by your death. And you did it, not out of timidity, but out of love for us. While always courageous in yourself, you felt timid out of anxiety in our behalf. When you were called home by the noble Symmachus,[22] your kinsman, because Italy was reported to be aflame with war, because you were hastening into peril, and because you might fall into the hands of the enemy, you replied that you were coming for this reason only, namely, that you might not fail us in our danger and that you might be a sharer in your brother's peril.

(33) You were fortunate, therefore, in such an opportune death and in not being saved to witness our present calamities. Certainly you have been more fortunate than your holy sister,[23] for she is deprived of your comfort and is in fear of violence to her modesty. Recently happy through having two brothers, she is now miserable because of both. She can neither follow the one nor leave the other. Your grave is her lodging, and your body's sepulchre her home. And would that even this lodging place were safe! Our food is in weeping and our drink is in tears.[24] For Thou hast given us the bread of tears for nourishment and Thou hast given us drink in tears in measure, or perhaps beyond measure.

(34) What am I to say of myself? I cannot die without leaving my sister, and I have no pleasure in life separated from you. For what can be pleasant to me without you, since you were ever the source of all my pleasure? What joy is there in remaining longer in this life, and in tarrying where we lived happily as long as we lived together? Even if there were anything which could give us delight here, it could not do so without your presence. If ever I rashly wished my life to

---

22 L. Avianius Symmachus, father of Symmachus the orator and opponent of St. Ambrose in the Altar of Victory controversy.
23 Marcellina.
24 Cf. Ps. 79.6.

be prolonged, now, at any rate, I would not wish to live without you.

(35) The present situation is unbearable. How can I bear to go on without you, the excellent companion of my life and the partner in all my labors and duties? I could not make his loss more bearable by reflecting on its possibility, so much did my mind dread even to think of such a thing! Not that I was unaware of his condition, but my constant prayer and desire had so dulled the sense of our common weakness that I could not think about him at all except in terms of continued happiness.

(36) Therefore, when I was recently quite ill—and would that it had been the end for me!—my sole regret was that you were not by my bedside to lend your fingers in assisting our holy sister in tenderly closing my lifeless eyes. What had I desired? What service am I not giving in return? What prayers and wishes lack fulfillment? What offices now follow? I was preparing for one thing; now I am compelled to carry out another. I am no longer the object of funeral rites, but their minister. Oh, what unfeeling eyes are mine, that could witness a brother dying! What rough and cruel hands, that closed the eyes in which I saw so much! What even more unfeeling neck, that could carry so sad a burden, however consoling a duty it was!

(37) You, brother, would have done these things more appropriately for me. I looked forward to these offices at your hands, and longed for them. But now, as the surviver of my own life, what comfort can I obtain without you? You alone were wont to comfort me in sorrow, arousing joy and dispelling sadness. How do I now look upon you, brother, no longer speaking to me, no longer giving me your kiss of affection? Yet our mutual attachment was always so deeply rooted that it was fostered rather by interior affection than

manifested by public displays of endearment. Having such a deep love for each other, we did not seek the testimony of others. The virile strength of our relationship as brothers permeated both of us to such a degree that we did not need to demonstrate our love by caresses. Since we were conscious of our mutual affection we were content with our internal love, and there appeared no need for outward parade of affection when even the very image of the other fostered our mutual love. Whether it was the way we both thought, or the way we both looked, we certainly seemed to be one in the other.

(38) Who looked at you and did not imagine he saw me? How often have I bade the time of day to persons who, having previously greeted you, would say that they had already been greeted by me? How many made some remark to you and mentioned that they had spoken to me? What amusement I would get, and what frequent delight, when I would perceive that they had mistaken us! What a pleasant mistake, what a delightful slip, what a harmless deceit, what a charming misrepresentation! For there was nothing for me to be embarrassed about in either your words or your deeds, and I was glad to have them ascribed to me.

(39) Upon occasion, when individuals would emphatically assert that they had discussed some matter with me, I would answer pleasantly and with a smile: 'Be sure you have not been talking with my brother.' But, while we had all things in common and were undivided in thought and affection, we never shared the confidences of friends, not out of any fear of danger resulting therefrom, but simply because we aimed to keep our pledged word. Yet, if it was necessary to consult together on some matter, our counsel was always in common, but the confidential element was not always shared. Although our friends conversed with either of us, hoping that what they said might reach the other, I know

that confidences by mutual agreement were usually kept so faithfully that they were not imparted even to a brother. This, indeed, was convincing proof that what had not been made known to a brother was certainly not betrayed to some stranger.

(40) Through the possession of so many benefits and enjoyments such as these I confess my mind was raised to a kind of ecstasy; I ceased to have any fear of surviving him, because I deemed him more worthy to live than I. Therefore, I have been dealt an intolerable blow. For the wounds inflicted by such deep anguish are more easily endured when there is a premonition than when they come without warning. Who will now console me in my grief? Who will lift me up from my affliction? With whom shall I share my troubles? Who will free me from the cares of this world? You were the manager of my business affairs, you took charge of the servants, you were the arbiter between a brother and a sister, an arbiter, not in strife, but in matters of affection.

(41) If there was ever any discussion between my holy sister and myself, we would choose you to judge which opinion seemed the better. You offended neither, and you aimed to satisfy both. You retained your loving affection and observed such moderation in judging that you sent each of us away pleased, and you gained the gratitude of both. And if you yourself presented some matter for discussion, how pleasantly did you argue, and how free was even your indignation from all bitterness! How mild your correction seemed to the servants themselves, since you were wont rather to defer to brethren than to be zealous in punishing! Our profession repressed our zeal for correcting. Or rather, you, brother, with your promise to punish and your eagerness to be lenient, turned me away from every intention to chastise.

(42) He gave proof, then, of no ordinary prudence. This virtue is defined by the wise as follows. The first of good things

is to know God and with pious mind to venerate that true and divine Being and with the whole affection of the soul to delight in the lovable and ardently to be desired beauty of eternal Truth. The second is to draw from that divine and heavenly source of nature love toward our neighbors. This teaching, also, the wise of this world have derived from our laws, for they could not have obtained these principles for the education of mankind except from the source of the divine Law in heaven.[25]

(43) What, therefore, shall I say about his reverence for the worship of God? Before he was initiated in the more perfect Mysteries, he experienced the dangers of shipwreck. The vessel upon which he was voyaging struck a rocky shallow, and the waves, tossing it hither and thither, were breaking it up. Though he did not fear death, he was, however, deeply concerned about dying without the Eucharist. So he asked members of the faithful, whom he knew were fully initiated, for the Blessed Sacrament,[26] not out of a prying curiosity to look upon it, but to obtain aid and assistance for his faith. He had it wrapped in a napkin, and tied the napkin around his neck, and so cast himself into the sea. He did not look for a plank loosened from the ship's structure, floating upon which he might save himself, for he had sought the arms of faith alone. And so believing that he was adequately protected and defended by these arms, he desired no other aid.

(44) We may look upon his courage at the same time, because as the ship was breaking up he did not, as a shipwrecked man, seize a floating piece of debris, but as a brave man he found support for his courage in himself. Nor did

---

25 Many of the Fathers regarded the Book of Wisdom, for example, as much earlier than Plato and as a definite but unacknowledged source of Platonic teaching on the cardinal virtues.

26 On the custom, still widespread in the fourth century, of reserving a portion of the Eucharistic Bread in private homes or of carrying it as a special protection on journeys, cf. *New Catholic Encyclopedia* 5.607 14.637.

his hope fail, nor his judgment deceive him. In short, he was the first rescued from the waves and brought ashore. He was fully conscious of his debt to the Protector to whom he had entrusted himself, and at once, when he had either rescued the rest of his servants or found that this had been done, without concern for his goods or regret for his losses, he sought out a church of God to return thanks for his deliverance and to be fully initiated in the eternal Mysteries. For he declared that no greater duty was incumbent upon him for returning thanks. If ingratitude to man has been likened to murder, what an enormous crime is ingratitude to God!

(45) It is the mark of a prudent man to know himself and, as the wise have put it, to live according to nature. But what is so much in accord with nature as to give thanks to the Creator? Look at the heaven over your head. Does it not render thanks to its Creator when we behold it? For 'the heavens show forth the glory of God, and the firmament declareth the works of his hands.'[27] The sea itself, when it is quiet and tranquil, gives proof of the divine tranquility; when it is in violent movement, the wrath on high causes terror. Do we not all rightly marvel at the thanks due to God when we observe that irrational nature checks its waves in a kind of rational manner and the waters know their own limits? And what shall I say of the earth, which in obedience to divine command gladly provides food for all living things, and of the fields, which, in payment of accumulating interest, as it were, make heaping and manifold returns for what they have received?

(46) In consequence, my brother, who under nature's guidance grasped with his vigorous and ardent mind the character of God's work, realized that his first duty was to render thanks to his Preserver. While he could not make full

---
27 Ps. 18.2.

recompense, he could at least have a sense of gratitude. For the quality of gratitude is this, that when a favor is returned it is felt, and through being felt it is returned. Hence, he gave thanks, and he received the gift of faith. For he who experienced such wonderful protection from the divine Mystery wrapped in a napkin realized how much it would mean to him if he could receive It with his mouth and consume It in the very depths of his heart. If It was so helpful to him when protected by a napkin, how much more profitable, he thought, It would be to him when taken into his inmost being.

(47) However, unlike so many overzealous souls, his zeal did not ignore caution. Convinced as he was that there is no genuine thankfulness outside the true faith, he summoned the bishop and asked him whether he was in union with the Catholic bishops, that is, with the Roman Church. The Church in that locality was possibly in schism, for at that time its bishop, Lucifer,[28] had separated from our communion. So, despite the fact that Lucifer had been an exile for the faith and had left heirs of his faith, my brother nevertheless thought there could be no true faith in schism. Although they had faith in God, they had no faith in the Church of God, for they suffered her limbs, as it were, to be divided and torn. Since Christ suffered for the Church, and since the Church is the Body of Christ,[29] it is apparent that they show no faith in Christ who repudiate His passion and tear His Body asunder.

(48) Consequently, even though he owed a debt of gratitude and feared to set sail as a debtor for so vast an amount, he thought it better to proceed to some place where he could make payment safely. For in his judgment payment for God's grace consists of love and faith. Nor did he put

---

28 The bishop was apparently an adherent of Lucifer of Cagliari, who had withdrawn from communion with the Roman Catholic Church.
29 Cf. Col. 1.18.

off making this payment the moment he had free access to a church. The grace of God, which he longed for, he received, and what he received he preserved. Nothing, therefore, evidences more wisdom than the type of prudence that distinguishes between divine and human matters.

(49) Why should I speak of his brilliant eloquence in the exercise of his forensic duties? What incredible admiration did he not attract to himself in the court of the highest prefecture? But I prefer to speak of those things which, once he received the Mysteries of God, he deemed of more importance than human affairs.

(50) Anyone wishing a fuller view of his courage should consider how often after shipwreck he crossed the sea with almost a dauntless disregard for this life. In his travels he covered widespread localities, and, to the very last, he did not seek an escape from danger but met it. I wish he had been as solicitous in taking precautions as he was patient when hurt or unconcerned about cold. But he was happy in this, that, so long as his bodily strength allowed and he could carry out what he wished to do, he spent his life performing tasks proper to youth and had no regard for his physical weakness.

(51) What words have I to describe his simplicity or, shall I call it, moderation in conduct and restraint of mind? If I allow myself to speak somewhat at length about one with whom I am no longer permitted to converse, kindly pardon me and forgive my show of grief. Surely, it is for your advantage also to observe that you are doing this kindness, not out of weakness and sympathy, but because you have been moved by sound judgment and honor for the deceased. Every simple soul is blessed. But his simplicity was so marked that, having become a child, as it were, he radiated the simplicity of that innocent age and was conspicuous as a living image of perfect virtue and as a mirror of blameless

life. Therefore, he has entered the kingdom of heaven, both because he believed the word of God and because, like a child,[30] he put aside the art of flattery. When some wrong was done to him, rather than avenge himself sharply he accepted it quietly. He was more disposed to listen to complaints that to tolerate deceit; he was easily conciliated, but was inaccessible to ambition; and he was so reverent toward modesty that sometimes it might be said he had more of that virtue than he needed.

(52) But we can never have more than enough of fundamental goodness. For modesty does not hinder, but rather graces, the performance of duties. A blush of virginal modesty suffused his countenance and betrayed his inward feeling whenever he suddenly chanced to meet some female relative. As if overwhelmed and cast to the gound—although his conduct was the same even in the company of men—he rarely lifted his head, or raised his eyes, or mingled in conversation. The bashful modesty of his mind was reflected in his actions, and with it the chastity of his body was in full harmony. He guarded unsullied the gifts of holy baptism, pure of body, but even purer of heart. He shrank no less from obscene speech as from bodily impurity, and he thought that respect should be paid to modesty no less by wholesome conversation than by personal chastity.

(53) Accordingly, he loved continence so much that he never sought a wife, partly because of his pursuit of chastity, partly, also, because of his love for us. It was astonishing how he concealed his true feeling and avoided any ostentation regarding his resolution. So carefully, indeed, did he veil his attitude that we, who encouraged him to marry, fancied he was putting it off rather than avoiding it. Accordingly, this was one matter he confided neither to his brother nor to his

---

30 Cf. Matt. 18.3.

sister, not out of any hesitation or doubt, but because of his retiring modesty.

(54) Who, therefore, does not wonder at a man situated in age between a sister and a brother, the one a virgin, the other a bishop, who although thus competing with the two highest callings, was so unexcelled in magnanimity that he reflected the chastity proper to the one and the holiness proper to the other, not under the bond of profession, but as an exercise in virtue? If, then, lust and anger produce the other vices, surely, I may say, chastity and gentleness are, as it were, the parents of virtues, allowing, as we do, that just as piety is the source of all good things, so it is also the seed bed of all the other virtues.

(55) What shall I say about his frugality, and his chaste restraints, as it were, regarding possessions. He who takes care of his own property does not seek other men's goods, nor is he puffed up by immoderate wealth who is content with his own. Therefore, he did not want to recover anything except his own, and that, too, because he did not relish being cheated rather than out of any desire to get richer. He rightly used to call those who seek other people's property 'money vultures.' But if covetousness is the root of all evils,[31] surely he strips himself of vices who does not seek money.

(56) Unless he invited friends, he never enjoyed elaborate meals or dinners with many courses. He sought to satisfy nature, not superabundance to gratify pleasure. Certainly he was not poor in this world's goods, but he was poor in spirit.[32] We ought have no doubt whatever about the happiness of a man who in wealth took no pleasure in riches, and in poverty did not consider what he had as scanty.

(57) To complete our treatment of his exemplification of

---

31 Cf. 1 Tim. 6.10.
32 Cf. Matt. 5.3.

the cardinal virtues, it remains for us to note in him the role of justice. Now, although virtues are closely interrelated, a distinct sketch of each is desirable, especially of justice. For this virtue, while somewhat grudging to itself, is devoted wholly to what is outside itself, and whatever it acquires through a kind of harshness toward itself, swept onward by its love for all, it pours forth upon its neighbors.

(58) This virtue expresses itself in many forms: in one, toward friends and acquaintances; in another, toward all men; in a third, toward the worship of God, or assistance to those in need. So, what he was toward all is quite patent through the affection of the provincials over whom he was governor. They used to say he was more like one's own father than a governor, a kind judge among devoted subjects, and a steadfast dispenser of equal justice.

(59) Although his good will embraced the whole human race, our undivided patrimony shows what kind of man he was in his attitude toward his brother and sister, for our inheritance was not distributed or lessened, but was preserved for us. For he refused to admit love as a reason for making a will. Indeed, he signified this in his parting remarks and final expressions of his desires to his loved ones. He said it was by his own free choice that he had not married, since he feared to be separated from us, and he did not want to draw up a will, lest our freedom of action might in some way be impaired. Accordingly, even after we had begged and pleaded with him, he remained convinced that he should make no testamentary dispositions. He did not forget the poor, but only asked that they be given as much as we thought just.

(60) By this alone he gave sufficient proof of his fear of God and furnished an example of the proper religious attitude toward men. What he gave to the poor he offered to God, since 'he that giveth bountifully to the poor, lendeth to

God.'³³ By earnestly requesting us to give what was just, he left to the poor, not a scanty portion, but all. That is the sum of justice, to sell what one has and to give it to the poor.³⁴ For he who 'hath distributed and hath given to the poor, his justice remaineth forever and ever.'³⁵ Therefore, he did not leave us heirs, but stewards. An inheritance is sought for an heir, but a stewardship entails an obligation to the poor.

(61) Hence, not unmeetly has the Holy Spirit declared today through the voice of the little reader³⁶ what a splendid man my brother was: 'The innocent in hands, and the clean of heart, who hath not taken his soul in vain, nor sworn deceitfully to his neighbor, this is the generation of them that seek God.'³⁷ Such a one, therefore, shall ascend into the mountain of the Lord, and shall dwell in the tabernacle of God.³⁸ For 'he that walketh without blemish and worketh justice, that hath spoken the truth and not deceived his neighbor.'³⁹ 'Nor did he put out his money to usury'⁴⁰ who always wished only to recover an inheritance. I recognize the voice of God: what no testamentary disposition provided for, the Spirit has revealed.

(62) Why should I recount how his affection carried him even beyond the requirements of justice? When he thought that, out of consideration for my being a bishop, something should be given to the unlawful possessor of our property, he lauded me as the author of the grant and the income from his own share he turned into the common fund.

(63) These as well as similar instances, once such a

---
33 Prov. 19.17.
34 Cf. Matt. 19.21.
35 Ps. 111.9.
36 On the admission of even young boys to the rank of lector in the fourth century, cf. Cabrol-Leclercq, *DACL* 82, col. 2247.
37 Ps. 23.4,5.
38 Cf. Ps. 23.3.
39 Ps. 14.2,3.
40 Ps. 14.5.

source of great pleasure to me, now through recollection sharpen my grief. But they abide with me and ever shall abide, and they never pass away like shadows. For the beauty of virtue does not die with the body, and natural life and supernatural merit do not have the same end, although natural life itself does not perish forever, but is at rest for a time by a kind of a release from its activities.

(64) Hence, I shall weep more out of longing than for the loss of a man who exemplified such virtues and has been rescued from dangers. The very timeliness of his death suggests that we attend his funeral rather with gratitude than with sorrow. For it is written that private grief should cease in time of public mourning.[41] Now, the Prophet does not make his recommendation to that one woman only who is figured there, but to each and every one, since he seems to have addressed the Church.

(65) Therefore, I too, am addressed, and holy Scripture asks: 'Is this what you teach? Do you not know that your example is a danger to others? Or is it possible that you are complaining that God has not heard your prayer? In the first place, your wish to merit alone what you know has been denied even to many saints is shameless arrogance, for everyone knows 'that God is not a respecter of persons.'[42] Even if God is merciful, were He always granting the prayers of all He would seem no longer to act freely, but, as it were, like someone under compulsion. Then, since all ask, if He were to hear all, no one would die. How many things do you not ask for daily? Must God's design be destroyed because of you? When you know that a petition cannot always be granted, why do you grieve that sometimes your petition is not obtained?

---

41 Cf. 4 Esd. 10.11. The fourth Book of Esdras was one of the most influential and widely used of the Apocrypha. Cf. C. Stahlmueller, "Apocrypha of the OT," *New Catholic Encyclopedia* 2.399.
42 Acts 10.34.

(66) 'Thou fool,' Scripture says, 'above all women seest thou not our mourning, and what has happened to us, how that Sion our mother is saddened with all sadness, and humbled with humbling? Mourn now, also very sore, since we all mourn, and be sad since we are all sad, and thou art grieved' for a brother. 'Ask the earth and she shall tell thee that it is she who ought to mourn, outliving so many that grow upon her. Out of her were all born in the beginning, and out of her shall others come, and behold they walk almost all into destruction. And a multitude of them is utterly rooted out. Who, then, ought to make more mourning than she that hath lost so great a multitude, and not thou, who art sorry but for one.'[43]

(67) So, let the common sorrow swallow up our sorrow and shut out the bitterness of our own grief. We ought not grieve for those whom we see have been set free, for we realize that it is with design at this time that such a number of holy souls have been released from the bonds of the body. For, seemingly by divine decree, we see that so many revered widows have died within the same short time that it is like a setting out upon a journey, not the stroke of death, lest their chastity, proven by long and faithful observance, should now fall into danger. What groans and what lamentation do not so bitter recollections arouse in me! Even if I had no time for grief, yet in private sorrow itself, and in the loss of the very flower of such noble merits, the common condition of nature consoled me, and the mourning, centered as it was on one, veiled the bitterness of a public funeral by the exhibition of a piety characteristic rather of the family circle.

(68) So, once again, O sacred Scripture, I seek your consolations, for I like to dwell upon your precepts and your sayings. How 'easier it is for heaven and earth to pass away than for one tittle of the Law to fail!'[44] But now let us hear

---
43 4 Esd. 10.6-11.
44 Luke 16.17.

what is written: 'Now,' it says, 'keep the sorrow to thyself, and bear with a good courage the things which have befallen thee. For if thou shalt acknowledge the determination of God to be just, thou shalt both receive thy son in time, and shalt be praised among women.'[45] If such advice is given to a woman, how much more so to a bishop? If such words are said about a son, it is surely not improper to regard them as applicable at the loss of a brother, who, had he been my son, could not have been dearer to me. For, just as when children die, the labors expended and the worries endured to no avail appear to increase grief, so, too, among brothers the long intimacy and close association accentuate the poignancy of sorrow.

(69) But again I hear Scripture saying: 'Do not continue this discourse, but allow yourself to be persuaded. For how great are the misfortunes of Sion! Be comforted out of regard for the sorrow of Jerusalem. For thou seest that our holy places are polluted and the name that was called upon us is almost profaned, and our sons have suffered shame. Our priests are burned, our levites gone into captivity, our wives are defiled, our virgins suffer violence, our just men carried off, our little ones given up, our young men made slaves, and our strong men made weak. And, which is the greatest of all misfortunes, the seal of Sion has lost her glory, because she is now delivered into the hands of men that hate us. Do thou, then, shake off thy great heaviness, and put from thee the multitude of sorrows, so that the Mighty One may be merciful to you again, and the Most High give you rest and surcease from sorrow.'[46]

(70) My tears, therefore, shall cease. I must accept wholesome remedies, since there must be some difference between believers and unbelievers. Let them weep, then, who cannot

---

45 4 Esd. 10.15,16.
46 4 Esd. 10.20-24.

have the hope of the resurrection. And they are deprived of it, not by divine decree, but by the hardness of faith. Let there be a difference between the servants of Christ and the worshipers of idols. Let idolaters mourn over their dead, convinced they have perished forever. Let them not cease from weeping, let them obtain no rest from sorrow, who believe that there is no rest for the dead. As for ourselves, however, death is not the end of our nature, but only of this life. Hence, since our nature indeed is restored in a better way,[47] let the coming of death wipe away all tears.

(71) Surely, if certain men found some consolation in thinking that death marks the end of consciousness and cessation of our nature, how much more should we have, to whom the knowledge of our good deeds gives the promise of better rewards after death? The heathen find satisfaction in looking upon death as a rest from all evils. And as they lack the fruit of life, so also they imagine they become freed from all sense or feeling of those heavy and continual sufferings which we endure in this life. But as for ourselves, as we are ennobled by our recompense, so we ought to be more patient through our consolation. For our dead do not seem to be lost but to be sent on before us, not to be swallowed up by death but to be received by eternity.

(72) My tears, therefore, shall cease, or, if they cannot cease, I will weep for you, my brother, in our public lamentation, concealing my personal anguish under the cloak of public grief. For how can my tears cease when at every mention of your name tears well up, either when habit itself recalls your memory, or when my affection brings back your likeness, or when remembrance renews my sorrow. For when are you separated from me, since you are present again in so many of my occupations? You are here, I say, and you are ever presenting yourself at my side. With my whole mind

---

47 Cf. 1 Cor. 15.44.

and soul I embrace you, I gaze upon you, I speak to you, I caress you, and I am aware of your presence in the very quiet of the night or in the clear light of day, when you vouchsafe to come back to see and console me in my grief. Hence, now, the very nights which, when you were alive, seemed irksome because they denied us opportunity to look upon each other, and now sleep itself, long the annoying interrupter of our conversations, have both begun to be sweet, for they restore you to me. Those whose mutual presence is never interrupted, whose concern for each other is not lessened, and whose esteem for each other is increased, are, therefore, not wretched, but happy. For sleep is the likeness and image of death.

(73) But if in the quiet of the night souls still held by the chains of the body, and fettered, as it were, behind the prison bars of their members, can nevertheless discern higher and more hidden things, how much more do they see these, when they now enjoy pure and ethereal mental powers and no longer suffer from the disabilities of bodily corruption? When, as a certain day was drawing to its close, I was justly complaining about your not coming to visit me in my rest, all the while you were so actually and undividedly present that, although I was sound asleep as regards my limbs, I was awake to you and you were alive to me, and I said: 'Brother, what is death?' Certainly you are not separated from me for an instant, for you will be so present to me everywhere that the enjoyment of each other which we could not have in this life we now possess without interruption and in all places. Previously, indeed, not everything was possible in our relations. Embraces, the sight of each other, and sweet caresses could not be enjoyed at all times and places. But even when we were not together physically, our images were always present in each other's minds. These have not disappeared even now,

but they constantly recur, and with greater frequency and clearness the more they are longed for.

(74) I still have you, then, brother, and neither death nor time shall tear you from me. Even tears are sweet, even weeping is pleasant, for they cool the burning longing of the soul, and pent up emotion is relieved and calmed. I cannot be without you, or ever forget you, or remember you without tears. O bitter days, that proclaim that the union with my brother has been broken! O tearful nights, that have taken from me such an excellent sharer of my rest and my inseparable companion! What tortures you would be inflicting upon me unless the image of him as if present were appearing to me, unless the visions of the mind were representing him who can no longer be seen with the eyes of the body!

(75) At last, brother most dear to my heart, although you have departed too early from this life, you are now nonetheless fortunate in escaping the burden of these sorrows. You do not have to mourn the loss of a brother from whom you could never long endure to be separated, and whom you hastened to see again as soon as possible. If in times past you used to hurry back to dispel my wearisome loneliness, and to relieve the sadness of a brother's heart, how much oftener ought you now revisit my afflicted soul and by so doing alleviate my sorrow begotten of your death!

(76) Yet my duties give me some respite, and devotion to my episcopal obligations occupies my mind. But what is to become of our holy sister? Although she tempers her affection because of her fear of God, she kindles the grief itself arising from her love by her religious zeal. She prostrates herself upon the ground, she embraces her brother's tomb, she is worn out from restless walking, she is constantly sad, and day and night she renews her grief. Even if conversation often stops her weeping, she weeps again at prayer. More-

over, although in her knowledge of Scripture she excels those who are wont to bring consolation, she offsets her longing to weep by her constant prayer, and then especially, when no one can interrupt her, she renews her heavy weeping. So in her we have an object of pity rather than of censure, for to weep at prayer is a mark of virtue. Young women, because they belong to the gentler sex and have greater tenderness in their affection, break out into tears, as we well know, at the sight of our common weakness, even when their own families are not mourning a loved one. Hence, when there is a greater cause for grieving, no limit can be set for that grief.

(77) The way of consolation, therefore, is wanting, since there is an abundance of good excuses. For we cannot forbid what we teach, especially when she bases her tears, not upon sorrow, but upon religious devotion, and for fear of shame hides the natural cause of her lamentation. Console her, then, brother, you who can visit her soul and enter her mind. Let her see that you are present; let her not think of you as dead. Thus, assured of your merit and having received your consolation, let her learn not to mourn so intensely for one who admonished us that he was not to be mourned.

(78) But why am I delaying, brother? Why am I waiting for my address to die with you and, as it were, be buried with you? Even though the sight and form of your lifeless body give solace, and your abiding and unchanging grace and beauty comfort my eyes, I will delay no longer, I repeat; let us proceed to the tomb. But first, in the presence of the people, I bid you the last farewell. I give you peace, and I pay the last kiss. Go before us to that common abode to which we must all go, and which I now long for beyond all others. Prepare a common dwelling for us, and just as here we had all things in common, so there let us also not know divided rights.

(79) Do not, I beg you, forsake one who pines for you;

expect one who is hurrying, help him as he hastens, and if you think he tarries too much, urge him on. Never, indeed, were we really long separated from each other, and you always came to us on your return. Now, since you can no longer come back to me, I will go to you. It is only fair that I should repay your kindness and now take my turn. There was never much difference in the way we lived, and we were always well or ill together. When one of us got sick, the other ran a fever, too, and when one recovered, both were up and about. Why have we lost our common right? Even recently we were both sick together. Why did we not both die together?

(80) To Thee, Almighty God, I now commend a guileless soul, to Thee I offer my oblation. Receive favorably and kindly a brother's gift, the sacrifice of Thy priest. By anticipation, I now offer these libations of myself. I am coming to Thee with my brother as a surety, not with a pledge of money but of a life. Do not make me remain in debt for so great a sum too long. The interest on a brother's love is high and nature's principal is large when both accumulate through increments of virtue. I can bear the burden if I shall be required to pay quickly.

SECOND ORATION

On Faith in the Resurrection

IN THE PRECEDING BOOK I indulged my longing somewhat, for I feared that the application of unduly severe remedies to a burning wound, as it were, might aggravate rather than lessen pain. At the same time, since I often addressed my brother and had him before my eyes, it was only proper to give natural emotion some outlet for a little while. Such emotion derives help from tears, is calmed by weeping, and is numbed by a heavy blow. For a soft and tender manner is of the essence of affection. It dislikes anything overbearing, harsh, or hard. On the contrary, patience is proved rather by enduring than by resisting.

(2) Hence, it was inevitable that a little while ago, on the day of death, a brother's mind should be distracted and wholly occupied. But now, since we are returning to the grave on the seventh day, a day symbolic of the future repose, it will be helpful to turn my mind from my brother for a short time and devote my attention to a general exhortation applicable to all. Thus, my thoughts and feelings will not be exclusively concerned with my brother. I shall not be over-

come suddenly by strong emotion, nor shall I be so lacking in appreciation for such great love and merit as to desert him whom we love. And surely I myself would increase the anguish of such an intense sorrow if again today I should make his death the theme of my discourse.

(3) That is why, dear brethren, I have made up my mind to find comfort out of common experience, and not to deem what awaits each and all as something hard. Therefore, death should not be regarded as a cause of grief, for, in the first place, death is common and is a debt which all must pay; secondly, it frees us from the calamities of this life; and finally, when under the appearance of sleep we obtain rest from the toils of this world, a stronger vigor is infused into us. What sorrow does not the gift of resurrection assuage! What grief can find entrance into the soul of man who believes that nothing perishes through death, but rather that through speedy death itself more is preserved from possible destruction! Therefore, dear brethren, as is proper in a general address of exhortation, we shall also pay a tribute of affection to my brother. Nor shall we seem to wander too far from him, if through our hope in the resurrection and the sweetness of future glory he should live again for us even in our discourse today.

(4) So, let us begin by showing that we should not mourn over the death of relatives. What, indeed, is more ridiculous than to deplore as something special what everybody knows is prescribed for all? That is tantamount to exalting the mind above the human state, to refusing to accept the universal law, to rejecting the fellowship of nature, to having a puffed up and carnal mind, and to being ignorant of the limitation of the flesh itself. What is more ridiculous than not to know who you are and to be affecting what you are not? What, too, is more lacking in foresight than to know what is going to happen, and, when it has happened, not to be able

to endure it? Even nature acts to restrain us and by her own method of consolation draws us away from grieving of this kind. For what grief is so heavy, and what sorrow so bitter, as never to have intervals of alleviation? For nature has a way whereby men, no matter how great their distress, provided only that they be men, can turn their minds from sorrow for a little while at least.

(5) It is said that there have been certain peoples who mourned at the births of men and celebrated their deaths with rejoicing. And in this they showed foresight, for they thought that they should mourn for all who entered upon the sea of this life, while they judged that it was only proper to hold joyful obsequies for those who had escaped from the storms and waves of this world. We ourselves, too, forget the birthdays of the dead, and, instead, celebrate annually the day on which they died.[1]

(6) Therefore, according to nature, we ought not give way to deep grief, lest we should seem to arrogate to ourselves some higher and exceptional nature or to refuse to accept the common law. For death is the equal lot of all, making no distinctions for the poor and no exception for the rich. Therefore, although through one man's sin death has passed unto all men,[2] accordingly, him whom we do not refuse to acknowledge as the father of the human race we cannot refuse to acknowledge also as the author of death.[3] And just as we have death through one, so also through One we have the resurrection. Let us not refuse tribulation if we wish to gain the divine reward. For, as we read, Christ came 'to save what was lost,'[4] and 'that he might be Lord

---
1 On this custom in the early Church, cf. L. C. Boyle, "Calendar, Christian," *New Catholic Encyclopedia* 2.1063.
2 Cf. Rom. 5.12.
3 Cf. *ibid.* 5.18.
4 Luke 19.10.

both of the dead and of the living.'[5] In Adam I fell, in Adam
I was cast out of paradise, in Adam I died. How shall God
call me back except He find me in Adam? For just as in
Adam I am guilty of sin and owe a debt to death, so in
Christ I am justified.[6] If, then, death is a debt, we ought to
endure its payment. But this topic must be reserved for treatment later.

(7) It is now proposed to show that death ought not to
cause too heavy a burden of sorrow, because nature itself rejects such grief. Thus, they say that the Lycians have a law
which requires men who give way to grief to wear feminine
apparel, because they deem display of grief in a man as soft
and effeminate. It is incongruous that men whose duty it is to
expose themselves to death for faith, religion, country, justice,
and the pursuit of virtue should grieve bitterly over something
which happens to another and which, if the situation should
require it, is to be desired for themselves. For how can one
avoid seeking escape from grief at his own lot when he is
unreconcilable in his grief at the death of others? Put aside
your sorrow, if you can; if you cannot, at least conceal it.

(8) Should we keep within ourselves or repress all grief?
Why should not reason rather than time lighten sadness?
Will not prudence alleviate better what the passage of time
will blot out? Truly, in my opinion, it is nothing short of an
act of impiety toward the memory of those whose loss we
mourn to prefer to forget them rather than to have our
sorrow allayed by consolation, or to recall them with a shudder
rather than to remember them with love, to fear the recollection of those whose likeness should be an object of delight,
to despair rather than hope regarding the merits of the dead,
and to consider our loved ones as being sentenced to punish-

---

5 Rom. 14.9.
6 Cf. Rom. 5.8,9.

ment rather than as entering upon an immortality which is their due.

(9) But someone may remark: We have lost those whom we loved. Is not this the lot we have in common with the world itself and its elements? We cannot retain forever things entrusted to us for a time. So that the earth may become productive and bring forth fruits annually she groans under the plow, is beaten by violent rains, is shaken by storms, is bound fast by the cold and is baked by the sun. After she has clothed herself in her rich and varied flowers she is stripped and despoiled of her own adornment. What countless plunders does she experience! Yet she does not complain about the loss of crops born to be lost. Nor does she refuse to bear the next harvest, aware, though she is, that it must be taken away from her.

(10) The sky itself is not always aglitter with the twinkling spheres of the stars which adorn it like coronets. It does not always grown bright at dawn and become ruddy with the rays of the sun. But in constant alternation that most pleasing countenance, as it were, of the world is darkened by the damp chill of night. What is more delightful than light; what is more cheering than the sun? Yet they come to an end daily. Still, their departure does not trouble us, because we assume that they will return. This teaches us what patience we should manifest in respect to our own lost ones. If the things above us pass away and do not cause us grief, why should we grieve when men pass away?

(11) Let our sorrow, then, be patient. Let that moderation demanded in happy circumstances be present in misfortune. If excessive rejoicing is not proper, is excessive grief? Inordinate grief, or dread of death, is not a minor evil. How many has it driven to suicide by rope or blade! In this they evidence their own folly: not enduring, yet seeking

death, and adopting as a remedy what they flee as an evil. Since they could not endure and suffer what is consonant with their nature, they incur the opposite of their desire: everlasting separation from those whom they wished to follow. But such occurrences are rare. Though their folly drives men headlong, nature itself restrains them.

(12) It is common, indeed, for women to make a public spectacle of weeping,[7] as if they were afraid that their misery might go unnoticed. They affect soiled garments, as though there were a feeling of grief in these. They wet their disheveled hair with filth. Finally, what seems to be the vogue in many localities, they rend their mantles, tear open their garments and make a public display of their nakedness, as though making a prostitute out of modesty itself because they have lost the rewards of their chastity. Thus they invite wanton eyes to lust after those naked limbs which, had they not been exposed, would not have been desired. And would that the sordid apparel concealed, not the bodies of such women, but their intentions. For, frequently under a veil of mourning, there lurks lasciviousness, and disorderly and repulsive dress is used as a cloak to hide the secret desires of wanton minds.

(13 A wife mourns the death of her husband with proper devotedness, not when she abandons her fidelity, but when she guards her modesty. She discharges her duty well when her deceased husband lives in her memory and affection. She who manifests that she is modest has not lost her husband. She who has not changed her husband's name has not been made a widow. And you have not lost an heir who help the co-heir, but in place of a successor in perishable things you have obtained a sharer in eternal. You have someone who can take the place of the heir. Give to the poor what is due the heir, so that there may be not only a survivor of a father or a mother, but also of your own life as well. You leave

---

7 Cf. Cicero, *Tusc. Disp.* 3.26.62.

more to your successor when his share is available, not for luxury in this life, but for the purchase of the things of heaven.

(14) But we long for our lost ones. There are two things especially which pain us: either, as in my own case, our longing for those whom we have lost, or the thought that they have been deprived of the pleasure of living and have been snatched away from enjoying the fruits of their toil. Love indeed arouses a tender feeling of pleasure which suddenly enkindles affection, thus leaving a mental disposition more capable of quieting than of dispelling pain. At the same time, since it appears proper to devotion to long for what has been lost, weakness increases under the guise of virtue.

(15) On what grounds do you argue that a wife ought to be more resigned after she has seen her husband off to a foreign country, either on a military or a diplomatic mission, or has learned that he has gone to sea on a commercial venture? Ought you not be as equally patient when you are left, not because of some chance decision or out of ambition for money, but because of nature's law? But you reply that for you hope of recovery is excluded. As if the hope for anyone's return were certain! Oftentimes, apprehensions are even more exhausting when the dread of danger is strong and constant. Again, it is a heavier burden to fear that something has happened than to endure what you know has really occurred. In the one case, apprehension mounts continually, while in the other an end of sorrow is being awaited.

(16) Have masters the right[8] to transport their slaves wherever they wish, and God not? We must not look for a man's return, but we are permitted to follow one who has gone before us. Certainly, the span of life is so brief that it does not seem to have taken much from one who has gone before, nor to delay very long the one who remains.

---
8 Cf. 1 Tim. 6.1,2.

(17) But, if you cannot soften your longing, does it not seem unbecoming to want the whole order of nature upset so that you may attain what you desire? When people are in love, their longing for one another is very ardent, yet they are controlled by a regard for necessity. If they grieve over having been forsaken, they do not usually mourn, but, having been cast aside, they feel embarrassed for falling in love too hastily. And so their patience in regret is more clearly recognized.

(18) But what shall I say of those who think the dead are deprived of the sweetness of life? No true enjoyment is possible in the bitter experiences and sorrows of this life which are caused either by the infirmities of the body itself or by the unpleasant things which happen outside of it. Anxious indeed, and forever in suspense even in desires for happier conditions, we are tossed about in a kind of uncertainty, putting our hopes in doubtful things in place of sure, in unsatisfactory in place of favorable, in transitory in place of permanent, having no power in our wills and no constancy in our wishes. But, if anything happens contrary to our intention, we think we are ruined. We are more broken by the sufferings caused by adversity than we are made happy through the enjoyments of prosperity. What advantages, then, do the dead miss in being rescued rather from misfortunes?

(19) Good health, I believe, is more beneficial to us than poor health is harmful. Wealth affords more pleasure than poverty annoys us. The gift of children is more lovely than their loss is sorrowful. Youth is more joyful than old age is sad. How often a man becomes tired of his desires when once attained and repents of what he has longed for, so that he is sorry for having obtained what he feared he would not obtain! What homeland, what pleasures, can truly compensate for exiles and for all other bitter penalties? Even when

pleasures are at our command, they become less attractive either because we are not disposed to enjoy them or because we fear to lose them.

(20) But let us suppose that the whole course of a man's life can continue unharmed, free from grief, and enjoying pleasures without interruption. What satisfaction can the soul obtain, enclosed within the walls of a body such as ours, and confined within the narrow compass of our limbs? If our flesh shuns a prison, if it loathes everything which denies it the power of free movement—and, as we know, it apparently tries to reach beyond itself with its limited senses of seeing and hearing—how much more is our soul filled with eager desire to escape from its bodily prison![9] When it is free, it has a motion like the air, and we know not whither it goes or whence it comes.[10]

(21) We know, however, that the soul survives the body and that, once it is freed from the shackles on its own faculties, it beholds in clear vision what previously, when dwelling in the body, it did not see. We can verify this fact through the experience which comes to men in sleep. When their bodies are, as it were, buried in sleep, their souls, being at peace, rise to higher things and relate to the body their visions of distant and even heavenly things. Therefore, if the death of our flesh frees us from the miseries of this world, it is certainly no evil, since it restores freedom and excludes pain.

(22) Here, accordingly, we must discuss the point that death is not an evil, since it is a refuge from all miseries and evils, a safe and secure anchorage, and a haven of rest. For what adversity do we not experience in this life? What storms and tempests do we not endure? By what troubles are we not disturbed? Whose merits are spared?

(23) The holy patriarch Israel, as a fugitive from his

---
9 Cf. Cicero, *Tusc. Disp.* 1.49.118.
10 Cf. John 3.8.

country, brother, and parents, exchanged his home for exile,[11] mourned over the violation of his daughter,[12] the murder of his son-in-law,[13] and suffered famine.[14] After he died, he lost his grave, for, lest he should rest even in death, he begged that his bones be translated.[15]

(24) Holy Joseph experienced the enmity of his brothers, the snares of the envious, the obsequiousness of servants, the orders of merchants,[16] the wantonness of his mistress, the stupid ignorance of her husband, and the miseries of imprisonment.[17]

(25) Holy David lost two sons. One was guilty of incest;[18] the other, of fratricide.[19] To have had them caused him shame; to have lost them brought him grief. He also lost a third, a child whom he loved. He wept over him while he was still alive, but he did not long for him after he died. For so we read[20] that, when the boy fell sick, David besought the Lord for him and fasted and lay upon sackcloth, and, although the elders approached him and tried to make him get up from the ground, he resolved neither to rise nor to eat. After he learned that the boy was dead, however, he arose from the ground, bathed upon the spot, anointed himself, changed clothing, worshiped the Lord, and took food.[21] Since this seemed strange to his servants, he answered that, while the child was still alive, he had rightly fasted and wept, because he justly thought that God might pity him, and was certain that He who could restore the dead to life could surely

---

11 Cf. Gen. 28.5ff.
12 Cf. Gen 34.2.
13 Cf. Gen. 34.30.
14 Cf. Gen. 42.2.
15 Cf. Gen. 48.30; 49.29.
16 Cf. Gen. 37.4ff.
17 Cf. Gen. 39.12ff.
18 Cf. 2 Kings 13.14.
19 Cf. 2 Kings 13.28,29.
20 Cf. 2 Kings 12.15ff.
21 Cf. 2 Kings 12.20.

preserve the life of one still living. But now that the child was dead, why should he fast, since he could not bring him back from death and restore him to life. 'I shall go to him rather;' he said, 'but he shall not return to me.'[22]

(26) What greater consolation to a mourner! What a true judgment from a wise man! What wonderful wisdom exhibited by a servant! Hence, no one should protest that some misfortune has befallen him and complain that he has been afflicted contrary to his merit. For who are you to proclaim your merit beforehand? Why do you desire to anticipate your Judge? Why do you snatch the verdict from the mouth of Him who is going to pronounce it? This was permitted not even to the saints, and never was it attempted by the saints with impunity. David confesses in one of his psalms that he was scourged on this account: 'Behold these are sinners; and yet abounding in the world they have obtained riches. Then have I in vain justified my heart, and washed my hands among the innocent. And I have been scourged all the day; and my accuser has come in the mornings.'[23]

(27) Peter, also, though filled with loyal devotion, but not yet fully conscious of our weakness, had rashly assured our Lord: 'I will lay down my life for thee.'[24] Before the cock crowed thrice, his presumption was put to the test.[25] Let Peter's trial be a salutary lesson for us so that we may learn not to disregard the weakness of the flesh, lest by so doing we should be tempted. If Peter was tempted, who should presume or who should assert that he cannot be, also? And, unquestionably, Peter was tempted for our sake, so that the temptation would not be exposed to failure in a stronger man than he, and that through him we might learn how to persevere under persecutions and, even if we should be

---
22 2 Kings 12.23.
23 Ps. 72.12-14 (Sepuagint).
24 John 13.37.
25 Cf. John 18.27.

tempted by our desire to save our lives, to overcome the stings of temptation by tears of patience.

(28) On the other hand, that same David, lest the difference in his conduct may perhaps trouble any one who follows Scripture closely, this same David, I repeat, who had not wept for his innocent son, wept for the parricide when he was killed. Accordingly, he broke out in lamentation and cried: 'My son Absalom, my son Absalom, who will grant me death in thy place?'[26] Therefore, not only is Absalom wept for, the parricide is wept for, Amnon is wept for, too.[27] Not only is the incestuous son wept for, but he is also avenged. Absalom saddened David by his contempt and revolt, and the murder of Amnon caused his brother's exile. The wicked son is wept for, but not the child whom he loved so much. Why is this? What is the reason for this? Prudent men are characterized by serious deliberation and the wise see their judgments confirmed. As a wise man, he is quite steady in his reasoning, for, in spite of marked differences in facts and actions, a consistency based on prudence and on a single faith is in evidence. David wept over the death of two of his sons, but he decided that he ought not weep for the dead child. He believed that those two were lost to him forever, but he hoped that the child would rise again.

(29) But more on the resurrection later. Let us now return to the point under discussion. We have already shown that even holy men, without any regard for their merits, have suffered many severe tribulations along with their heavy toils in this world. Hence, David, returning to himself, says later: 'Remember, Lord, that we are dust, and man, his days are like grass';[28] and elsewhere: 'Man is like to vanity: his days pass away like a shadow.'[29] What, indeed, is more

---

26 2 Kings 18.33 (Septuagint).
27 Cf. 2 Kings 13.36.
28 Ps. 102.15.
29 Ps. 143.4.

miserable than we human beings who are cast into this life, as it were, stripped and naked, with fragile bodies, deceitful hearts, and weak minds, anxious with respect to cares, indolent toward work, and prone to pleasure?

(30) Not to be born, therefore, is by far the best, according to the saying of Solomon. For those, also, who seemed to themselves to be superior in philosophy have followed him[30]. 'And I praised all the departed who have already died rather than the living, as many as are living up to now. And happier than them both is he that is not yet born, nor hath seen the evil work that is done under the sun. And I saw all the labor and all the excellence of this work, that a man becomes envied by his neighbor, and this too is vanity and presumption of spirit.'[31]

(31) Who said this but the very man who asked for and obtained wisdom to know the arrangement of the world, the power of the elements, the revolutions of the year, the dispositions of the stars, the natures of living creatures, the rage of wild beasts, the force of the winds, and to understand the thoughts of men?[32] How, then, could mortal matters escape the knowledge of a man from whom heavenly things were not hidden? The man who found out the thought of the woman claiming the child of another as her own,[33] the man who, although he had not investigated and studied the nature of living things, knew them under the inspiration of divine grace,[34] could he err or lie concerning the state of his own nature which he knew through his own personal experience?

---

30 St. Ambrose is alluding to a widespread view in Christian antiquity that all the books of the Old Testament assigned to Solomon actually went back to him and, therefore, antedated the great Greek philosophers and influenced their teachings.
31 Eccle. 4.2-4 (Septuagint).
32 Cf. Wisd. 7.7,17-20.
33 Cf. 3 Kings 3.16-27.
34 Cf. Wisd. 7.20; 3 Kings 4.29,33.

(32) But even if Solomon alone gave formal expression to this feeling, he was not the only one who had it. He had read the words of holy Job: 'Let the day perish wherein I was born,'[35] and he had learned that being born is the beginning of all evils. Consequently, he desired the day on which he was born to perish, so that the origin of his troubles might be taken away, and he desired the day of his birth to perish, so that he might receive the day of the resurrection.[36] Again, Solomon had heard his father say: 'O Lord, make me know my end. And what is the number of my days? that I may know what is wanting to me.'[37] For David knew that what is perfect cannot be comprehended here, and so he hastened toward the things to come. For now we know in part, and understand in part. But then we shall be able to comprehend what is perfect, when, not the shadow, but the reality of the majesty and eternity of God shall begin to shine and to reveal itself unveiled before our eyes.[38]

(33) No one, however, would hasten to the end, unless he were fleeing the disadvantages of this life. And, therefore, even David explained why he hastened to the end, when he said: 'Behold thou hast made my days old: and my substance is as nothing before thee. And indeed all things are vanity: every man living.'[39] Why, then, do we put off fleeing from vanity? Or why do we wish to be troubled to no purpose in this world, accumulating money and not knowing for what heir we gather it? Let us pray that tribulations be removed from us, that we be taken out of this foolish world, that our pilgrimage may be shortened, and that we may return to our true country and natural home. For upon this earth we are strangers and foreigners.[40] We must return to the place

---

35 Job 3.3.
36 Cf. Job 19.25.
37 Ps. 38.5.
38 Cf. 1 Cor. 13.9-12.
39 Ps. 38.6 (Septuagint).
40 Cf. Eph. 2.19.

from which we descended. We must beg and beseech, not in lukewarm fashion, but most earnestly, to be delivered from the deceit and wickedness of babblers.[41] David, who knew the remedy, bemoaned that his stay upon earth was prolonged and lamented that he had to dwell among the unjust and sinners.[42] What shall I do, who am both a sinner and know not the remedy?

(34) Jeremias, likewise, laments that he was born, and in these words: 'Woe is me, my mother, why has thou borne me a man of contention in all the earth. I have not helped anyone, nor has anyone helped me: my strength has failed.'[43] If, then, holy men shun life, men whose life, though useful to us, is judged useless to themselves, what ought we to do, who are not able even to profit others, and who know that, as borrowed money becomes difficult to pay as interest mounts, so this life of ours becomes more heavily burdened daily by its debt of sin.

(35) 'I die daily,'[44] says the Apostle. That, certainly, is superior to the attitude of those who said that meditation on death is true wisdom. For they only praised the contemplation of death, while Paul practiced the actual experience of dying. Moreover, they were concerned for themselves alone, but Paul, perfect though he was, died, not for his own weakness, but for ours. And what is meditation upon death except a kind of separation of body and soul, since death itself is defined as nothing else than the separation of body and soul? This at least is the common opinion.

(36) According to the Scriptures, however, we learn that there are three kinds of death.[45] The first is when we die to sin and live unto God.[46] Blessed, then, is that death which, fleeing

---
41 Cf. Eccli. 19.5.
42 Cf. Ps. 119.5.
43 Cf. Jer. 15.10 (Septuagint).
44 1 Cor. 15.31.
45 Cf. Rom. 6.10.
46 Cf. also, St. Ambrose, *De bono mortis* 9, and *Expos. in Lucam* 7.35.

sin and devoted to God, separates us from what is mortal and consecrates us to Him who is immortal. The second is the soul's liberation from the bonds of the body and its departure from this life. By this death the patriarch Abraham and the patriarch David died, when they were buried with their fathers. The third kind of death is that of which it is said: 'Leave the dead to bury their own dead.'[47] In that death not only does the flesh die, but the soul dies, also, 'For the soul that sinneth, the same shall die.'[48] For it dies to the Lord, not through natural infirmity but through the sickness caused by guilt. This type of death is not the release from this life, but is the fall resulting from sin.

(37) One type of death, then, is spiritual, a second natural, and a third penal. But natural death and penal death are not identical. For the Lord did not give death as a penalty, but as a remedy. Hence, when Adam sinned, one thing was prescribed as a punishment, and another as a remedy. The punishment is contained in the words: 'Because you have listened to your wife, and have eaten of the tree, of which alone I commanded thee that thou shouldest not eat, cursed be the ground in your work; in toil shalt you eat of it all the days of your life. Thorns and thistles shall it bring forth to you; and you shalt eat the plants of the field. In the sweat of your brow you shall eat bread, till you return to the ground, out of which you were taken.'[49]

(38) Here we have freedom from punishment, for these words contain the penalty decreed against the thorns of this life, the cares of the world, and the pleasures of riches which shut out the Word.[50] Death has been given as a remedy, as an end of evils. For God did not say: 'Because you listened to your wife, you shall return to the ground.' This would

---
47 Matt. 8.22.
48 Ezech. 18.4.
49 Gen. 3.17-19.
50 Cf. Luke 8.12.

have been a penal sentence, as is this: 'Cursed be the ground. Thorns and thistles shall it bring forth to you.' But He said: 'In the sweat of your brow you shall eat bread, till you return to the ground.' You see that death is rather the limit of our punishment, because by it the course of this life ended.

(39) Therefore, death, far from being an evil, is even a good. Accordingly, it is sought as a good, for it is written: 'Men will seek death and will not find it.'[51] For they will seek it who will begin to say to the mountains: 'Fall upon us; and to the hills: Cover us.'[52] And the soul also that sins will seek it. The rich man lying in hell, who wishes to have his tongue cooled by the finger of Lazarus, he, too, seeks it.[53]

(40) So we see that this kind of death is an advantage, while this life is a punishment. Hence, Paul says: 'For me to live is Christ and to die is gain.'[54] What is Christ but the death of the body, the spirit of life? Therefore, let us die together with Him, that we may live with Him. Let us have daily a kind of experience in and longing for death, so that, by that separation from bodily desires which we have mentioned, our soul may learn to withdraw itself and, having placed itself on high, as it were, whither earthly lusts cannot approach and attach it to themselves, it may assume the likeness of death, lest it incur the penalty of death. For the law of the flesh wars against the law of the mind and subjects it to the law of error, just as the Apostle revealed when he said: 'I see another law in my members, warring against the law of my mind and making me prisoner in the law of sin.'[55] We are all attacked, and we all know this, but we are not all delivered. And, therefore, I am an unhappy man unless I shall seek the remedy.[56]

---

51 Apoc. 9.6.
52 Luke 23.30.
53 Cf. Luke 16.24.
54 Phil. 1.21.
55 Rom. 7.23.
56 Cf. Rom. 7.24.

(41) But what remedy? 'Who will deliver me from the body of this death? The grace of God, by Jesus Christ our Lord.'[57] We have a physician: let us follow his remedy. Our remedy is the grace of Christ, and the body of death is our body. Let us, therefore, be exiled from the body lest we be exiles from Christ.[58] Even if we are in the body, let us not follow what is of the body. Let us not neglect the rights of nature, but let us desire rather the gifts of grace. For to depart and to be with Christ is by far the better; yet to stay on in the flesh is necessary for your sake.'[59]

(42) But it is not necessary for all, Lord Jesus. It is not so for me, who am of no use to anyone. For to me, to die is a gain, so that I may sin no more. To die is a gain for me, who in this very book wherein I am attempting to console others I am driven by a powerful impulse into longing for my lost brother, since it does not allow me to forget him. Now I love him more and long for him more intensely than ever. I long for him when I speak, I long for him when I read again what I have composed. And therefore I think this must be written primarily in order that I may never free myself from remembering him. What I am doing is not contrary to Scripture, namely, that I should grieve more patiently, but long more ardently.

(43) You, my brother, have taken from me all fear of death, and would that my soul might die in your soul! That is what Balaam desired as the greatest of goods for himself, when endowed with the spirit of prophecy he said: 'Let my soul die in the souls of the just, and let my seed become like their seed.'[60] And truly he desired this according to prophecy. For he who had seen the birth of Christ saw also His triumph, saw His death, and saw in Him the everlasting resurrection of

---

57 Rom. 7.24,25.
58 Cf. 2 Cor. 5.6,8.
59 Phil. 1.23.24.
60 Num. 23.10 (Septuagint).

mankind. Consequently, since he was to rise again, he had no fear of death. Let, then, my soul not die in sin, nor admit sin into itself. But let it die in the soul of the just man, that it may receive his justice. Accordingly, he who dies in Christ becomes through baptism a sharer in His grace.[61]

(44) Death, therefore, is not to be dreaded. It is not bitter to the needy, nor especially grievous to the rich, nor oppressive to the old, nor cowardly for the brave, nor eternal to the faithful, nor unexpected to the wise. How many have made their lives immortal solely by the renown of their deaths! How many have been ashamed to live and have found it a benefit for them to die! We have learned that often by one man's death great nations have been freed, and that by the death of a general hostile armies have been put to flight, which, while he lived, he had not been able to conquer.

(45) By the death of the martyrs, religion has been defended, the faith spread, and the Church strengthened. The dead have been victorious, and the persecutors have been vanquished. Accordingly, we celebrate the deaths of those of whose lives we know nothing. So, too, David in prophecy rejoiced at the departure of his own soul, saying: 'Precious in the sight of the Lord is the death of the saints.'[62] He held death in more esteem than life. The death itself of the martyrs is the prize of life. Furthermore, even the hatreds of enemies are dissolved by death.

(46) Are further illustrations required? By the death of One the world was redeemed. For, had Christ so willed, He had it in His power not to die.[63] But He did not think death should be shunned as though it were a cowardly thing, and He could not have saved us in a better way than by dying.[64] Hence, His death is the life of all. We sign ourselves with the

---
61 Cf. John 3.5; Rom. 6.3 ff.
62 Ps. 115.15.
63 Cf. John 10.18.
64 Cf. John 15.13.

sign of His death, when we pray we announce His death, when we offer the Sacrifice we proclaim His death. His death is a victory, His death is a mystery, His death is an annual feast of the world. What more need we say of His death after we show by the divine example that death alone has gained immortality and death itself has redeemed itself? Death, then, should not be lamented, since it is the source of salvation for all. Death must not be shunned, for the Son of God neither disdained nor shunned it. The order of nature must not be destroyed. Exceptions cannot be made for individuals in what is common to all.

(47) Death, in fact, was not in nature, but it became a part of nature. God did not establish death in the beginning, but gave it as a remedy. Let us then consider it, lest it seem the opposite. For, if death is good, why is it written that 'God made not death? but by the evil of men death came into the world'?[65] Death was really not necessary to the divine plan, since for those placed in paradise a continual succession of all good things flowed forth. But after the transgression of Adam and man's condemnation to long labors and unbearable sorrow, his life became wretched. Consequently, an end had to be established for evils, so that death might restore what life had lost. For, unless grace should breathe upon it, immortality would be rather a burden than an advantage.

(48) If we consider the matter carefully, this death is not that of our nature but of evil, for our nature remains, but evil dies. That which was rises again, and would that, as it is free from sinning, so it may be without former guilt! But this itself is a proof that there is no death of our nature, namely, that we shall be the same as we were. Hence, we shall either pay the penalty for our sins, or we shall obtain a reward for our good deeds. For the same nature will rise

---

65 Wisd. 1.13; 2.24. The Septuagint and Vulgate have 'by the evil of the devil' in place of St. Ambrose's 'by the evil of men.'

again, all the more distinguished for having completed its service to death. Accordingly, 'the dead in Christ will rise up first. Then we who live, who survive, shall be caught up together with them in clouds to meet Christ in the air, and so we shall ever be with the Lord.'[66] The dead will be first, and the living will be second; the dead with Jesus, and the living through Jesus. For the dead, life will be sweeter after rest. But while the shortening of their life on earth will be welcome to the living, they will have no knowledge of the remedy.

(49) There is nothing, therefore, which we should fear in death, nothing over which we should grieve. Let the life which was received be returned to nature when she requests it, or let it be sacrificed to the call of duty which is concerned with the practice of religion or virtue. No one, moreover, has ever wished that he should remain in his present state. Such a promise is thought to have been made to John, but this is not true. We adhere strictly to his words, and base our position on them. In his own Gospel he asserts that he never received any promise that he would not die,[67] lest anyone through his example might be filled with a vain hope. But, if such a wish is presumptuous, how much more presumptuous is it to grieve beyond measure over something that has not happened beyond measure?

(50) The pagans usually console themselves either by the thought that death is a common calamity, or by a recognition of the rights of nature, or by a belief in the immortality of the soul. I wish that their opinions were consistent, and that they did not convert the unfortunate soul into many ridiculous monstrosities and forms. What, therefore, ought we to do, whose reward is the resurrection? While many cannot deny this gift, they refuse to believe. Therefore, let us establish our faith in the resurrection, not by some one argument only, but in as many ways as possible.

---

66 1 Thess. 4.16,17.
67 Cf. John 21.23 and St. Ambrose *In Ps. 108* 20.12.

(51) All things are accepted as true, either on the basis of experience, or reason, or concrete example, or because it is fitting that they are as they are, and each of these factors supports our belief. Experience teaches us that we move; reason, that whatever moves us must be considered as belonging to another power; example, that the land has produced crops, and consequently we assume that it will continue to do so; fitness, because even where we do not count on a return for our efforts, yet we do not believe that it is fitting to abandon the practice of virtue.

(52) One argument, therefore, strengthens another. Belief in the resurrection, however, is based most clearly on three main arguments, and these include the rest. These are: reason, universal example, and the testimony furnished by the fact that many have risen. Reason is clear. For, since our life as such functions through a union of body and soul, and since the resurrection entails the reward of good conduct and the punishment of evil, it is necessary that the body rise again, since its conduct is to be weighed. For how shall the soul be called to judgment without the body, since it must render an account of its companionship with the body?

(53) Rising again is a common attribute of all life, but it is difficult to believe this, because it does not result from our merit but is a gift of God. The first argument for belief in the resurrection, therefore, is the activities of the world, and the state of all things; the series of generations, successive changes and alternations, the risings and settings of constellations, the daily endings of day and night, and their recurring rebirths, as it were, daily. No other explanation, furthermore, can be found for the productive capacity of this earth unless it be admitted that the divine economy replaces by the dew of night the same amount of moisture, so necessary for all growing things, which is absorbed by the daily heat of the

sun. And what shall I say about the fruits? Do they not seem to die when they fall and to rise again when they grow green again? What has been sown rises again, and what has died rises again, and assumes again the same class and species as before. The earth first gave back her fruits, and in these our nature first sought the pattern of the resurrection.

(54) Why should we doubt that body will rise again from body? Grain is sown, grain comes up again. The fruit falls to earth, the fruit forms again. But the grain decks itself with blossoms and is clothed with a husk. 'And this mortal body must put on immortality, and this corruptible body must put on incorruption.'[68] The blossom of the resurrection is immortality; the blossom of the resurrection is incorruption. What is richer than everlasting rest? What is a source of greater gain and satisfaction than perpetual security? Here is the manifold fruit, the harvest, whereby man's nature waxes more vigorous and productive after death.

(55) But some may wonder how decayed bodies can become sound again, scattered members brought together, and destroyed parts be restored.[69] Yet no one wonders how seeds softened and broken by the dampness and weight of the earth grow and become green again. Such seeds, of course, are rotted and dissolved by contact with the earth. But when the generative moisture of the soil imparts life to the buried and hidden seeds by a kind of life-giving heat, they emit the animating force, as it were, of the growing plant. Then, gradually, nature rears from the stalk the tender life of the growing ear and, like a careful mother, wraps it in a sheath as a protection against its being nipped at this immature stage by the frost or scorched by the sun when the kernels are emerging, as it were, from babyhood. Later, nature usually surrounds the fully developed ear with a fence of beard, so

---
68 1 Cor. 15.53.
69 Cf. 1 Cor. 15.35,36.

the rain cannot beat it to pieces, the wind scatter it, or small birds devour it.

(56) Why, therefore, should we wonder whether the earth will restore human beings which she has received, since she gives new life to, rears, clothes, protects, and defends whatever seeds are sown in her? So all doubts should be dropped whether the dependable earth, which restores with compound interest, as it were, the seed entrusted to her, will also return her deposit of mankind. Need I mention the various kinds of trees which grow from the planted seed? When their fruit has ripened and fallen with repeated fecundity, they produce a new crop similar in all respects to the old. And certain kinds of trees restore themselves and have many renewed periods of life, so that they outlast the very centuries. We see a grape decay and a vine shoot forth. A graft is inserted and a tree is reborn. Is there a divine providence for renewing trees and no concern for men? He who has given these things for man's use has not allowed them to perish. Will He allow man to perish whom He has made to His own image?

(57) But it appears incredible to you that the dead should live again. 'Senseless man, what thou thyself sowest is not brought to life, unless it dies.'[70] Sow any dried seed you please, and it comes to life again. But, you reply, seed has a vital fluid in it. Yet our body has its blood, and it has its moisture. That is the vital fluid in us. Therefore, the argument advanced by those who deny that a dry shoot revives, and try to employ this alleged fact to the prejudice of the flesh, is, I think, to be rejected, since all flesh comes from clay. Clay comes from moisture, and moisture is from the earth. Accordingly, many plants grow even when there is no rainfall and the soil is dry and sandy, since the earth itself provides enough moisture. So, we cannot assume that the earth, which

---

70 1 Cor. 15.36.

is wont to restore all other kinds of life, will fail in this function as regards mankind. Hence, it is clear that we must not doubt what is more in accord with nature than against it. For it is as natural that all things living should rise again as it is unnatural that they should perish.

(58) Now we come to a point which frequently disturbs the pagans. How is it possible for the earth to restore those whom either the sea has swallowed up or wild beasts have torn limb from limb or devoured? This objection leads strictly to the conclusion that there is doubt, not regarding belief in the resurrection, but in respect to a part of mankind. For, granted that the bodies of those torn to pieces will not rise again, the rest shall. The resurrection as a fact is not to be rejected because of an exceptional situation. Yet, since all things earthly return and crumble into the earth, I wonder how there can be any doubt even concerning the instances noted.[71] For the most part, the sea itself also casts up on neighboring shores whatever human bodies it has swallowed. And if this were not so, it surely would not be difficult for God to join what has been scattered, and to unite again what has been dispersed. Could it be maintained for a moment that God, whom the universe and the silent elements obey and nature serves, did not perform a greater miracle in giving life to clay than in joining it together?

(59) There is a bird in Arabia called the phoenix. After it dies, it comes back to life, restored by the renovating fluid in its own flesh. Shall we believe that men alone are not restored to life again? Now, from the many oral and authoritative reports written on this matter,[72] we know that the bird

---

71 Cf. Eccle. 3.20.
72 The story of the phoenix was introduced into Western literature by Hesiod and particularly by Herodotus. It was widely believed to be true, although questioned in part by Pliny the Elder and others. The story naturally had a special appeal for Christians, and the phoenix became a common symbol of immortality in Christian literature and art. The phoenix theme received its most elaborate treatment in the

in question has a fixed life span of five hundred years, and that when by a sort of natural premonition it knows that the end of life is at hand, it provides itself with a casket of frankincense and myrrh and other perfumes, and, when its preparations and its appointed period are completed, it enters the casket and dies. Presently, a worm comes forth from its moisture, gradually grows birdlike in form, assumes a bird's habits, and, borne aloft on the oarage of its wings, faithfully takes up again the duties of its renewed life. For it carries the box or tomb of its body or cradle of its resurrection, in which in departing from life it dies and after dying rises again, from Ethiopia to Lycaonia. Thus, through the resurrection of the phoenix the inhabitants of those regions know that five hundred years have elapsed. Therefore, for that bird the five-hundredth year is that of its resurrection, and, for us, the thousandth year.[73] His resurrections occur within the period of this world, but our resurrection will come at the consummation of the world. Many are also of the opinion that this bird sets fire to its own funeral pyre and rises again from its embers and ashes.

(60) Perhaps, however, a more thorough investigation of nature will give us a more solid foundation for our belief. Let us, then, turn our thoughts back to the origin and beginning of human procreation. You are men and women and are not ignorant of what pertains to human nature. But if some are so, do you imagine that we are born from nothing? From what tiny beginnings do we grow so large. And if I am not more plainspoken, you understand what I mean or,

---

poem, *De ave phoenice*, ascribed to Lactantius. For the Latin text of this work, accompanied by a good introduction and translation, see J. W. Duff and A. M. Duff, *Minor Latin Poets* (Loeb Classical Library, London and Cambridge, Mass. 1935), pp. 643-665.

73 Hardly an allusion here to the millenial reign of Christ. The term 'thousandth' is used rather to signify completeness, the fulfillment of time. See F. H. Dudden, *The Life and Times of St. Ambrose* (Oxford 1935) II 668.

rather, what I do not wish to say. Whence comes this head and this wonderful countenance fashioned for various functions and uses? We see the work, but we do not see its maker. How explain the origin of this erect figure, dignified posture, capacity for action, quickness of mind, and ability to walk erect? We are certainly ignorant of the tools of nature, but the effects of their work are evident. You, too, were once a seed and your body is the seed of that which shall rise again. Listen to Paul and learn that you are such a seed: 'What is sown in corruption shall rise in incorruption, what is sown in dishonor shall rise in glory. What is sown in weakness shall rise in power. What is sown a natural body shall rise a spiritual body.'[74] So you are sown as are all other things. Why, then, do you wonder whether you will rise again like the rest? You believe the first fact because you see it; you do not believe the second because you do not see it. 'Blessed are they who have not seen, and yet have believed.'[75]

(61) Yet, before the proper season arrives, not even that first fact is believed. For not every season is suitable for seeds to grow. Wheat is sown at one time, and it comes up at another. At one time, the vine is grafted; at another, shoots begin to grow, foliage becomes luxuriant, and the grape takes form. At one time, the olive tree is planted; at another, as though heavy with child and burdened with a progeny of berries, it is bent low under the abundance of its own fruit. But before the proper time arrives for each its production is restricted, nor does the tree or plant which bears have the time of bearing within its own power. At one season, we see the mother of all exhibiting an unsightly appearance; at another, bare of crops; at another, fresh with blossoms; at another, brown and withered. If she had her own way, the earth would like to dress herself up in season and out, and never

---
74 1 Cor. 15.42-44.
75 John 20.29.

lay aside the golden garments of her fields of grain, or the fresh green-tinted attire of her meadows, instead of being in want of herself and without benefit from the gains of her own produce which she has transferred to others.

(62) Therefore, if you will not believe in our resurrection through faith, if you will not believe through parallel examples, you are going to believe it through experience. For, just as the end of the year is a fitting time for the ripening of many other products, such as those of the vine and the olive and the various fruits, so for us, also, the consummation of the world, like the end of the year, has set a fitting time for our rising again. And it is well that the resurrection of the dead occurs at the consummation of the world, since we are thus protected from falling back, after the resurrection, into this evil age. Christ suffered to deliver us from this evil world, so that the temptations of this world might not again overthrow us. For being reborn would cause us harm, if we should be reborn to a life of sin.

(63) Consequently, we have both a reason and a time for the resurrection. We find a reason in the fact that nature in all its productions remains consistent with itself and does not show inconsistency in the case of mankind alone. We have a time, in that all things are produced at the end of the year. For the seasons of the world make up one year. And why is it strange that the year is one when the day is one? For on one day the Lord hired laborers for His vineyard, saying: 'Why do you stand here, all day idle?'[76]

(64) The causes of the origins of all things are seeds. That the human body is a seed has been stated as a fact by the Apostle of the Gentiles.[77] Whenever seed is sown, therefore, there is present a basic substance or cause for rising again. But even if there were not such a substance or cause,

---
76 Matt. 20.6.
77 Cf. 1 Cor. 15.42.

who would fancy it difficult for God to make a man anew whence or how He might wish? For He ordered the world to come into existence out of no matter or substance, and the world was made. Look up at the heavens, look at the earth. Whence have come the fiery stars; whence, the ball and rays of the sun? Whence, the globe of the moon? Whence, the mountain peaks, hard rocks, and woods teeming with foliage? Whence, the widely diffused air, and the waters poured into and spread over the earth? Now, if, as David says, God made all things out of nothing, 'For he spoke and they were made: he commanded and they were created,'[78] how can we doubt whether what has been can be born again, when we see that that has been given existence which did not exist before.

(65) It is a strange fact that pagan philosophers, although not believing in the resurrection, nevertheless, for fear the race should perish, provide for this contingency with an indulgent kindness, as it were. Therefore, they say that souls pass and enter into other bodies in order that the world may not perish.[79] But let them tell us which is the more difficult, for souls to migrate or to return, to go back to their old abodes or to seek new ones.

(66) But let them doubt who have not been taught. For us, however, who have read the Law, the Prophets, the Apostles, and the Gospel, it is forbidden to doubt. For who can doubt, when he reads: 'And at that time shall all thy people be saved, that is written in the book. And many of those that sleep in the graves of the earth shall rise at one opening, some unto life everlasting, and others unto reproach and everlasting confusion. And they that understand shall shine as the brightness of the firmament, and of the just

---

78 Ps. 148.5.
79 Transmigration was a typical doctrine of Pythagoreanism and Orphism and thence passed into Platonism. Vergil reflects a compound of ideas on the subject in *Aeneid* 6.713ff.

many shall be as stars for all eternity.'⁸⁰ Well, therefore, has the Prophet spoken of the rest of those who sleep, for thus we are given to understand that death is not eternal, but, like sleep, it is entered upon for a time and then, at an appointed time, is put aside. He has shown, too, that the course of the life which is to be after death will be better than that which before death is passed in pain and sorrow. For the life after death is compared to the stars, while our life here is condemned to misery.

(67) Why should I need to bring in what is written in another place: 'You will raise me up and I will praise you?'⁸¹ Or that other passage in which holy Job, after experiencing the miseries of this life and overcoming every adversity by his virtuous patience, anticipated the compensation for his present evils afforded by the resurrection, when he said: 'You will raise up this body of mine which has suffered many evils'?⁸² Isaias, too, proclaiming the resurrection to the people, says that he is the announcer of the Lord's message. For we read: 'For the mouth of the Lord hath spoken it, and they shall say in the day.'⁸³ What the mouth of the Lord stated, therefore, that the people should say, is set forth later on, where it is written: 'Because of our fear, O Lord, we have conceived and have brought forth the Spirit of Thy salvation, which Thou hath poured forth upon the earth. They that inhabit the earth shall fall, they shall rise that are in the graves. For the dew which is from Thee is health for them, but the land of the wicked shall perish. Go, my people, enter into thy chambers, shut thy doors upon thee, hide thyself a little for a moment, until the anger of God pass away.'⁸⁴

(68) How well did he signify that the chambers are the

---

80 Cf. Dan. 12.1-3 (Septuagint).
81 Ps. 17.49,50 (freely quoted).
82 Job 19.26 (Septuagint).
83 Isa. 25.8,9.
84 Isa. 26.18-21 (Septuagint).

tombs of the dead, in which we are hidden for a little while, the better to be able to pass to the judgment of God, which will claim the right of just anger according to the extent of our wickedness. Therefore, he who is hidden and rests is still alive, but, as it were, withdrawing and departing from our midst. Thus, he escapes the misery of being entangled more tightly in the snares of this world. Through the voice of the Prophets heaven speaks and gives assurance that the joy of the resurrection is reserved for the dead and that health will be restored to their dissolved bodies by divine dew. Dew is a well-chosen sign, for by it all the living seeds of the earth are made to grow. Why marvel, then, if the ashes and embers of our disintegrated body also grow vigorous through the richness of dew from heaven, and, upon receiving the life-giving moisture, our members are again connected and assume their former appearance?

(69) Again, in minute detail the holy Prophet Ezechiel teaches[85] and describes how strength will be restored to our dry bones, feeling return, and motion be added; how, with the return of sinews, the whole structure of the human body will grow strong, and how the driest bones will be clothed with restored flesh, and the openings of the veins and the streams of the blood will be concealed by a veil of skin drawn tautly over them. At the very words of the Prophet, as we read, the crop of human bodies seems to rise up again to life, and one may see the wide expanses of the fields sprouting with a novel kind of growth.

(70) It is established that seed of one sort cannot become another kind of plant, much less produce issue so essentially different as men springing from serpents and flesh from teeth, although wise men of old believed that a harvest of armed men bristled up from the teeth of the hydra sown at Thebes. How much more credible it is, indeed, that whatever has

---
85 Cf. below, Ch. 71.

been sown rises again in its own nature, that crops do not differ from their seed, that soft things do not spring from hard or vice versa, that poison does not become blood, but that flesh is restored from flesh, bone from bone, blood from blood, and humor from humor? Can you, you pagans, deny a restoration of nature, then, when you maintain your belief in metamorphosis? Since you believe in idle fables, how can you not believe the word of God, the Gospels, the Prophets?

(71) But let us hear the words of the Prophet himself: 'The hand of the Lord was upon me, and the Lord brought me forth in the spirit: and set me down in the midst of a plain, and this was full of human bones. And he led me about through them on every side: now there were very many upon the face of the plain, and they were exceeding dry. And he said to me: Son of man, dost thou think these bones shall live? And I answered: O Lord God, thou knowest. And he said to me: Prophesy concerning these bones; and say to them: Ye dry bones, hear the word of the Lord. Thus saith the Lord God to these bones: Behold, I shall send the spirit of life into you. And I will give you sinews, and I will cause flesh to grow over you, and I will cover you with skin; and I will give you my Spirit and you shall live, and you shall know that I am the Lord. And I prophesied as he had commanded me; and as I prophesied all these things, behold there was a great movement of the earth.'[86]

(72) Now, notice how he shows that there is hearing and movement in the bones before the spirit of life is again infused into them. For, above, the dry bones are commanded to hear, as if they were endowed with a sense of hearing, and here it is indicated by the Prophet that each bone went to its proper joint, for we read: 'And the bones came together each one to its joint. And I saw, and behold the sinews and

---

86 Ezech. 37.1-7 (Septuagint).

the flesh came up upon them: and the skin was stretched out over them, but there was no spirit in them.'[87]

(73) Great is the favor shown us by the Lord in making use of a Prophet as a witness of the future resurrection, in order that we, too, should see it through his eyes. For all could not have been employed as witnesses, but we are all witnesses in one. For a lie does not suit a holy man, nor error befit so great a Prophet.

(74) Nor should it seem improbable that bones, at God's command, should again enter their bodily structure. Actually, we have countless examples in which physical nature has obeyed the commands of heaven. When the earth was ordered to bring forth vegetation, it did so.[88] When Moses struck the rock with a rod, water for a thirsting people gushed out, and the hard rocks poured forth streams through God's mercy for those parched by the heat.[89] What else did the rod changed into a serpent[90] signify than that, should God so will, animate beings can be produced from inanimate? If bones come together when bidden, is that conceivably less credible than streams turning back or the sea fleeing? For so the Prophet testifies: 'The sea saw and fled: Jordan was turned back.'[91] Nor can there be any doubt about the certainty of the facts concerning the destruction of the Egyptians and the preservation of the people of Moses. The waters of the sea were held back, yet, at the same time, surrounding the Hebrews. They then poured back and brought death upon the Egyptians, so that they destroyed one people and saved the other.[92] What, too, do we find in the Gospel itself? Did not our Lord show there that the sea grew calm at His word, that

---
87 Ezech. 37.7,8.
88 Cf. Gen. 1.11.
89 Cf. Num. 20.11.
90 Cf. Exod. 4.3.
91 Ps. 113.3.
92 Cf. Exod. 14.22ff.

the storm clouds of heaven were scattered, that the blasts of the winds subsided, and that the dumb elements obeyed Him and the shores were quieted?[93]

(75) But let us consider these matters in further detail, so that we can see how the dead will be restored by the spirit of life, how those lying in their graves will arise, and the sepulchres be opened. 'And he said to me: Prophesy to the spirit, O Son of man, and say to the spirit: Thus saith the Lord: Come, spirit, from the four winds of heaven, and blow upon these dead, and let them live. And I prophesied as he had commanded me: and the spirit came into them, and they lived: and they stood up upon their feet, an exceeding great multitude. And the Lord said to me: Son of man: These bones are all the house of Israel. They say: our bones are dried up, our hope is lost, and we shall be cut off. Therefore, prophesy, and say to them: Thus saith the Lord: Behold I will open your graves, and will bring you out of your sepulchres, O my people: and will bring you into the land of Israel. And you shall know that I am the Lord, when I shall open your sepulchres, and shall bring you, my people, out of your graves. And will put my spirit in you, and you shall live, and I will set you down upon your own land: and you shall know that I am the Lord. I have spoken and I will do it, saith the Lord.'[94]

(76) We note how contact with the vital spirit is again resumed and we learn how the graves will open and the dead will arise. Or should we wonder that the sepulchres of the dead are unsealed at the bidding of the Lord, when the entire earth to its utmost limits is shaken by a single peal of thunder, when the sea overflows its bounds, and then checks the course of its waves? Hence, he who has believed 'that in a moment, in the twinkling of an eye, at the last trumpet'—

---

93 Cf. Matt. 8.26,27.
94 Ezech. 37.9-14.

for the trumpet shall sound—that the dead shall rise again,[95] shall be caught up amongst the first in the clouds to meet Christ in the air.[96] He who has not believed shall be forsaken, and by his disbelief he shall bring upon himself his own condemnation.

(77) The Lord shows also in the Gospel, to come to specific instances, how a person will rise again. He not only quickened Lazarus, He quickened the faith of all. For if a person believes, as he reads, his spirit, which was dead, also is quickened with that same Lazarus. For, when the Lord went to the sepulchre and loudly cried out: 'Lazarus, come forth,'[97] what other meaning is there in this except that He wished to give visible proof, to exemplify our future resurrection? Why did He cry out loudly? Was it because He was not used to working through the Spirit, or because He was not wont to command in silence? No, He intended rather to emphasize the Scriptural statement 'that in a moment, in the twinkling of an eye, at the last trumpet, the dead shall rise again incorruptible.'[98] For the lifting of His voice corresponds to the peal of trumpets. When He cried out: 'Lazarus come forth,' why did He add the specific name, except, perhaps, lest one might be raised instead of another, or lest the resurrection might seem to be accidental rather than something commanded?

(78) The dead man, therefore, heard and came forth from the tomb. He was bound hand and foot with bandages, and his face was covered with a cloth.[99] Imagine, if you can, how he picks his way with eyes closed, moves forward with his feet tied, and makes progress without taking separate steps. Although the bands remained, they did not hold him back.

---

95 1 Cor. 15.52.
96 Cf. 1 Thess. 4.16.
97 John 11.44.
98 1 Cor. 15.52.
99 Cf. John 11.43.

Although his eyes were covered, they saw. Accordingly, he who arose walked, and left his sepulchre, and had sight. For, where the power of a divine command was operating, nature had no need of its own functions, and, as if in a kind of trance, no longer followed its own course, but obeyed the divine will. The bonds of death were broken before those of the tomb. Walking was practiced before it was prepared for.

(79) If anyone is astonished at this, let him inquire who gave the command and his astonishment will cease. It was Jesus Christ, the Power of God, the Life, the Light, the Resurrection of the dead. The Power lifted up a man lying in the grave; the Life made him walk; the Light dispelled the darkness and restored his sight; the Resurrection renewed the gift of life.

(80) Perhaps you are concerned by the fact that Jesus took away the stone and loosened the bands,[100] and you are worried that there will be no one to take away the stone from your grave. As if He who could restore life could not remove a stone, or that He who made a bound man walk could not break bonds, or that He who shed light upon covered eyes could not uncover a face, or that He who could renew nature could not split a rock! But in order that they who refused to believe in their hearts might at least believe their eyes, they removed the stone, they saw the corpse, they smelled the stench, they broke the bands. They could not deny that he was dead whom they saw rising again. They saw the marks of death and the proofs of life. What wonder if, as they worked, they had a change of heart in the process, and, as they heard, they at least believed their ears! What wonder if, as they looked, they were forced to believe their eyes, and, as they broke the bonds, they loosened the shackles of their minds! What wonder if, as Lazarus was being unbound, the people

---

100 Cf. John 11.41,44.

were set free, and, as they allowed him to go off, they themselves returned to God! Therefore, many who had come to Mary, seeing what was done, believed.[101]

(81) Nor was this the only instance our Lord Jesus Christ afforded us, but he raised others, also, that we might believe at least on the basis of more numerous examples. Moved by the tears of a widowed mother, He raised up a young man. Approaching and touching the stretcher, He said: 'Young man, I say to thee, arise. And he who was dead, sat up, and began to speak.'[102] The moment he heard, he sat up and spoke. The gift of power, then, is one thing, and the order of nature another.

(82) And what shall I say about the daughter of the ruler of the synagogue, at whose death the people were mourning and the flute players were playing their music? In the belief that she was indeed dead, solemn funeral services were being performed. The spirit returned immediately at the voice of the Lord, she arose with revived body, and she partook of food to furnish proof that she was alive.[103]

(83) And why should we wonder that a soul is restored at the word of God, and flesh returns to bones, when we recall that a dead person was restored to life by physical contact with the body of a Prophet?[104] Elias prayed and restored a dead child to life.[105] Peter, in the name of Christ, bade Tabitha rise and walk.[106] The poor rejoiced that she was restored to them and believed on account of the food she gave them. Shall we still not believe at the risk of our salvation? They purchased the resurrection of another by their tears. Shall we doubt that ours was purchased by the Passion of Christ? When He gave up His spirit to show that He had

---
101 Cf. John 11.45.
102 Luke 7.14,15.
103 Cf. Mark 5.38-43.
104 Cf. 4 Kings 4.34; 13.2.
105 Cf. 3 Kings 17.21-23.
106 Cf. Acts 9.36-41.

died for our resurrection, He exemplified the course of the resurrection itself. For, as soon as He again cried out with a loud voice and gave up His spirit, the earth quaked, and the rocks were rent, and the tombs were opened, and many bodies of the saints who had fallen asleep arose, and, coming forth out of the tombs after His Resurrection, they came into the holy city and appeared to many.[107]

(84) If these things occurred when He gave up His spirit, why should we think them incredible when He returns for the judgment, especially since this earlier resurrection is a proof of that future resurrection, a pattern of the reality to come? Indeed, it is less a pattern than it is the truth itself. Who, then, at our Lord's Passion, opened the graves and assisted the dead to rise and showed them how to find their way to the holy city? If there was no one, it was certainly Divine Power working in the bodies of the dead. Does one seek human aid when he clearly sees the work of God?

(85) God has no need of human assistance. God commanded the heavens to come into existence, and it was done. He decided to create the earth, and it was created.[108] Who carried the stones upon his shoulders? Who paid the cost? Who helped Him at the work? These thing were done in a moment. Do you want to know how quickly? 'He spoke and they were made.'[109] If the material universe sprang into being at a word, why should not the dead also rise again at a word? Although they are dead, yet they once were alive, they had the sense of feeling and knowing, and they had the power of acting. Furthermore, there is the greatest difference between not being capable of life and remaining lifeless. The Devil said: 'Command this stone to become a loaf of bread.'[110] When he confesses that, at God's command, material nature

---

107 Cf. Matt. 27.50-53.
108 Cf. Gen. 1.6ff.
109 Ps. 148.5.
110 Luke 4.3.

can be transformed, do you not believe that, at God's command, nature can be made anew?

(86) Philosophers discuss the course of the sun and the system of the heavens, and there are some who think that they should be believed although they are ignorant of what they are discussing. For they have neither visited the heavens, nor measured the sky, nor visually examined the universe. And none of them was with God in the beginning, and none has said of God: 'When he prepared the heavens, I was present. I was fashioning with him. I was the one at whom he rejoiced.'[111] If, therefore, such men are believed, why is not God believed, who says: 'For as the new heavens, and the new earth, which I will make to stand before me, saith the Lord: so shall your name stand and your seed. And there shall be month after month, and sabbath after sabbath: and all flesh shall come before my face, to adore in Jerusalem, saith the Lord God. And they shall go out and see the limbs of men who have transgressed against me: their worm shall not die, and their fire shall not be quenched: and they shall be a loathsome sight to all flesh.'[112]

(87) If heaven and earth are renewed, how can we doubt the possibility of man's renewal, for whom heaven and earth were made? If the transgressor is kept for punishment, why should not the just man be preserved for glory? If the worm of sinners does not die, how shall the flesh of the just perish? For the resurrection, as the very form of the word indicates, is this: What has fallen shall rise again, what has died shall live again.

(88) It is in full accord with the nature and course of justice that, since body and soul possess activity in common, the body carrying out what the mind has planned, both should come into judgment and both be committed to

---
111 Prov. 8.27.30 (Septuagint).
112 Isa. 66.22-24 (Septuagint).

punishment or preserved together for glory. For it would seem almost absurd that, whereas the law of the mind strives against the law of the flesh and under pressure of the sin dwelling in man, often does what is odious to it, the mind, guilty only through another's fault, should be subject to punishment, while the flesh, the author of the evil, should obtain rest. Since the mind has not sinned alone, it should not be punished alone; since with the aid of grace it has not fought alone, it should not alone gain glory.

(89) Unless I am mistaken, the reason is full and adequate, but I do not demand a reason from Christ. If I am convinced by reason, I deny faith. Abraham believed God.[113] Let us also believe, so that we who are the heirs of his race may likewise be heirs of his faith. David, too, believed, and so he spoke.[114] Let us also believe, so that we can speak in the knowledge that 'he who raised up Jesus, will raise us up also with Jesus.'[115] For God, who never deceives, promised this. The Truth, too, promised this in His Gospel when He said: 'Now this is the will of him who sent me, that I should lose nothing of what he has given me, but that I should raise it up on the last day.'[116] And He did not consider it sufficient to have said this once, but He expressly repeated it also in what follows: 'For this is the will of my Father who sent me, that whoever beholds the Son, and believes in him, shall have everlasting life, and I will raise him up on the last day.'[117]

(90) Who said this? It was He, of course, who, when He died, raised up many bodies of the departed. If we do not believe God, shall we not even believe evidence? Shall we not believe what He promised when He actually accomplished even what He did not promise? Why would He

---
113 Cf. Gen. 15.6; Rom. 4.3.
114 Cf. Ps. 115.10.
115 2 Cor. 4.14.
116 John 6.39.
117 John 6.40.

have died, unless He also had a reason for rising again? For, since God could not die, Wisdom could not die. Yet what had not died could not rise again. So our mortal flesh was assumed, which could die, so that, while that died which was wont to die, that which had died might rise again. For the resurrection was not possible save through man. 'For since by a man came death, by a man also comes resurrection of the dead.'[118]

(91) Therefore, man arose, because man died. Man was raised up again, but it was God who raised him. Then He was man according to the flesh; now, God is in all.[119] Now we no longer know Christ according to the flesh,[120] but we have the grace of His flesh, so that we know Him as the first fruits of those who rest,[121] the firstborn from the dead.[122] Unquestionably, the first fruits are of the same species and nature as the rest of the fruits. The first fruits are offered to God to beg a richer increase, as a holy gift for all gifts, and a kind of libation, as it were, from restored nature. Christ, then, is the first fruits of those who rest. But is He the first fruits of His own who rest, and who, freed from death, as it were, are held in a kind of sweet slumber, or is He the first fruits of all the dead? On the contrary, 'For, as in Adam all die, so also in Christ all will be made to live.'[123] Therefore, as the first fruits of death were in Adam, so also the first fruits of the resurrection are in Christ.

(92) All men will arise again, but let no just man become discouraged and be troubled at the common lot of resurrection, since he awaits the chief reward for his virtue. All, indeed, shall rise, 'but,' as the Apostle adds, 'each in his

---
118 1 Cor. 15.21.
119 Cf. 1 Cor. 15.28.
120 Cf. 2 Cor. 5.16.
121 Cf. 1 Cor. 15.20.
122 Cf. Col. 1.18.
123 1 Cor. 15.22.

own turn.'[124] The fruit of the divine mercy is common to all, but the order of merit differs. The day gives light to all, the sun warms all, and the rain in bountiful showers makes fruitful the fields of all.

(93) We are all born, and we shall all rise again; but in the state both of living and of living again there will be a difference in grace and condition. 'In a moment, in the twinkling of an eye, at the last trumpet. For the trumpet shall sound, and the dead shall rise incorruptible, and we shall be changed.'[125] Yes, even in death some rest, and some live. Rest is good, but life is better. And so the Apostle arouses the man who is at rest to life, saying: 'Awake, sleeper, and arise from among the dead, and Christ will enlighten thee.'[126] Therefore, he is aroused that he may live, that, like Paul, he can say 'that we who live, shall not precede those who have fallen asleep.'[127] Here, he is not speaking of the common manner of life and the breath we all enjoy, but of the merit of the resurrection. For, after saying: 'And the dead in Christ will rise up first,' he adds: 'And we who live, who survive, shall be caught up together with them in clouds to meet Christ in the air.'[128]

(94) Paul died, certainly, and by his noble sufferings he exchanged the life of the body for immortal glory. Was he mistaken, then, in writing that while yet alive he would be caught up in the clouds to meet Christ? For we read this of Henoch and of Elias.[129] But you, too, will be caught up in the spirit. Behold the chariot of Elias, and the fires! Even if they are not seen, they are ready, that the just man may ascend, the innocent be transported, and that your life may not know death. Accordingly, the Apostles did not

---

124 1 Cor. 15.23.
125 1 Cor. 15.53.
126 Eph. 5.14.
127 1 Thess. 4.15.
128 1 Thess. 4.16,17.
129 Cf. Gen. 5.24; 4 Kings 2.11.

know death. And, therefore, it also was said: 'Amen, amen, I say to you, many of those standing here will not taste death, till they have seen the Son of Man coming in his kingdom.'[130] For he lives, who does not have in him what can die, who does not have some shoe or bond from Egypt, but put off such before laying aside the service of this body. So not Henoch alone lives, since not he alone was caught up. Paul, too, was caught up to meet Christ.

(95) The patriarchs also live. For, unless the dead were living, God would in nowise be called the God of Abraham, the God of Isaac, and the God of Jacob. 'For He is not the God of the dead, but of the living.'[131] And we, too, shall live, if we have the will to imitate the deeds and conduct of our fathers. We wonder at the rewards of the patriarchs: let us imitate their submissiveness. We proclaim the grace which they received: let us follow their obedience; let us not, enticed by our appetites, fall into the snares of the world. Let us seize our present opportunity, let us cleave to the commandment of the Law, the mercy of our calling, and the desire of suffering. The patriarchs went forth from their own land: let us go forth in our resolve from the dictatorship of the body;[132] let us go forth in resolve as they in exile. But they did not regard as exile what was undertaken out of devotion to God, or required by necessity. They changed their native land for another: let us change earth for heaven. Theirs was a change in dwelling: let ours be a change in spirit. Wisdom showed them the heavens bright with stars:[133] let It brighten the eyes of our soul. Thus the type agrees with truth, and truth with the type.

(96) Abraham, who was glad to receive strangers, faithful to God and tireless in His service, and prompt in fulfilling his

---
130 Matt. 16.28.
131 Luke 20.38.
132 Cf.1 Peter 2.11.
133 Cf. Gen. 15.5.

duty, saw the Trinity typified.¹³⁴ He added religious devotion to hospitality, for, although he beheld Three, he adored One, and, while keeping a distinction of the Persons, yet he called One, Lord, thus giving honor to the Three but signifying one Power. For, not knowledge, but grace, spoke in him. And he believed better what he had not learned than we who have been taught. No one had falsified the type of truth, and, therefore, he saw Three, but worshiped their unity. He brought out three measures of meal, but slaughtered one calf,¹³⁵ believing one sacrifice was sufficient, but a threefold offering; one victim, but a threefold gift. Furthermore, in the account of the four kings,¹³⁶ who does not understand that Abraham subjected to himself the elements of material nature and all earthly things in prefiguration of the Lord's Passion? He was loyal in war, and was not grasping in victory,¹³⁷ for he preferred to be enriched with the gifts of God, not of men.

(97) As an old man he believed that he could beget a son,¹³⁸ and as a father he judged that he could sacrifice him. And his paternal love did not cause him to hesitate when reverence for God aided his aged hand,¹³⁹ for he knew that his son would be more pleasing to God as a sacrifice than as alive and unharmed.¹⁴⁰ Therefore, he brought his beloved son to be sacrificed, and him whom he had begotten so late he offered without delay. Nor was he held back by being addessed as father, when his son called him 'father' and he answered 'my son.'¹⁴¹ Names, indeed, are tender assurances of love, but the commands of God are worthy of even greater love. And so, while both felt mutual compassion in their hearts, there was no faltering in resolution. The hand of a

---

134 Cf. Gen. 18.1ff.
135 Cf. Gen. 18.6,7.
136 Cf. Gen. 14.1ff.
137 Cf. Gen. 14.23.
138 Cf. Gen. 15.6.
139 Cf. Gen. 22.10.
140 Cf. Gen. 22.2.
141 Cf. Gen. 22.7.

father lifted the knife over his own son, and, lest the sentence fail of execution, in his paternal love he was in the act of striking the blow. He was afraid the stroke would miss, that his right hand would weaken. He felt as a father would, but he did not shrink from his duty to God. He was hurrying to obey, even as he heard God's voice.[142] Therefore, let us, too, put God before all those whom we love, whether father, or brothers, or mother, so that He can keep safe our loved ones for us, just as in Abraham's case we see the generous Rewarder rather than the servant.

(98) The father, indeed, offered his son, but God was appeased not with blood but with religious obedience. In place of the body, God showed the ram in the bush,[143] that He might restore the son to his father and yet that a victim should not be lacking to the priest. Consequently, neither was Abraham stained with the blood of his own son, nor was God deprived of a victim. When the Prophet saw the ram, he did not assume a boastful attitude, he did not persist obstinately in his resolve, but took the ram in place of the boy. His conduct shows all the more how piously he offered the son whom he received back so gladly. If you, likewise, make an offering to God, you do not lose it. But we are selfish. God sacrificed His only-begotten Son for us,[144] but we refuse ours. Abraham saw this and recognized the mystery, that our salvation would be on a tree.[145] And it did not escape his notice that in one and the same sacrifice there was one thing which seemed to be offered and another which could be slain.

(99) Let us imitate Abraham's devotion to God, let us imitate Isaac's goodness, let us imitate his purity. Isaac was certainly a good and virtuous man, devoted to God, and

---

142 Cf. Gen. 22.11,12.
143 Cf. Gen. 22.13.
144 Cf. Rom. 8.32.
145 I.e., on the Cross.

faithful to his wife. He did not return evil for evil. He yielded to those who drove him out, but he received them again when they were sorry, being neither harsh to insolence nor obdurate to kindness. When he went away from others, he fled to avoid strife. When he received them again, he readily forgave them, and he was exceptionally kind when he pardoned. Men sought to associate with him, and he added a delightful feast.[146]

(100) In Jacob, also, let us imitate a type of Christ. Let there be in us some likeness of his action. If we imitate him, we shall have fellowship with him. He obeyed his mother, he yielded to his brother, he served his father-in-law, and he looked for his wages, not from a division, but from an increase in the flock. And there was no avaricious division, where the portion was so lucrative.[147] Nor was that sign of the ladder from earth to heaven for no purpose,[148] for by that vision was made evident the future fellowship of men and angels through the Cross of Christ. And the thigh of Jacob was paralyzed, so that in his thigh he might recognize his lineal Heir and that the paralysis of his thigh might prophesy his Heir's Passion.[149]

(101) We see, then, that heaven is open to virtue and that this is not the prerogative of a few. 'For many will come from the east and the west,' the north and the south, 'and shall sit down with Abraham, and Isaac, and Jacob in the kingdom of heaven,'[150] as, with all agitation of mind removed, they give expression to the joy of eternal rest. Let us follow Abraham in our conduct, so that he may receive us into his bosom and cherish us with loving embrace even as he did Lazarus, the heir of his humility, and surrounded with his

---

146 Cf. Gen. 26.1-31.
147 Cf. Gen. 30.27-43.
148 Cf. Gen. 28.12.
149 Cf. Gen. 32.24.
150 Matt. 8.11.

own virtues.¹⁵¹ For the generation of the holy patriarch approved by God cherishes us, not in a corporeal bosom, but in the garment, as it were, of our good deeds. 'Be not deceived,' says St. Paul, 'God is not mocked.'¹⁵²

(102) We realize how grave an offense it is not to believe in the resurrection of the dead. For, if we do not rise again, Christ, then, died in vain and did not rise again.¹⁵³ For, if He did not rise for us, He did not rise at all, because there was no reason why He should rise for Himself. The universe rose again in Him, the heaven rose again in Him, the earth rose again in Him. For there shall be a new heaven and a new earth.¹⁵⁴ Furthermore, what need had He of resurrection who was not bound by the chains of death? For, even though He died as man, He was free even in hell itself.

(103) Do you wish to know how free? 'I am become as a man without help, free among the dead.'¹⁵⁵ And well is He called free who was able to raise Himself up, according to what is written: 'Destroy this temple, and in three days I will raise it up.'¹⁵⁶ Well, too, is He called free who had come down to redeem others. He was made as a man, not in appearance merely, but actually fashioned as such, for He is man and who shall know Him?¹⁵⁷ For, 'being made like unto men, and appearing in the form of a man, He humbled himself, becoming obedient to death,'¹⁵⁸ so that precisely through that obedience we might see His glory, 'the glory as of the only-begotten of the Father,' as St. John says.¹⁵⁹ For thus the representation of Scripture is preserved, since the glory of the

---

151 Cf. Luke 16.22.
152 Gal. 6.7.
153 Cf. 1 Cor. 15.13-15.
154 Cf. Apoc. 21.1.
155 Ps. 87.5.
156 John 2.19.
157 Cf. Jer. 17.9 (Septuagint).
158 Phil. 2.7,8.
159 John 1.14.

Only-begotten and the nature of perfect man are thus preserved in Christ.

(104) Therefore, He needed no helper. For, as He needed no aid when He made the world, neither did He need any when He redeemed it. No legate, no messenger, but the Lord Himself saved the world. 'He spoke and they were made.'[160] The Lord Himself saved the world; He is everywhere because all things are through Him. For who could have helped Him by whom all things were created and in whom all things hold together?[161] Who could have helped Him who makes all things in an instant, and at the last trumpet raises the dead?[162] At the last trumpet, not that He could not raise them at the first or the second; order is preserved, not that a difficulty be finally overcome, but that the proper number be completed.

(105) Since my discourse is drawing to a close, it is time now to say something about the nature of the trumpets, so that the trumpet may also be the sign of the completion of my address. In the Apocalypse of St. John we read of seven trumpets which seven angels received.[163] There, too, we read that when the seventh angel blew a trumpet, there was a loud voice from heaven, saying: 'The kingdom of this world has become the kingdom of our Lord and of his Christ, and he shall reign forever and ever.'[164] The word trumpet also means a voice, for we read: 'For, behold, a door was opened in heaven and the first voice which I heard, as it were, a trumpet speaking with me and saying: Come up hither and I will show thee the things which must come to pass.'[165] We also read: 'Blow up the trumpet on the new moon,'[166] and again, elsewhere: 'Praise him with sound of trumpet.'[167]

---

160 Ps. 32.9.
161 Cf. Col. 1.17.
162 Cf. 1 Cor. 15.52.
163 Cf. Apoc. 8.2.
164 Apoc. 11.15.
165 Apoc. 4.1.
166 Ps. 80.4.
167 Ps. 150.3.

(106) We should, therefore, observe as carefully as possible the signification which the trumpets have, so as not to run the risk of looking upon this matter as an old wives' tale, and of thinking of it as unworthy of spiritual teaching and out of accord with the dignity of the Scripture. For when we read that our warfare is not against flesh and blood, but against spiritual forces of wickedness on high,[168] we ought not to think of carnal weapons, of course, but such as are powerful before God.[169] It is not enough that we see a trumpet or hear its sound, unless we understand the meaning of its sound. 'For, if the trumpet gives forth an uncertain note, how shall anyone get ready for war?'[170] Hence we ought to know the meaning of the trumpet's sound, lest we should seem to be barbarians,[171] when we either hear or speak of trumpets of this kind. And, therefore, when we speak of them, let us pray that the Holy Spirit will interpret their meaning for us.

(107) Let us consider what we have read in the Old Testament concerning trumpets, realizing that the festivals prescribed for the Jews by the Law are a shadow of celebrations above and heavenly feasts. For here is the shadow, and there is the truth.[172] Let us endeavor to arrive at the truth by means of the shadow. Certainly, in another place the figure of truth has been presented in this fashion, for we read that God spoke to Moses, saying: 'Say to the children of Israel: the seventh month, on the first day of the month, there shall be a rest for you, a memorial of the blowing of trumpets, and you shall call it holy. You shall do no servile work therein, and you shall offer a holocaust to the Lord.'[173] And in Numbers: 'The Lord spoke to Moses, saying: make thee two trumpets of beaten silver wherewith thou mayest

---

168 Cf. Eph. 6.12.
169 Cf. 2 Cor. 10.4.
170 Cf. 1 Cor. 14.8.
171 The barbarians employed horns and drums rather than trumpets.
172 Cf. Col. 2.16,17.
173 Lev. 23.24,25 (Septuagint).

call together the multitude and when the camp is to be removed. And when thou shalt sound the trumpets among them, all the multitude shall gather unto thee to the door of the tabernacle of the covenant. If thou sound one trumpet, all the princes and leaders of Israel shall come to thee. And with the trumpet you shall blow a first signal, and they shall move the camp forward and shall establish themselves on the East. And with the trumpet you shall blow a second signal, and they shall move the camp forward, and shall establish themselves towards Libanus. And with the trumpet you shall blow a third signal, they shall move the camp forward which shall be established towards the North. They shall blow a signal with the trumpet in their moving forward. And the sons of Aaron, the priests, shall sound the trumpets: and this shall be an ordinance forever for your generations. If you go forth to war into your land against the enemies that fight against you, you shall sound a signal with the trumpets, and you shall be remembered before the Lord and you shall have deliverance from your dead. And on the days of your joy and on your festival days, and on the first days of your months, sound the trumpets, and at your holocausts and at your peace offerings, and there shall be a remembrance of you before the Lord, saith the Lord.'[174]

(108) Shall we, then, think of festival days in terms of eating and drinking? On the contrary, let no one call us to account in respect to eating, 'For we know that the Law is spiritual.'[175] 'Let no one, therefore, call you to account for what you eat or drink or in regard to a festival or a new moon or a Sabbath. These are a shadow of things to come, but the body is of Christ.'[176] So let us seek the body of Christ which the voice of the Father from heaven, the last trumpet,

---

174 Num. 10.1-10 (Septuagint, but with some marked deviations).
175 Rom. 7.14.
176 Col. 2.16,17.

as it were, showed to you on that occasion when the Jews said that it thundered for Him.¹⁷⁷ Let us seek, I repeat, the body of Christ which the last trumpet will again reveal to us, 'For the Lord himself with cry of command, with voice of archangel, and with trumpet of God will descend from heaven; and the dead in Christ will rise up first.'¹⁷⁸ For, 'Wherever the body is, there will the eagles be gathered together.'¹⁷⁹ Wherever the Body of Christ is, there will be the truth.

(108bis) The seventh trumpet, then, seems to signify the weekly day of rest, which not only is computed in days and years and periods—and for this reason the jubilee number, too, is sacred—but also includes the seventieth year, when the people returned to Jerusalem after having been in captivity for seventy years. In hundreds also and in thousands, the observance of the sacred number is by no means neglected, for not without purpose has God said: 'And I will leave me seven thousand men in Israel whose knees have not been bowed before Baal.'¹⁸⁰ Therefore, the shadow of future rest is represented in days, months, and years, the time of this world. That is why Moses gave the children of Israel a commandment that in the seventh month, on the first day of the month, rest should be observed by all, a memorial of the blowing of trumpets, and that no servile work should be done, but sacrifice should be offered to God,¹⁸¹ because at the end of the week, the Sabbath of the world, as it were, spiritual, and not bodily, work will be required of us. For what belongs to the body is servile, because the flesh serves the spirit. Innocence makes a man free, but sin makes him a slave.

(109) It was necessary, therefore, that spiritual things

---
177 Cf. John 12.28,29.
178 1 Thess. 4.15.
179 Luke 17.37.
180 3 Kings 19.18.
181 Cf. Lev. 23.24,25 (Septuagint).

should be revealed as through a mirror and in an obscure manner. 'For, we see now through a mirror but then face to face.'[182] Now we make war according to the flesh;[183] then in spirit we shall behold the divine mysteries. Hence, let the character of the true law be expressed in our lives and actions, we who walk in the image of God, for the shadow of the Law has now passed away. The carnal Jews had the shadow, we have the likeness, and they who are to rise again will again have the reality. For we know that according to the Law there are these three: the shadow, the image, and the reality. The shadow is in the Law; the image is in the Gospel; the reality shall be in the Judgment. All things are Christ's, and all are in Him. We cannot see Him now according to reality, but we see Him in a kind of image of future things, of which we saw the shadow in the Law. Christ, therefore, is not the shadow but the image of God,[183a] not the mere image only, but the reality. And, therefore, the Law was through Moses because the shadow was through man, the image was through the Law, and the truth or reality through Jesus. For the Truth could not have proceeded from any other source save Truth.

(110) If anyone, therefore, desires to behold this image of God, he must love God so as to be loved by Him, no longer as a servant but as a friend who observes His commandments, that he may enter the cloud where God is.[184] Let him fashion for himself two spiritual trumpets of pure and beaten silver,[185] that is, composed of and adorned with precious speech. And let them not emit harsh and raucous tones inspiring fear, but let them pour forth thanks in the highest to God in continuous exultation. By the call of such trumpets

---

182 1 Cor. 13.12.
183 Cf. 2 Cor. 10.3.
183a Cf. 2 Cor. 4.4.
184 Cf. Exod. 24.15,16.
185 Cf. Num. 10.2.

the dead are raised. They are aroused, of course, not by the sound of the metal but by the word of Truth. And perhaps these are the two trumpets whereby Paul, through the divine Spirit, cried out, saying: 'I will pray with the spirit, but I will pray with the understanding also; I will sing with the spirit, I will sing with the understanding also.'[186] For the one without the other seems quite incapable of giving forth a perfect call.

(111) It is not every one's prerogative, however, to sound both trumpets, nor is it everyone's prerogative to call together the whole assembly; that privilege is granted to the priests and ministers of God who are the trumpeters.[187] Thus, whoever hears the sound and follows it to where the glory of God is, and with early resolve hastens to the tabernacle of the testimony, will be able to see the works of God, and will merit for all his posterity that appointed and eternal home. When the grace of the Spirit and the energy of the soul act in unison, then, indeed, is the battle won and the enemy put to flight.

(112) These are also salutary trumpets, if we believe with the heart and confess with the mouth. 'For with the heart a man believes unto justice, and with the mouth confession is made unto salvation.'[188] Accordingly, with these twin trumpets we arrive at that holy land, namely, the grace of resurrection. So let them always sound together in harmony for us, that we may always hear the voice of God. Let the utterances of the Angels and Prophets arouse us and move us to hasten to higher things.

(113) David was considering this resolution in his heart when he said: 'For I shall go over into the place of the wonderful tabernacle, even to the house of God: with the voice

---
186 1 Cor. 14.15.
187 Cf. Num. 10.8.
188 Rom. 10.10.

of joy and praise; the noise of one feasting.'[189] For not only are enemies vanquished by the sound of these trumpets, but without them there cannot be rejoicings, festivals, or new moons either. For no one, unless he drinks in the promises of the word of God and believes the resounding oracles of Scripture, can exult with joy or keep festivals or new moons, in which, freed from corporeal pleasure and worldly concerns, he longs to fill himself with the light of Christ. And sacrifices themselves cannot be pleasing to Christ, unless vocal confession accompanies them. For at the oblation offered by the priest this usually moves the people to implore God's favor.

(114) Let us, therefore, be preachers of the Lord and let us praise Him with sound of trumpet.[190] And not minimizing or despising the power of this instrument, let us consider it as one of the things which can fill the ear of the mind and enter into the depths of our inmost consciousness. Let us not imagine that what suits the body is applicable to the Godhead. We must not measure the greatness of divine power by standards of human strength nor inquire how or with what kind of a body anyone will rise again, or how separated parts will be united and lost elements restored. For all these things are accomplished by the divine will the moment they are decided upon. Nor do we look for a physical hearing of trumpets, since it will be the invisible power of the majesty of heaven which will be exercised. For with God to will is to do. And we need not inquire into the effort involved in rising again, but should rather seek its fruits. The resurrection will be accomplished more easily if, emptied of our sins, we attain the fullness of the spiritual mystery, and renewed flesh receives grace from the Spirit, and the soul obtains from Christ the brightness of eternal light.

---

189 Ps. 41.5,6.
190 Cf. Ps. 150.3.

(115) These mysteries pertain not only to individuals, but also to the whole human race. For note that the order of grace is according to the figure of the Law. When the first trumpet sounds, it collects those from the East, as the leaders and the elect.[191] When the second sounds, it gathers together those nearly on a par in merit who, being situated in the direction of Libanus, have abandoned the follies of the nations. When the third trumpet sounds, it summons souls who, as upon a sea, have been tossed about by the storms of this world and have been turned hither and thither by the waves of this life. When the fourth sounds, it calls those who in no way were able to soften the hardness of their hearts in accordance with the admonitions of God's word. That is why they are said to be toward the North, for, according to Solomon, the north is a hard wind.[192]

(116) Therefore, although in a moment [192a] all are raised up again, all, however, are raised in the order of their merits. And so, the first to rise are those who, through an early influence of piety, going forth before the rising dawn of faith, as it were, received the rays of the eternal Sun. I believe that this may be said rightly of the patriarchs in the course of the Old Testament, or of the Apostles under the Gospel. The second to rise are those who abandoned pagan rites and passed from sacrilegious error to embrace the teaching of the Church. So, then, the first came from the Fathers, and the second from the Gentiles, for the light of the faith had its origin from the former and, having been received by the latter, it will remain among them to the end of the world. The third and fourth groups to rise are those who are in the South and the North. Into these four is the earth divided, of these four is the year comprised, with these four is the universe filled, and from these four is the Church

---

191 Cf. above, Ch. 107.
192 Cf. Prov. 27.16 (Septuagint).
192a Cf. 1 Cor. 15.52.

gathered together. For all who are united with Holy Church and enrolled under the designation of the divine Name will obtain the privilege of the resurrection and the grace of eternal bliss. 'They will come from the east and from the west, from the north and from the south, and will feast in the kingdom of God.'[193]

(117) Christ fills His world with copious lights, since 'His going out is from the end of heaven, and his circuit even to the end thereof; and there is no one who can hide himself from his heat.'[194] Benignly He gives light to all, wishing not to repel the foolish but to correct them, and desiring not to exclude the hard of heart from the Church but to soften them. Hence, the Church in the Canticle of Canticles and Christ in the Gospel invite them, saying: 'Come to me, all you who labor, and are burdened, and I will give you rest. Take my yoke upon you, and learn from me, for I am meek and humble of heart.'[195]

(118) And recognize also the voice of the Church inviting us when she says: 'Arise, O north wind, and come, O south wind, blow through my garden and let my ointments flow forth. Let my brother come down into his garden and eat the fruit of his apple trees.'[196] For knowing even then, O Holy Church, that from these also you would have fruitful works, you promised to your anointed One the fruit from such as these. It was you who first said that you were brought into the King's chamber, loving His breasts above wine.[197] For you loved Him who loved you, you sought Him who nourished you, and you despised dangers for religion's sake.

(119) Then, O spouse, you are asked to come from Libanus, in the Lord's judgment still all fair and all blameless.

---

193 Luke 13.29.
194 Ps. 18.7.
195 Matt. 11.28,29.
196 Cant. 4.16; 5.1 (Septuagint).
197 Cf. Cant. 4.10 (Septuagint).

For it is written: 'Thou art all fair, O my love, and there is no blame in thee. Come hither from Libanus, my spouse, come hither from Libanus.'[198]

(120) Afterwards, no longer fearing rushing waters or violent torrents descending from Libanus, you call the north and south winds, and you desire them to blow upon your garden so that your ointments may flow forth upon others, and that you may, in them, offer to Christ the manifold fruits of your fertility.

(121) Therefore, 'Blessed is he who keeps the words of this prophesy'[199] which has revealed the resurrection to us with the clearest testimony, saying: 'And I saw the dead, the great and small, standing in the presence of the throne, and they opened the scrolls. And another book was opened, which is the book of life; and the dead were judged out of those things which were written in the scrolls, according to their works. And the sea gave up the dead that were in it, and death and hell gave up the dead that were in them.'[200] We must not, therefore, question how they will rise again whom hell casts up again and the sea restores.

(122) Let us hear also when the future reward of the just is promised. 'And I heard,' John says, 'a loud voice from the throne saying: Behold the dwelling of God with men, and he will dwell with them. And they will be his people; and God himself will be with them as their God. And he will wipe away every tear from their eyes. And death shall be no more; neither shall there be mourning, nor crying, nor pain any more.'[201]

(123) Please compare now and contrast this life with that, and choose, if you can, an unending existence of the body spent in toil, in the wretched misery of the marked

---

198 Cant. 4.7,8.
199 Apoc. 22.7.
200 Apoc. 20.12,13.
201 Apoc. 21.3,4.

vicissitudes of life, in the satiety of fufilled desires, and in the aversion that follows pleasures. If God were willing to let such things last forever, would you choose them? For, if life in itself is to be fled from, that there may be an escape from troubles and rest from miseries, how much more should we look forward to that rest which will be succeeded by the eternal pleasure of the resurrection to come, and in which there will be no longer any succession of grave faults or allurements to sin?

(124) Who is so patient in sorrow that he does not pray for death? Who is so firm in sickness that he does not wish to die rather than live as an invalid? Who is so brave in grief that he does not desire to have done with it even through his own death? Now, if we are dissatisfied while we live, although we know that a limit has been set for our life, how much more disgusted would we be with this life if we saw that the troubles of this body would be with us without end? Who, then, would wish to be free from death? Or what would be more unendurable than a miserable immortality? 'If,' says St. Paul, 'with this life only in view we have had hope in Christ, we are of all men the most to be pitied.'[202] He said this, not because to hope in Christ is miserable, but because Christ has prepared another life for those who hope in Him. For this life is liable to sin; the life above is reserved for our reward.

(124bis) How much dissatisfaction do we see that even the brief courses of our lives bring upon us! The boy longs to be a young man; the young man counts the years when he will be older; the mature man, ungrateful for the blessing of being in the prime of life, eagerly desires the honor associated with old age. Thus, to all there comes naturally a desire for change, simply because we become dissatisfied with what we now are. Therefore, even the very things which we have wished for

---
202 1 Cor. 15.19.

become wearisome to us upon their enjoyment, and what we have desired to obtain we reject upon its attainment.

(125) Consequently, holy men have not without reason lamented their prolonged sojourning here. David lamented it,[203] Jeremias lamented it,[204] Elias lamented it.[205] If we can believe wise men, even those in whom the divine Spirit spoke were hastening to better things. If we inquire into the judgments of others in order to learn that all held a single view, what great men have not preferred death to sorrow; what great men have not preferred it to fear! Clearly, they judged the fear of death worse than death itself! So, when the departure of the dying is longed for and the dread of the living is avoided, death is not feared for its evils but is preferred to the miseries of life.

(126) Well, then, let it be granted that the resurrection is to be preferred to this life. But what if the philosophers themselves have found a type of existence after death which will give us greater pleasure than rising again?[206] Even those, indeed, who say souls are immortal do not mollify me, since they allow me only partial redemption. For what happiness can that be in which I have not entirely escaped? What life, if the work of God dies out in me? What justice, if death as the end of natural existence is common to saint and sinner? What truth is that, that the soul, because it moves itself and

---
203 Cf. Ps. 119.5.
204 Cf. Jer. 20.16,17.
205 Cf. 3 Kings 19.4.
206 The problem of the immortality of the soul was much debated by the representatives of all the ancient schools of philosophy, and various answers were given to this question as well as to the related one concerning the condition or life of the soul after its separation from the body. Most of the common pagan views on these matters are discussed in Cicero's *Tusculan Disputations* 1, a work undoubtedly familiar to St. Ambrose. The philosophical proof of the soul's immortality based on self motion which St. Ambrose mentions here is treated at length in *Tusc. Disp.* 1.53-54, Plato's *Phaedrus* being cited as an authority.

is always in motion, should be considered immortal? What the state or activity of what we have in common with animals in our bodies is before the body exists is uncertain, and the truth cannot be gathered from contrary views, but would be destroyed.

(127) But can we accept the opinion of those who say that our souls, after they have departed from our bodies, enter the bodies of wild beasts and various other kinds of animals?[207] The philosophers themselves, at any rate, usually explain that these are the ridiculous creations of poets, such as might be produced by the deceitful potions of Circe.[208] They observe further that not so much they, who supposedly underwent such things, as the senses of those who invented these stories were turned by Circe's cup, as it were, into various beasts and monsters. For what is closer to the marvelous than to believe that men could possibly be changed into the form of beasts? How much more truly marvelous would it be that the soul which governs man should be able to assume the nature of beasts, so opposed to that of mankind, and, though capable of reason, pass into an irrational animal, than that the forms of bodies might have been changed! You yourselves who teach such things destroy what you teach. For you have entrusted these monstrous changes to magicians and their spells.

(128) The poets voice such ideas in sport and the philosophers censure them. But what they believe to be mere fictions they hold to be true about the dead. The poets who invented such fictions did so, not, indeed, because they wanted to prove their own fable, but to ridicule the errors of the philosophers, who fancy that the same soul, which was wont to control anger by a meek and humble resolve, to be

---

207 There is a vivid discussion and strong repudiation of transmigration, for example, in Tertullian, *De anima* 28-35. Cf. above, note 79.
208 Cf. Homer, *Odyssey* 10.210ff.; Ovid, *Metam.* 14.1ff.

patient, and to abstain from bloodshed, can now be inflamed with the mad violence of a lion, and, with ungovernable anger and unbridled rage, can thirst for blood and seek for slaughter; or that the same soul, which, by kinglike counsel, used to restrain the varied storms of popular outbreaks and to calm them with the voice of reason, can now endure to howl in pathless and desert places in the manner of wolves; or that the soul, which, groaning under an excessive burden, used to low in wretched complaint over the harsh labors of the plow, can now, being changed into human form, look for horns on her smooth brow;[209] or that the soul, which once used to be carried swiftly up to the heights of heaven on the oarage of its wings,[210] can no longer think of such flights and must grieve over the sluggishness caused by the weight of a human body.

(129) On this account, perhaps, you destroyed the famous Icarus,[211] for the youth, led on by your arguments, possibly imagined that he was once a bird. In similar fashion, many old men also have been deceived and died in great grief because they foolishly believed swan fables,[212] even imagining that by comforting themselves with sad strains they could change their gray hair into soft down.

(130) How incredible these things are! How disgusting! How much more appropriate to believe in conformity with nature, to believe in conformity with the process observed in all kinds of fruits, to believe in conformity with many actual examples, the oracles of the Prophets, and the heavenly promise of Christ! What is more excellent than to be convinced that the work of God does not perish and that those made after the likeness and image of God cannot be changed into the forms of beasts! It is the soul, of course, and not the

---
209 Cf. Vergil, *Ecl.* 6.51.
210 A Vergilian phrase; cf. *Aeneid* 1.301.
211 Cf. Ovid, *Metam.* 8.195ff.
212 Cf., e.g., the story of Cygnus in Ovid, *Metam.* 2.365-380.

body, which is according to the image and likeness of God. For how could man migrate, to whom all other living creatures whatsoever are subject, if the better nature does not allow this? And if nature were to do so, grace would not.

(131) But I have seen enough, pagans, of what you think about yourselves. For it ought not seem so strange that you who worship beasts believe that you can be changed into beasts. I, however, would like to see you have a better opinion of your merits and be convinced that you are destined, not for mingling with the herds of the animal kingdom, but for association with angels.

(132) The soul has to depart from the tortuousness of this life and the defilements of the earthly body. It must hasten to those heavenly gatherings, although it is granted to the saints alone to reach them. There it shall sing praise to God. For in the lesson taken from the Prophet[213] we hear of those singing praise to God to the accompaniment of their harps.[214] 'Great and marvelous are thy works, O Lord God Almighty, just and true are thy ways, O King of the ages. Who will not fear thee, O Lord, and magnify thy name? For thou only art holy: for all nations will come and worship before thee.'[215] And it shall see thy marriage feast, O Lord Jesus, wherein the bride is led from earthly to heavenly dwellings, as all sing in joyous accord, 'All flesh shall come to thee,'[216] now no longer subject to the world but espoused to the Spirit, and shall look upon bridal chambers adorned with linen, roses, lilies, and garlands. For whom else are the nuptials so adorned? For they are adorned with the purple stripes of confessors,[217] the blood of martyrs, the lilies of virgins, and the crowns of priests.

---

213 I.e., St. John.
214 Cf. Apoc. 14.2.
215 Apoc. 15.3,4.
216 Ps. 64.3.
217 For the symbolism here, cf., also, St. Ambrose, *Expos. in Lucam* 7.128

(133) Holy David desired this for himself above all else, that he might behold and see these things. Therefore, he says: 'One thing I have asked of the Lord, this will I seek after; that I may dwell in the house of the Lord all the days of my life; that I may see the delight of the Lord.'[218]

(134) It is a pleasure to believe this, and a delight to hope for it. Certainly, not to have believed it is a penalty, and to have hoped for it a grace. If, however, I am wrong in preferring to be associated after death with angels rather than with beasts, I am glad to be wrong in this, and I will never allow myself to be deprived of this opinion as long as I live.[219]

(135) For what comfort have I left save realization of the hope that I shall come to you, brother, very soon, and that the separation between us caused by your departure will not be a long one? And through your intercessions, I hope that I, who long for you, may obtain the favor of being called to you the more quickly. For everyone ought to desire for himself above all else that 'this corruptible body put on incorruption, and this mortal body put on immortality,'[220] so that we who now succumb to death through the frailty of the body, being placed above nature, may no longer have even the possibility of fearing death.

---
218 Ps. 26.4.
219 In this statement St. Ambrose adopts the form and language of a passage in Cicero, *De senectute* 23.85.
220 Cf. 1 Cor. 15.53.

SAINT AMBROSE

CONSOLATION ON THE DEATH OF EMPEROR VALENTINIAN

Translated by
ROY J. DEFERRARI, Ph.D.
The Catholic University of America

INTRODUCTION

THE CONSOLATION ON THE DEATH of Valentinian is, substantially, the funeral sermon delivered by St. Ambrose at the burial of the remains of the youthful Valentinian II, Emperor of the West.

One of the first acts of Theodosius, Emperor of the East, after his victory over Maximus had been to send one of his generals, a pagan Frank named Arbogast, to Gaul. Arbogast had been a soldier in the army of Gratian, Valentinian's older brother and his predecessor as Emperor of the West, and had remained loyal to him during the defection of his troops. He had also served ably under Theodosius in the campaign against Maximus. Theodosius made him *magister militum* of all the imperial troops in Gaul, and he ruled alone there from 388 until 391. In the summer of that year Theodosius returned to Constantinople, and Valentinian, now twenty, took up his residence at Vienne in Gaul, as Emperor of the West. The situation was an impossible one for Valentinian. All recognized Arbogast as master, and Arbogast recognized only Theodosius, who had appointed him to his post and now named him 'protector' of the young Emperor of the West. Furthermore, Arbogast resented the very presence of Valentinian.

On Saturday, May 15, 392, Valentinian was found strangled with his own handkerchief. Whether Valentinian killed himself, as Arbogast made public, or whether, as many believe, he was murdered at the instigation of Arbogast, if not by his own hand, is not definitely known. St. Ambrose, our chief and best source on this question, clearly points to murder, but he apparently had no proof. He did not openly accuse Arbogast; in fact, he did not even mention his name. Without clear evidence, he had need to be circumspect.

The corpse of Valentinian, temporarily interred at Vienne on Pentecost, the day after his death, was removed to Milan, where his sisters, Justa and Grata, went to mourn beside it daily for two months. Theodosius, as usual, was undecided as to what course to follow. In Gaul, Arbogast took advantage of this hesitancy. After overcoming the reluctance of the creature of his choice, he had his soldiers proclaim an imperial courtier, Eugenius, as Emperor of the West on August 22, 392. Arbogast apparently expected Theodosius to ratify this action. But Theodosius was evasive even to a special embassy sent to his court to announce formally the suicide of Valentinian and the consequent creation of Eugenius as emperor by the army in Gaul.

More than two months after the death of Valentinian, word came from Theodosius authorizing the burial at Milan. The body was placed in a tomb of porphyry, next to that of Gratian. Mass was offered, and in the presence Valentinians's sisters St. Ambrose preached this eloquent and touching funeral sermon.

The year of the delivery is known, 392, but the month is still a matter of some controversy, and the exact day is impossible to determine from the existing sources. All indications point to the month of August. Beyond that one cannot be more precise.

ON THE DEATH OF VALENTINIAN

ALTHOUGH IT MAY MEAN an increase of grief to write[1] about a subject over which we grieve, yet, because we often find solace in recalling the one over whose loss we grieve for the reason that he seems to live again in our discourse, while, as we write, we direct our minds to him and fix our attention on him, it has been a task of love to make known something of the last moments of Valentinian the Younger. It has been such, moreover, lest we should seem by our silence either to have blotted out the memory of a loved one who merited well of us and to have left it unhonored, or to have avoided an incentive to grief, since to grieve is often a consolation to him who grieves. Furthermore, when I speak about him or to him, let my discourse be about a man who, as it were, is present to me, or even before me.

(2) What, then, shall I lament first? What shall I first deplore with bitter complaint? The days of our desires have been turned into tears for us,[2] since Valentinian has come to us, but not as he was hoped for. Yet even by his death he wished to fulfill his promise, but most bitter has become his presence, which was so desired. Would that he were still absent

---

1 The sermon was prepared for circulation in a revised, written form.
2 Cf. Tob. 2.6.

from us, that for his own sake he might still be living! But he could not endure to be inactive when he heard that the Italian Alps were infested by a barbarian foe,[3] and he preferred to encounter danger by wholly forsaking Gaul than to fail us in our peril. A grave crime on the part of the emperor do we acknowledge this to be, that he wished to come to the rescue of the Roman Empire! This was the cause of his death, a cause full of glory. Let us pay the noble prince a tribute of tears, since he has paid us the tribute even of his death.

(3) Yet the exhortation to weep is not necessary. All are weeping: they weep who did not know him, even they weep who feared him, even they weep who do not wish to weep, even barbarians weep, even they weep who seemed to be his enemies. What great lamentations among the peoples were caused by the course of his entire journey from Gaul hither? For all lament, not so much that their emperor is dead, but with a family grief, as it were, that a common parent has died, and all bewail his death as a death of one of their own. For we have lost an emperor whom we lament bitterly for two reasons: for immaturity of years[4] and ripeness of age in counsels. For these things, then, do I weep, as the Prophet has said: 'My eyes are clouded by weeping, because he who consoled me has departed from me.'[5] The eyes, not only of my body but also of my mind, have been dimmed, and every sense has been enveloped by a kind of blindness, because he has been snatched from me who turned my soul and recalled it from the depths of despair to the highest hope.[6]

(4) 'Hear all ye people and see my sorrow. My virgins,

---

[3] An incursion of barbarians into Pannonia early in 382 had frightened Italy.
[4] Valentinian was only twenty years old at the time of his death.
[5] Lam. 1.16.
[6] This probably refers to Ambrose's struggle with the court, particularly with the mother of Valentinian II, concerning the transfer to the Arians of a basilica, first the Portian Basilica, later the Basilica Nova.

and my young men are gone into captivity';[7] but once it was known that they were from the regions governed by Valentinian, they returned free. A barbarian foe made war on the youthful emperor, and the foe, forgetting his own victory, was mindful of the imperial dignity. Of his own accord he freed those whom he had captured, giving as an excuse that he did not know that they were Italians. We were preparing even to add a rampart to the Alps, but the majesty of Valentinian did not wait for a palisade of the Alps, for flooding rivers, for deep banks of snow, but, crossing over Alps and rivers, he protected us by the rampart of his imperial power. Therefore, it seems that I should use the exordium of the Prophet's lamentation: How does Italy mourn, who hath abounded in joys?[8] 'Weeping she hath wept in the night, and her tears are on her cheeks. There is none to comfort her among all them who love her. All they who love her have despised her. All her people sigh.'[9]

(5) And because it has been said of Jerusalem 'she hath wept,' our Jerusalem, that is, the Church, also 'hath wept in the night,' because he who was making her more resplendent by his faith and devotion has died. Fittingly, therefore, 'weeping she hath wept, and her tears are still on her cheeks.' Truly, the suffusion of a tear-stained countenance is wont to show the abundance of weeping, when the cheeks are bedewed with tears, but because it is written: 'Her cheeks are as vials of aromatical spices begetting perfume, her lips lilies dropping full myrrh,'[10] the mystical grace of the weeping Church is meant, which at the death of Valentinian has poured forth the good ointment of her sorrow and honors his life by praising it. To her his death could not have been an affliction, since the fragrance of his praise, worthy to be proclaimed by the lips of all, has taken away all stench of death.

---
7 Lam. 1.18.
8 Cf. Lam. 1.1-2.
9 Lam. 1.11.
10 Cant. 5.13.

(6) The Church, therefore, mourns her beloved one and 'her tears are on her cheeks.'[11] Hear what is meant by the cheek: 'To him who strikes thee on the one cheek, offer the other also,'[12] because she is patient under pain, that the one who strikes may repent. You were struck, O Church, on your cheek when you lost Gratian;[13] you offered the other also when Valentinian was snatched from you. Rightly have you tears, not on one cheek but on both, because you piously bemoan both brothers. You mourn, therefore, O Church, and from weeping your cheeks are flooded, as it were, with flowing tears of affection. What are the cheeks of the Church of which the Scripture elsewhere says: 'Thy cheeks are as the bark of pomegranates'?[14] They are the cheeks on which modesty is wont to shine, beauty to sparkle, on which there is either the flower of youth or the distinguished mark of perfect age. Therefore, at the death of her faithful emperors faith experiences a feeling of shame, the Church blushes, as it were; and at such untimely deaths of her pious princes the whole beauty of the Church becomes sorrowful.

(7) The Church mourns in her wise men, who are, as it were, the head of the Church: 'For the eyes of a wise man are in his head.'[15] She mourns in her eyes, that is, in her faithful, because it is written: 'Thy eyes are as doves apart from thy reticence,'[16] because they see spiritually and know how to keep silent about the mysteries which they have seen. She mourns in her priests, who are as the cheeks of the Church, on which is the beard of Aaron, that is, the beard of the priesthood upon which the ointment descends from the

---

11 Lam. 1.2.
12 Luke 6.29.
13 Of the three emperors—Valentinian, Gratian, Theodosius—St. Ambrose had greatest affection for Gratian.
14 Cant. 6.6.
15 Eccles. 2.14.
16 Cant. 4.1.

head.¹⁷ These are the ones in whom the beauty of the Church exists, in whom her flower is more pleasing, in whom age is more perfect, who, like the pomegranates, display beauty outwardly by their bodily abnegation, but inwardly with spiritual wisdom nourish the people of every age and sex who have been committed to them, subjected indeed by the world to injuries, but dispensing inner mysteries. She mourns in her virgins who are as lilies and lilies full of myrrh, exhibiting the whiteness of purity and the glory of the mortified pleasures of the body.

(8) In these, therefore, she weeps, as it is written: 'The ways of Sion mourn, her priests mourn, her priests sigh, her virgins are taken away, and she herself is indignant within herself.'¹⁸ And within herself she is indeed indignant, and to Valentinian she says: 'I will take you up and bring you into my mother's house, into the chamber of her who conceived me. I will give you to drink of a wine made with much labor of spices,'¹⁹ that is, made with much labor of spices of strong odor from the juice of my pomegranates, that he may drink the 'wine' which 'cheers the heart of man'²⁰ and that there may flow over him the juice of the pomegranates in which there is much and varied fruitfulness. For discourse of many meanings and abounding in various texts of Scripture, the discourse of angels, the discourse of Apostles and of Prophets, whom the holy Church envelops as by a single bark, is the juice of the pomegranates.

(9) Valentinian, seeing these things filled with perfect grace, replies: 'The mercies of the Lord that we are not consumed; because His mercies have not been consummated, I have renewed them like the morning light.'²¹ 'Many are my

---

17 An adaptation of Ps. 132.2.
18 Lam. 1.4.
19 Cant. 8.2.
20 Ps. 103.15.
21 Lam. 3.22,23.

groanings and my heart has failed.'²² 'The Lord is my lot, I said, therefore will I wait upon Him. The Lord is good to those that wait upon Him, to the soul that seeketh Him. It is good to hope in the salvation of God. It is good for a man when he hath borne the heavy yoke in his youth; he shall sit solitary and hold his peace, because he hath borne a heavy yoke.'²³ And he surely is consoling himself with the reward of his virtues, because in his youth he endured labors, bore many trials; he preferred to carry on the proud neck of the mind the heavy yoke of the purpose of amendment rather than that soft yoke full of pleasures.

(10) Blessed, indeed, is he who even in his old age has corrected his error; blessed he who even at the point of death turns away his mind from vice. For 'blessed are those whose sins are covered,'²⁴ because it is written: 'Cease from evil and do good, and dwell forever and forever.'²⁵ Whoever, therefore, shall turn away from sins, and shall be converted to better things at whatever age, shall obtain forgiveness of his past sins, which he has either confessed with a penitent disposition or from which he has turned with a purpose of amendment. But in meriting this forgiveness he shares the companionship of many; for there are many who have been able to recall themselves from sin both in the slippery path of youth and in old age, but rare is he who in his youth has borne the heavy yoke with earnest sobriety. This is the yoke of which the Lord speaks in the Gospel: 'Come to Me all you who labor and are burdened, and I will give you rest; take My yoke upon you.'²⁶ If anyone, therefore, before he is burdened with a heavy load of sins, has borne the yoke in his youth, he

---

22 Lam. 1.22.
23 Lam. 3.24-28.
24 Ps. 31.1.
25 Ps. 36.27.
26 Matt. 11.28,29.

shall sit alone; he is not to be compared with the many, but with him who can say: 'For Thou hast singularly settled me in hope.'[27]

(11) But perhaps you may say: How does Jeremias call the yoke heavy, when the Lord in the Gospel has said: 'For My yoke is sweet, and My burden light'?[28] Now, first understand that the Greek has 'yoke' only, and has not added 'heavy.' Notice this, also, that, although it was so in Lamentations, in the Gospel He said 'sweet yoke' and 'light burden,' not 'light yoke.' For the yoke of the Word can be heavy, yet sweet; heavy to the youth, heavy to the young man whose age is in fuller flower, so that he is unwilling to offer the neck of his mind in subjection to the yoke of the Word. The yoke of the Word can seem heavy because of the burdens of discipline, the rigor of amendment, the weight of abstinence, and the curbing of lust, yet it is sweet because of the fruitfulness of grace, the hope of eternal reward, the sweetness of a purer conscience. Still, He called the yoke of the Word 'sweet' and the burden of conscience 'light,' because for him who has taken up the yoke of the Word with a patient neck the burden of discipline cannot be heavy.

(12) He, therefore, who has borne the yoke in his youth will sit alone and will hold his peace,[29] rejoicing in the eternal mysteries of divine recompense which have been revealed to him. Or, surely, he will hold his peace, having no need of obtaining a pardon for sin, when he has anticipated this need by a timely confession and has removed it by a speedy amendment. For it will not be said to him: 'The things that thou hast not gathered in thy youth how shalt thou find them in thy old age?'[30] But it can also be understood thus, that he who has borne the yoke of the Word early, that is, from his

---
27 Ps. 4.10.
28 Matt. 11.30.
29 An adaptation of Lam. 3.27,28.
30 Eccli. 25.5.

youth, will not mingle with young men, but will sit apart and will hold his peace until he trains himself in the full perfection of virtue; and he will put upon his mind the cloak of great patience, and he will give his cheek to the persecutor,[31] even content with the outrage, that he may obey heavenly commands.

(13) For it is a great thing either to abstain from the vices of youth or to leave them at the very threshold of youth and to turn to more serious things, for the ways of youth are treacherous and confusing. Therefore, Solomon says: 'Three things are impossible for me to understand, and a fourth which I do not know: the footprints of an eagle in flight and the tracks of a serpent on a rock and the paths of a ship that is sailing, and the ways of a man in his youth.'[32] And David says: 'The sins of my youth and of my ignorance do not remember.'[33] For a young man not only falls because of the frailty of his unstable age, but he also fails frequently because of his ignorance of heavenly commands; he quickly wins pardon, however, who offers ignorance as an excuse. And so the Prophet says: 'The sins of my youth and of my ignorance do not remember.' He does not say: 'The sins of my old age and of my wisdom do not remember.' But like the Prophet, who has quickly corrected and amended the vices of his youth, he offers age and ignorance as an excuse.

(14) Valentinian, also, like the Prophet even in sin, says: 'The sins of my youth and of my ignorance do not remember.' He not only said this, but also corrected his error before he learned that there was a fall into any error. And so he says: 'The amendment of my youth do not remember.' Error is in many; in few, correction.

(15) And what shall I say further of one who thought that he ought to abstain even from the sports of youth, that

---

31 Cf. Luke 6.29; Isa. 50.6.
32 Prov. 30.18,19.
33 Ps. 24.7.

the joyfulness of this age ought to be restricted, that the harshness of official severity ought to be softened, that the leniency of old age, out of keeping with his years, ought to be granted to one who was summoned to render judgment for a proven crime? It was rumored at first that he took delight in the games of the circus. He removed this charge so completely that not even on the publicly observed birthdays of princes nor in honor of the imperial dignity did he think that the games of the circus should be celebrated. Some said that he was engaged in the hunt of wild beasts and that his attention was distracted from the affairs of state; immediately he ordered all the beasts to be slain.[34]

(16) You could have seen the young man listening to the business of the consistory[35] and truly in the spirit of Daniel rendering a just and mature decision where old men might have hesitated or been influenced by consideration of some person. The envious taunted him because he sought dinner early. He then began to make such a practice of fasting that often he gave his courtiers an elaborate banquet though he himself ate nothing, so that in this way he might satisfy both the obligations of religion and the good manners of a prince.

(17) Word was brought that the young nobles of Rome were desperately in love with the beauty and charm of a certain actress. He ordered her to come to court. The messenger, seduced by a bribe, returned without having executed the command. He sent a second, lest he might seem to have wished to amend the vices of the youths yet could not. An occasion for calumny was given to some; yet when she was brought to court, he never gazed or looked upon her. Afterwards, he ordered her to leave, so that all might know that his command was not without effect and that he might teach

---

[34] The conversion of the younger Valentinian described here can be dated from his return to Italy in the summer of 388 after the fall of Maximus.

[35] The emperor's council.

the youths to refrain from the love of a woman whom he himself, who could have had her in his power, had spurned. And this he did when he was still without a wife, yet he gave proof of his chastity as though bound by wedlock. Who is so much a master of a servant as he was of his own body? Who so much a judge of others as he was the censor of his own age?

(18) What shall I say of his piety? When an informer accused men born of noble ancestry and wealthy by inheritance—things which easily arouse envy—of desiring the throne, and when the prefect prosecuted them, he replied: No sentence of capital punishment would be imposed, especially on holy days. And when some days later the charge of the informer was being read, he pronounced it a calumny and gave orders to regard the accused as free until the prefect should hear the case. Neither before nor afterwards did anyone, as long as the young man was emperor, fear the envy of so serious a charge. The young man smiled at what strong emperors fear.

(19) Rome had sent legates[36] to recover the rights of the temples, the unholy prerogatives of the priests, and of their sacred cults; and, what is more serious, the legates were making their representations in the name of the Senate. And when all who were present in the consistory, Christians and pagans alike, said that these privileges should be restored, he alone, like Daniel,[37] with the Spirit of God aroused within him, denounced the Christians for lack of faith and resisted the pagans by saying: 'How can you think that what my pious brother took away should be restored by me?' since

---

36 During the reign of Valentian II, four deputations were sent to one or the other of the emperors regarding the restoration of the state subsidies to the pagan religion and of the Altar of Victory to the Senate. This passage probably refers to the fourth made in 391. Cf. E. K. Rand, *Founders of the Middle Ages* (Cambridge, Mass. 1929) 14-21.

37 Cf. Dan. 13.35.

thereby both his religion and his brother, by whom he was unwilling to be surpassed in piety, would be offended.

(20) And when he was confronted with the example of his father, that during his father's regime no one had taken away these rights and privileges,[38] he replied: 'You praise my father because he did not take them away; neither have I taken them away. Did my father restore them so that you might insist that I should restore them? Finally, even if my father had restored them, my brother took them away, and in this matter I should prefer to be an imitator of my brother. Or was my father Augustus, and my brother not? Equal respect is due to both, and equal was the good will of both toward the state. I shall imitate both, so that I will not restore what my father could not have restored, because no one had taken it away, and I am resolved to maintain what has been established by my brother. Let Mother Rome demand whatever else she may desire. I owe love to a parent, but still more I owe obedience to the Author of salvation.'

(21) What shall I say of the love of the provincials,[39] either of that with which he himself embraced them, or of that which was paid in return to their protector by those upon whom he never permitted any imposition to be visited? 'Old taxes,' he said, 'they cannot pay; will they be able to endure new ones?' For this the provinces praise Julian. But the latter, indeed, was in the full vigor of life, in early manhood; the latter found much and exhausted all, the former found nothing and abounded in everything.

(22) While stationed in the country beyond the Alps, he heard that the barbarians[40] had advanced toward the boundaries of Italy. Anxious lest his kingdom be attacked by a

---

38 Ambrose here refers without comment to the policy of non-interference in religious affairs, either Christian or pagan, adopted by Valentinian I.
39 Valentinian's special subjects in Gaul.
40 In this work Ambrose refers to barbarian invasions on three occasions. Although Italy was threatened, it was not invaded at this time.

foreign foe, he made haste to come, eager to put aside his leisure in Gaul and to assume our dangers.

(23) All that is common knowledge, but this is personal, that he often summoned me when absent and declared that I especially must initiate him into the sacred Mysteries. Furthermore, in truth, when a rumor reached the city of Vienne that I was hastening thither to invite him to Italy, how he rejoiced, how pleased he was that I should be with him as he desired! The delay of my arrival seemed to him too prolonged. And would that no message of his coming had arrived first!

(24) I had already promised[41] that I would set out, replying both to the persons of high rank and to the prefect, as they begged me to consult the interests of the peace of Italy, that, although I could not with propriety intrude without need, I would not fail them in their necessities. My journey was decided upon. Behold, after three days a letter on preparing stations was received, the royal accoutrements were brought in, and other things of this kind were done which indicated that the emperor was about to set out on a journey. For these reasons the mission was abandoned by the very ones by whom it had been demanded.

(25) I seemed to myself to be responsible for my expected but unrealized appearance. But would that I owed this debt to you while still alive! I would make excuse that I had heard nothing of your perils, had received none of your letters, that I could not have come to meet you with my own horses even if I had undertaken the journey. And so, sure of pardon, while I was subtracting the days and was picking the road of your arrival, behold I received a rescript that I should con-

---

41 Because of anxiety at Milan, high officials asked Ambrose to go to Vienne and to request the emperor to come to the defense of Italy. Ambrose promised to go, although very reluctant to interfere between Valentinian and Arbogast. A report, probably false, that the emperor was already on his way caused Ambrose to cancel his trip.

sider it necessary to set out without delay because you wished to have me as a surety of your fidelity with your count. Did I object? Did I delay? It was added that I should hasten quickly and that I should not consider as a reason for my journey a synod of Gallic bishops, because of whose repeated dissensions I had frequently excused myself for not going, but that he himself might be baptized.

(26) At the very moment of my departure I could have perceived indications of what had already taken place, but because of my eager haste I was unable to notice anything. I was already crossing the peaks of the Alps, and behold there came a message, bitter for me and for all, of the death of so great an emperor. I retraced my journey and bathed myself in tears. With what prayers from all did I set out! With what lamentation from all did I return! For they thought not an emperor, but security, had been snatched from them. How deeply was I torn with grief, above all, because so great a prince, because a dear friend of mine, because one so exceedingly fond of me had died! What emotions did I discover to have been his during those two days in which he survived the letter that he had sent me! In the evening a silentiary set out; on the morning of the third day he was already inquiring whether he had yet returned, whether I was coming. Thus did he think that some security would come to him.

(27) O most noble youth, would that I could have found you still living, would that some delay had preserved you until my arrival! I make no promise about any power on my part, none as regards my ability and prudence, but with what great care and with what great zeal would I have restored concord and good feeling between you and your count! How I would have offered my very self as a pledge for your fidelity, how I would have pledged myself as a surety for those of whom the count said he was afraid! Surely, if the count were not unyielding, I would have remained with you.

I took for granted on your part that you would hear me, if you should see that I was not heard in your behalf.

(28) Much had I to keep; now I have nothing but tears and weeping. Daily are you greater unto my sorrow, you become greater unto my grief. All testify how much you have done for me; all declare that my absence was the cause of your death. But I am not Elias, I am not a prophet, that I could have known the future, but I am the voice of one crying in lamentation[42] that I may be able thereby to bewail the past. For what better have I to do than to make return to you in tears for your great affection toward me? I took you up a mere child in my arms when as an envoy I went to your enemy; I embraced you when you were entrusted to me by the hands of your mother. As your envoy I went to Gaul a second time[43] and sweet to me was that service in behalf of your safety first of all, and secondly in behalf of peace and the piety with which you were requesting the remains of your brother. Not yet were you without anxiety for yourself, but already were you anxious for the honorable burial of your brother.

(29) But let us return to Lamentations and enter the very bowels of sorrow: 'What shall I testify to thee,' he says, 'or what shall I liken to thee, O daughter of Jerusalem? Who shall save thee and who shall console thee, virgin daughter of Sion? For great destruction hath been wrought upon thee. Who shall heal thee?'[44] But who will console me from whom others seek the office of consolation? 'He hath filled me with bitterness, he hath inebriated me with gall.'[45] 'My bowels are

---

42 Cf. Isa. 40.30; Matt. 3.3; Mark 1.3; Luke 3.4; John 1.23.
43 The purposes of Ambrose's second mission to Maximus in 386 were: to secure the safety of Valentinian, threatened by the usurper; to preserve peace in the Western Empire between Maximus in Gaul and Valentinian in Italy; and, finally, to effect the return to Milan of the remains of Gratian for burial.
44 Lam. 2.13.
45 Lam. 3.15.

in pain,'⁴⁶ to use the words of the Prophet, because I have lost him whom I was about to beget in the Gospel.

(30) But he has not lost the grace for which he asked, he who today has risen before us in the sermon which I preached to the people. For when in my treatment of the assigned lesson I happened upon this, that the poor people blessed God, I began to ask who this people was, and to distinguish between two peoples, the one rich, the other poor. The rich is the people of the Jews, the poor, that of the Church: the one, rich in the revelations entrusted to it; the other, poor and borrowing revelations from others. Rightly poor, because it was gathered by a poor Man, namely, by Him who, being rich, became poor that through His poverty we might be enriched,⁴⁷ for 'he emptied Himself'⁴⁸ that He might fill all.

(31) But how is He poor who had the riches of eternity and 'the fullness of divinity'?⁴⁹ Therefore, He was in the flesh, and He said: 'Hereafter you shall see the Son of Man sitting at the right hand of the Power.'⁵⁰ And elsewhere He says to Peter: 'To thee I will give the keys of the kingdom of heaven.'⁵¹ Was He, then, poor who was giving away the kingdom of heaven? But hear how He is poor: 'Take up,' He says, 'My yoke upon you, because I am meek and humble of heart.'⁵² Therefore, even His people, whom I see to be richer than the rich people mentioned, are poor, but not through want, for they have merited to have not only the revelations of the Prophets but also the precepts of the Apostles which were infused by the divine Spirit.

(32) Not, then, through want is he poor, but poor in spirit, to whom it was said: 'Blessed are the poor in spirit for

---

46 Jer. 4.19.
47 Cf. 2 Cor. 8.9.
48 Phil. 2.7.
49 Col. 2.9.
50 Matt. 26.64.
51 Matt. 16.19.
52 Matt. 11.29.

theirs is the kingdom of heaven.'[53] Truly blessed are the poor who received what the rich did not have. Of this number is that poor Prophet of whom it is written: 'This poor man cried and the Lord heard him.'[54] Of this people is he who says: 'Silver and gold I have none, but what I have I give thee; in the name of Jesus of Nazareth arise and walk.'[55] Therefore, that poor Founder of a poor people says: 'O God, be not Thou silent in my praise, for the mouth of the wicked and the mouth of the deceitful man is opened against me. They have spoken against me with a deceitful tongue, and they have compassed me about with words of hatred, and have fought against me without cause. Instead of making me a return of love, they detracted me, but I gave myself to prayer.'[56] Prayer is a good shield whereby all the fiery darts of the Adversary are repelled.[57] Therefore, the Lord Jesus prayed, and His follower, Valentinian, prayed.

(33) But perhaps it may be said: What did his prayer profit him? Behold, he died in the first stage of life's course. Of the suddenness of his death, not of its manner, do I speak, for I employ not the word of censure but of sorrow. But the Lord also prayed and was crucified; for He prayed further that He might take away the sin of the world. Let us hear, therefore, what the disciple of Christ prays for—certainly, for what his Master taught him. Now He taught us to watch and pray that we enter not into temptation, that is, that we fall not into sin. For this is the temptation of a Christian, if he fall into danger to his soul, but to fear death is not a part of perfection.

(34) But one should pray also for his enemies, pray even for his persecutors, as the Lord Himself prayed, saying:

---

53 Matt. 5.3.
54 Ps. 33.7.
55 Acts 3.6.
56 Ps. 108.2-4.
57 Cf. Eph. 6.16.

'Father, forgive them, for they know not what they do.'[58] Behold His great clemency. They persecuted their own Author; He forgave even the grave sins of His adversaries; rather, He even excused their offenses by covering them with the cloak of ignorance, saying: 'For they know not what they do.' For if they had known, they would not have persecuted their Lord[59] on whose power and jurisdiction they believed that their salvation depended. And because the persecutors of Christ were not satisfied by His death alone, they added curses and insults. And He Himself says: 'They will curse and Thou wilt bless.'[60] He taught us that we should not fear in the least curses of persecutors, since we possess the Author of blessing, and that insults should not move us when there is a Protector who can remove curses.

(35) What of the fact that he did not fear to die? Nay, rather he offered himself up for all, saying that the innocent were subjected to hatred to no purpose, that to no purpose were others being endangered on his account. And he desired death for himself rather than that he himself should be a cause of death to others. Such is the Gospel teaching of our Lord, who at the very time of His arrest said: 'If you seek me, let these go their way.'[61] And so he died for all whom he loved, a man in whose behalf his friends thought it of little account if they should all perish.

(36) We have noted his attitude of mind toward his friends. Let us consider the affection which he had for his sisters. In them he found repose, in them he obtained consolation, in them he found relaxation for the mind and soothing for his heart wearied by cares. He begged of them that if through some lapse of boyhood, if through some word, they seemed to have been offended by their brother, they

---

58 Luke 23.34.
59 Cf. 1 Cor. 2.8.
60 Ps. 108.28.
61 John 18.8.

should forgive and should beseech pardon for him of the Lord God. The hands and heads of his sisters he was wont to kiss, unmindful of his imperial dignity, but mindful of his kinship, and the more he stood above others by right of power, the more humble did he show himself to his sisters. He begged of them not to remember injury but to remember kindness.

(37) It happened that he heard a case regarding a possession of theirs. For so great a man was he that even in the suit of his sisters he was thought by the provincials to be a just judge. Although from love he inclined toward his holy relatives, he tempered his piety with justice. He heard the case, not regarding a right, but regarding the possession of an estate. On the one hand, brotherly love struggled in behalf of his sisters; on the other, mercy for the cause of an orphan, so that he interceded with his own sisters for him. He remitted the case to a public judge, lest he might offend against justice or brotherly love. In secret, however, as we learn from the final disposition made by the noble maidens, he so impressed his pious love on his holy sisters that they were willing to relinquish the estate and to make this known. Sisters truly worthy of so great a brother, who preferred of their own accord to surrender what their mother had left them rather than subject their brother to shame on their account!

(38) This inheritance of a brother's praise and glory is for you, holy souls, a more precious bequest, and by it a devoted brother has rendered you nobler and richer. For he adorned your head not with jewels but with kisses, and he did not so much encircle your hands with royal insignia as he caressed them with his imperial lips. In the enjoyment of your presence he placed all his solace, so that he did not even long exceedingly for a wife. Therefore he deferred marriage because he was sustained by the pious affection of your graciousness. Let all this, then, be more a source of pleasure

than of grief to you, so that your brother's glory may refresh your minds more than sorrow torment them. Tears often both sustain and relieve the mind; weeping cools the heart and consoles a sorrowful affection.

(39) You are indeed looking upon painful obsequies, but even blessed Mary stood by the cross of her Son, and the Virgin watched the passion of the Only-begotten. I read of her standing; I do not read of her weeping. Wherefore, her Son said to her: 'Women, behold thy son,' and to the disciple He said: 'Behold thy Mother,'[62] leaving to them the heritage of His love and His grace. Hence I desire, devoted children, to show you fatherly affection, since because of my sins I was not worthy to save your brother. Your brother I behold in you, to your brother I cling, your brother I consider to be present to me; nay rather, both brothers, whom I regard as my plucked-out eyes. More happily do emperors persecute bishops than love them. How much more fortunately for me did Maximus threaten me! In his hatred there was praise, in the love of these brothers is the heritage of suffering caused by death. My sons, would that I might have been allowed to pour out this life of mine for you! A curtailment of sorrow would I have found, and more glorious would it have been for me to die for such dear friends!

(40) But, holy daughters, let me return to consoling you, although the bitterness of what has happened takes away all the force of consolation. If consolation be brief, it offers nothing wherewith to soothe a sorrowing love, but, if it be too diffuse, it brings a longer remembrance of sorrow. For the more diffuse you are, the more, while in the very act of consoling, will you affect him whom you wish to console, and the longer will you make his sorrow.

(41) Therefore, I shall not wipe away your tears by my discourse as with a sponge. I would not wish to do this even if

---

62 John 19.26,27.

I could. For pious affections find a kind of pleasure in weeping, and usually a heavy sorrow is dispelled by tears. But I make this request, that by your deep grief you do not pluck out the brother who has been implanted in your hearts, or turn him away by your lamentations, or disturb him as he rests. Let him remain in your hearts, let him live in your breasts, let him cling to your pious embraces as he used to, let him imprint his brotherly kisses, let him be always in your sight, always on your lips, always in your speech, always in your minds. His state is now such that you need not fear for him as before. Forget his misfortune, hold fast to his virtue. Hope in him as one who will help you, let him stand by as a protector at night, let not even sleep now exclude him from your presence. For his sake let repose delight you, that he may return to you more loved than ever. It is in your power, daughters, to prevent anyone now from taking your brother from you.

(42) But you wish to keep his body. Throwing yourselves upon his tomb, you cling to it. Let that tomb be for you a brother's habitation, let it be the hall of his palace, in which the members dear to you will repose.

(43) But if you again remind me of your grief because he departed so early from life, I certainly do not deny that he died at an untimely age, one whom we would have wished to support with time taken from our own life, that he might live out of our own years who could not complete his own.

(44) But I ask whether or not there is any consciousness after death? If there is, he is alive; nay, rather, because there is, he now enjoys eternal life. For how does he not possess consciousness whose soul lives and flourishes and will return to the body, and will make that body live again when it has been reunited with it? The Apostle cries out: 'We would not, brethren, have you ignorant concerning those who are

asleep, lest you should grieve, even as others who have no
hope. For if we believe that Jesus died and rose again, so with
him God will bring those also who have fallen asleep through
Jesus.'[63] Life, therefore, awaits them for whom resurrection
awaits.

(45) But if the Gentiles, who have no hope of resurrection, are consoled by this alone, in that they say that after
death the departed have no consciousness and because of this
no sense of pain remains, how much the more should we
receive consolation because death is not to be feared, since it
is the end of sin, and because life is not to be despaired of
which is restored by the resurrection? Job also says that death
is not to be feared, but rather to be desired by the just, when
he says: 'Would that Thou mayest protect me in hell and hide
me until Thy wrath pass and appoint me a time when Thou
wilt remember me. For if a man is dead, he shall live. Completing the days of my life I shall survive until I be made
again. Then Thou shalt call and I shall obey Thee; and the
works of Thy hands Thou wilt not despise.'[64]

(46) Granted that one should grieve that he died at an
early age, nevertheless one should rejoice that he departed a
veteran in the campaigns of virtue. For so great was the
amendment of his life in the period of youth, which is perilous
for all, so great the praise of his morals, that they overshadow
every remembrance of grief. For, that he died is a mark of
frailty; that his character was such, a mark of admiration.
How happy would the State have been, if it could have kept
him longer! But since the life of the saints is not this life on
earth, but that in heaven—for to the just 'to live is Christ,
and to die is gain,' since 'to depart and be with Christ is a lot
by far the better,'[65]—we should grieve that he was so sud-

---
[63] 1 Thess. 4.12-14.
[64] Job 14.13-15 (Septuagint); cf., also, Ps. 137.8.
[65] Phil. 1.21.23.

denly snatched from us, but we should be consoled that he has passed on to better things.

(47) Thus David wept for his son who was about to die; he did not grieve for him when dead.[66] He wept that he might not be snatched from him, but he ceased to weep when he was snatched away, for he knew that he was with Christ. And that you may know that what I declare is true, he wept for his incestuous son Amnon[67] when he was killed, and he mourned for the parricide Absalom when he perished, saying: 'My son Absalom, my son Absalom!'[68] He did not think the innocent son should be mourned, because he believed that the others had perished for their crime but that the latter would live on account of his innocence.

(48) Therefore, you have no reason for grieving excessively over your brother. He was born a man, he was subject to human frailty. No one redeems himself from death, neither the rich man, nor even kings; nay rather, they themselves are subject to more grievous death. Job said: 'The years of the mighty one are numbered, but fear is in his ears; when he seems to have peace, then will come his destruction.'[69] As for you yourselves, you, too, should bear patiently that such trials have befallen you which you see you have in common with the saints. David also was left deserted when he lost his sons. He would have wished, then, to die as your brother was snatched from you; he bewailed the crimes, not the death of his sons.

(49) But, granted that we must mourn. How long may the time of our grief be extended? You have finished a period of two months in the daily embracing of your brother's remains. The daughter of Jephte alone in the Scriptures demanded a definite time for her weeping, when she learned

---
66 Cf. 2 Kings 12.15-17,19-23.
67 Cf. 2 Kings 13.28,29.
68 2 Kings 18.33.
69 Job 15.20-22 (Septuagint).

that her father as he was about to set out for battle had vowed that, if successful, he would offer to the Lord whatever should meet him first. As he returned home after the victory, his daughter, aware of his love, but unaware of his vow, ran to meet him. Her father saw her and groaned, saying: 'Woe is me, daughter, that thou hast ensnared me, thou hast become a goad of pain to me. For I have opened my mouth to the Lord concerning thee, and I shall be unable to retract.' She said to him: 'Father, if thou hast opened thy mouth against me, do with me as it hath gone forth from thy mouth.' And again she said: 'Grant me two months, and going I shall bewail my virginity in the mountains, I and my companions.' And so after the two months had elapsed, she returned and fulfilled the obligation of the sacrifice. By a decree of the people of Israel for four days every year she was lamented by the women of that nation.[70]

(50) Therefore, for bewailing the flower of her virginity the daughter of Jephte judged two months to be sufficient, and the resurrection had not yet come. And in that space of time she thought that she had been sufficiently bewailed by a few. With you all peoples have wept, all provinces mourned, and do you still think that this mourning of yours is too short? If you could redeem your brother by your death he still would be unwilling to be brought back to life by your affliction, for he believes that he lives better in you. He desired rather that he himself should die than that he should see any injury to you, he was ready to offer himself willingly for you, and on the very day of our sorrow he is said to have uttered these words only: 'Alas for my poor sisters!' And so he grieved more for your bereavement than for his own death.

(51) But I hear that you grieve because he did not receive the sacrament of baptism. Tell me: What else is in

---

70 Judges 11.35-40.

your power other than the desire, the request? But he even had this desire for a long time, that, when he should come into Italy, he would be initiated, and recently he signified a desire to be baptized by me, and for this reason above all others he thought that I ought to be summoned. Has he not, then, the grace which he desired; has he not the grace which he requested? And because he asked, he received, and therefore is it said: 'By whatsoever death the just man shall be overtaken, his soul shall be at rest.'[71]

(52) Grant, therefore, O holy Father, to Thy servant the gift which Moses received, because he saw in spirit; the gift which David merited, because he knew from revelation. Grant, I pray, to Thy servant Valentinian the gift which he longed for, the gift which he requested while in health, vigor, and security. If, stricken with sickness, he had deferred it, he would not be entirely without Thy mercy who has been cheated by the swiftness of time, not by his own wish. Grant, therefore, to Thy servant the gift of Thy grace which he never rejected, who on the day before his death refused to restore the privileges of the temples although he was pressed by those whom he could well have feared. A crowd of pagans was present, the Senate entreated, but he was not afraid to displease men so long as he pleased Thee alone in Christ. He who had Thy Spirit, how has he not received Thy grace?

(53) Or if the fact disturbs you that the mysteries have not been solemnly celebrated, then you should realize that not even martyrs are crowned if they are catechumens, for they are not crowned if they are not initiated. But if they are washed in their own blood, his piety and his desire have washed him, also.

(54) Do not, I beseech, O Lord, separate him from his brother, do not break the yoke of this pious relationship. Now Gratian, already Thine, and vindicated by Thy judg-

---

71 Wisd. 4.7.

ment, is in further peril, if he be separated from his brother, if he deserve not to be with him through whom he has deserved to be vindicated. What hands he now raises aloft to Thee, O Father! What prayers does he pour forth for his brother! With what an embrace does he cling to him! How he does not suffer him to be snatched from him!

(55) Your father also is present, who under Julian spurned imperial service and the honors of the tribunate out of his love for the faith. Give to the father his son, to the brother his brother, both of whom he imitated, the one by his faith, the other equally by his devotion and piety, in refusing to restore the privileges of the temples. What had been lacking in his father, he added; what his brother established, he preserved. And I also assume the role of intercessor for him for whom I anticipate reward!

(56) Offer the holy mysteries with your hands, with devoted love let us ask for his repose. Offer the heavenly sacraments, let us accompany the soul of our son with our oblations. 'Lift up with me, O people, your hands to the holy place,'[72] so that at least through this service we may repay him for his deserts. Not with flowers shall I sprinkle his grave, but I shall bedew his spirit with the odor of Christ. Let others scatter lilies in basketfuls. Christ is our lily, and with this lily I shall bless his remains, with this I shall recommend for his favor. Never shall I separate the names of the devoted brothers nor make a distinction in their merits. I know that this joint remembrance will conciliate, and that this union will delight, the Lord.

(57) Let no one think that there has been any detraction from their merits because of their early deaths. Henoch was snatched away lest wickedness should alter his heart;[73] Josias in the eighteenth year of his reign so celebrated the Pasch

---
72 Ps. 133.2.
73 Cf. Gen. 5.24; Eccli. 44.16; Heb. 11.5; Wisd. 4.11.

of the Lord that he surpassed all the princes of the past in devotion, and he did not survive longer through the merits of his faith. Nay, rather, because grievous destruction threatened the Jewish people, the just king was taken away beforehand.[74] I fear that you, too, were snatched away from us because of some offense on our part, so that, as a just man, you might escape in the eighteenth year of your reign the bitterness of impending evil.

(58) But now I shall embrace the remains that are dear to me, and shall deposit them in a fitting sepulchre, yet I shall gaze on each member. My Valentinian, 'my youth white and ruddy,'[75] having in himself the image of Christ, for with such words the Church honors Christ in the Canticles. Do not think this an impropriety, for with the sign of their lord even servants are branded, and soldiers are marked with the name of their emperor. Therefore, the Lord Himself also says: 'Touch ye not My anointed,'[76] and 'you are the light of the world.'[77] And Jacob has said: 'Juda, thee let thy brethren praise.'[78] To his own son he spoke and revealed the Lord. And of Joseph it was said: 'My son is grown, my son Joseph is grown,'[79] and he signified Christ.

(59) Therefore it is permitted me also to mark the servant with the sign of the Lord: 'My young man is white and ruddy, chosen from among ten thousand.'[80] My son was chosen when, after the death of his father, as a mere child he attained imperial power. 'His head is a rock of gold, his eyes like doves upon a flood of waters.'[81] For 'There we sat and wept,'[82] they said who came thence.

---

74 Cf. 4 Kings 23.21-24.
75 Cant. 5.10.
76 Ps. 104.15.
77 Matt. 5.14.
78 Gen. 48.8.
79 Gen. 49.22.
80 Cant. 5.10.
81 Cant. 5.11,12.
82 Ps. 136.1.

(60) 'His belly is an ivory casket,'[83] which had received the oracles of the Scriptures, so that he could say: 'My bowels are in pain,'[84] as the Prophet has said. For he says this who is an imitator of Christ.

(61) 'His cheeks are as vials of aromatic spices,'[85] upon which the ointment of Christ poured.

(62) 'His lips are as dripping lilies, full of myrrh. His hands are turned and as of gold, full of Tharsis,'[86] because in his words justice shone forth, and in his works and deeds grace was resplendent. And in him speech was full of power and royal authority, and constancy was unchanged by any fear of death, and precious and faultless was his correction of actions, for every good laborer is the hand of Christ.

(63) 'His throat is sweet and he is all desire.'[87] For how sweetly have all his judgments clung to the throats of all men! With what great affection is his every word repeated! How greatly, my son, are you longed for by the multitudes! Upon me, certainly, you impressed those last words which I hold in my heart, the words in which you asked me to become your surety. You yourself sought of me the testimony of a glorious judgment. I was not able to present myself as a surety for you, as I was preparing to do. Yet, though absent, I declared my intention, and Christ heard me state that I was a surety in your behalf. My consent is binding in heaven, even though it is not binding on earth. I have put myself under an obligation to God, although I could not put myself under obligation to men.

(64) I have spoken of your body. Now I shall address your soul, which is worthy of the adornments of the Prophet. I shall use, therefore, the Prophet's exordium: 'Who is she

---
83 Cant. 5.14.
84 Jer. 4.19.
85 Cant. 5.13.
86 Cant. 5.13,14 (Septuagint).
87 Cant. 5.16.

that looketh forth as the dawn, fair as the moon, bright as the sun?'[88] I seem to see you in your splendor, I seem to hear you saying: 'The dawn is mine, O Father, the night of earth has passed, the day of heaven is at hand.'[89] Therefore, you look forth on us, O holy soul, looking back from a region above, as it were, on things below. You have gone forth from the darkness of this world, and you shine like the moon, you are resplendent like the sun.[90] And rightly as the moon, because even before, although in the shadow of this earthly body, you shone and illumined the darkness of earth, and now, borrowing light from the Sun of Justice, you enjoy bright day. Therefore, I seem to see you withdrawing, as it were, from the body, and, having thrust aside the darkness of night, rising at dawn like the sun, approaching God, and, in swift flight like an eagle, abandoning earthly things.

(65) 'Turn, O Solamitess, turn, turn, and we shall look on thee.'[91] Turn to us, O peaceful soul, that you may show your glory to your sisters and that they may begin to console themselves with the security of your repose and happiness. Turn to us once only, that we may see you, and turn again and hasten with all speed to that great Jerusalem, the city of the saints. Or indeed, since Christ says this to the pious soul, He commands it to turn for a little while, that its glory and its future repose with the saints may be manifest to us, and then He commands it to hasten to the company of the saints on high.

(66) 'What will you see in the Solamitess,' he says, 'who comes like the companies of camps?'[92] that is, in her who has

---

88 Cant. 6.9.
89 Cf. Rom. 13.12.
90 Cf. Eccli. 50.7.
91 Cant. 6.12.
92 Cant. 7.1.

fought much and against many in the flesh. For she fought against external foes, she fought against the treacherous changes of the world, she fought against the weaknesses of the body, against manifold passions. She heard from the Lord: 'Turn, O Solamitess.' She turned once to peace in the world, she turned, through renewed communion, to the favor of Christ; and thus beautiful is her turning in the world, most beautiful her stately departure and flight into heaven.

(67) And therefore she deserves to hear: 'Beautiful are become thy steps in shoes, daughter of Aminadab,'[93] that is, daughter of a prince. For beautiful was the progress which you made in the body, since you used this as a shoe, not as a cloak, so that, taller and higher, as it were, you might turn your steps wheresoever you wished without any stumbling; or, in truth, that you might put off the body like a shoe, as Moses did, to whom it was said: 'Put off the shoes from thy feet.'[94]

(68) Therefore, your father Aminadab, that prince of the people, now says to you: 'Hearken, O daughter, and see, because the king hath desired thy beauty.'[95] 'Beautiful,' therefore, 'are become thy steps in shoes, O daughter of Aminadab. The joints of thy thighs are like crowns,'[96] that is, a grace consistent with itself in all its acts and moderation equaled the insignia of great triumphs. Therefore, because of your moderation and peaceful serenity, not even Gaul experienced an enemy, and Italy repulsed an enemy who threatened her borders. Moreover, that crowns are the insignia of victory cannot be doubted, since those who have fought bravely in war are honored with crowns.

(69) 'Thy navel is like a round bowl, not wanting tempered wine. Thy belly is like a heap of wheat, set about

---
93 Cant. 7.1.
94 Exod. 3.5.
95 Ps. 44.11,12.
96 Cant. 7.1.

with lilies. Thy neck is like a tower of ivory. Thy eyes a pool in Esebon.'[97] The good navel of the soul, capable of receiving all virtues, is like a bowl, fashioned by the Author of faith Himself.[98] For in a bowl Wisdom has mixed her wine, saying: 'Come, eat my bread and drink the wine which I have mingled for you.'[99] This navel, therefore, fashioned with all the beauty of the virtues does not lack mixed wine. His belly also was filled not only with the wheaten food of justice, as it were, but also with that of grace, and it bloomed with sweetness like a lily.[100] His neck also was white and pure, subjected willingly to the yoke of Christ. Thoughts governed by reason, the glory of faith, and the mark of circumcision were the glorious adornment of his head, which was crowned not with royal diadems but with the insignia of the blood of the Lord.

(70) Rightly like a king, victorious over sin, and with his head encircled with a heavenly crown, does he ascend, and to his soul God the Word says: 'How beautiful and sweet art thou become, my love, in thy delights!'[101] Beautiful through the glory of virtue, sweet through grace, tall like a palm, which is the prize of the victor.

(71) His brother Gratian runs to meet this soul as it ascends, and embracing it he says: 'I to my brother and his turning to me,'[102] either because he desires him to cling closely to himself or because with brotherly love he stands at his side as an advocate, saying that his turning is to be preferred even to his favor.

(72) 'Come, my brother,' he says, 'let us go forth into the field, let us find rest in the villages, let us get up early to

---

97 Cant. 7.2-4.
98 Cf. Heb. 12.2.
99 Prov. 9.5.
100 Cf. Isa. 35.1.
101 Cant. 7.6.
102 Cant. 7.10.

the vineyards,'[103] that is, you have come here where the fruits of the different virtues are conferred according to the merits of each of us, where the rewards of merits abound. Let us go forth, then, into a field in which our labor is not in vain, but where there is a rich harvest of graces. What you have sown on earth reap here; what you have scattered there gather here. Or at least come into the field which is the odor of Jacob, that is, come into the bosom of Jacob, so that, like poor Lazarus in Abraham's bosom,[104] you also may find rest in the tranquility of Jacob the patriarch, for the bosom of the patriarchs is a kind of retreat of eternal rest. Fittingly, therefore, is Jacob a fruitful field, as the patriarch Isaac testified, when he said: 'Behold the fragrance of my son is as the fragrance of a plentiful field which the Lord has blessed.'[105]

(73) 'Let us find rest,' he says, 'in the villages,' showing that repose there is more secure which, protected and walled about by the hedge of heaven's refuge, is not disturbed by the attacks of the beasts of the world.

(74) 'In our gates,' he says, 'are all the fruits of the trees; the new and the old, my brother, I have kept for thee. Who shall give thee to me, my brother, for my brother, sucking the breasts of my mother. Finding thee without, I shall kiss thee; I shall take thee up and bring thee into my mother's house, and into the chamber of her who conceived me. I will give thee to drink wine scented with great labor from the juice of my pomegranates. His left hand under my head, and his right hand shall embrace me.'[106] Gratian promises his brother of august memory that the fruits of the various virtues are at hand for him. For he himself was also

---
103 Cant. 7.11,12.
104 Cf. Luke 16.22.
105 Gen. 27.27.
106 Cant. 7.13-8.3.

faithful in the Lord, pious and meek and pure of heart; he was also chaste in body who knew not intercourse with any woman other than his wife.

(75) Thus in the gates of his house he has fruits prepared, and not far to seek. He offers the new and the old which he has kept for his brother, that is, the mysteries of the Old Testament and of the Gospel, and says: 'Who shall give thee to me, O brother, for a brother, sucking the breasts of my mother?'[107] that is, no ordinary person but Christ Himself enlightened you with spiritual grace. He baptized you, because the ministry of men was lacking you. Greater things have you gained, who believed that you had lost lesser. What are the breasts of the Church except the sacrament of baptism? And well does he say 'sucking,' as if the baptized were seeking Him as a draught of snowy milk. 'Finding thee without,' he says, 'I shall kiss thee,' that is, finding you outside the body, I embrace you with the kiss of mystical peace. No one shall despise you, no one shall shut you out, I will introduce you into the inner sanctuary and hidden places of Mother Church, and into all the secrets of mystery, so that you may drink the cup of spiritual grace.

(76) After he had embraced his brother, therefore, he began to conduct him to his own mansion, and, since he had proceeded beyond the ordinary in his service, he began to ascend with his brother, praying that a greater increase of love might there be granted to his brother and to himself, because the human failings, envy and pride, which in most men are wont to make void the laws of fraternal love, had been absent from them.

(77) Both the angels and other souls, on seeing them, inquire of those who by their company and office, as it were, were escorting the brothers, saying: 'Who is this that as-

---
107 Cant. 8.1.

cendeth shining, leaning on her brother?'[108] We have indeed no doubt concerning the merits of Valentinian, but let us now believe the testimony at least of the angels, that, with the stain of sin wiped out, he ascended cleansed whom his faith had washed and his petition had sanctified. Let us believe also, as others hold, that 'he ascended from the desert,' that is, from this arid and uncultivated place to those flowery delights, where, united with his brother, he enjoys the bliss of eternal life.

(78) Blessed are you both, if my prayers will avail aught!'[109] No day will pass you over in silence, no prayer of mine will pass you by unhonored, no night will hurry on its course without your receiving some participation in my prayers. I will repeatedly remember you in all by oblations. Who will prevent me from mentioning the innocent? Who will forbid my embracing you with continuous remembrance? 'If I forget thee, holy Jerusalem,' that is, holy soul, devoted and peaceful brethren, 'let my right hand forget me, let my tongue cleave to my jaws, if I do not remember thee, if I do not remember Jerusalem in the beginning of my joy.'[110] I shall sooner forget myself than you; even if my speech ever becomes silent, my love will speak; even if my voice fails, the love which is implanted in my heart will not fail.

(79) 'How are the mighty fallen!'[111] How both are fallen by the rivers of Babylon!'[112] How much swifter for both men have been their courses of life than the waters of the Rhone itself! O Gratian and Valentinian, beautiful and most dear to me, in what a narrow limit you have enclosed your lives! How close have been the confines of your deaths! How near your burials! Gratian and Valentinian, I say, it is

---

108 Cant. 8.5.
109 Cf. Vergil, *Aeneid* 9.446-447.
110 Ps. 136.5,6.
111 2 Kings 1.19,25,27.
112 Cf. Ps. 136.1.

a pleasure to hang upon your names, and it is a delight to find rest in the remembrance of you. O Gratian and Valentinian, beautiful and most dear to all! Inseparable in life, and in death you are not separated.[113] The tomb has not separated you whom love did not separate. The causes of your deaths have not parted you whom a single affection joined together. A diversity of virtues did not render you unlike whom a single religion fostered; you who were simpler than doves, swifter than eagles, meeker than lambs, more guileless than calves.[114] 'The arrow' of Gratian 'was not turned back,' and the justice of Valentinian 'was not in vain'[115] nor his authority empty. 'How' without battle 'are the mighty fallen!'

(80) 'I grieve for you,' Gratian my son, most sweet to me. Many are the proofs you gave of your devotion. In the midst of your perils you sought me; in your last moments you called me by name; you grieved the more at my grief for you. 'I grieve for you,' also, Valentinian my son, 'most beautiful to me. Your love has come to me as the love'[116] of a dear one. You thought that through me you were being rescued from peril; you not only loved me as a parent but you hoped in me as your redeemer and liberator. You said: 'Do you think I shall see my father?' Noble was your desire of me, but ineffectual your presumption. Woe to me for your vain hope in man!'[117] But you sought the Lord in His bishop. Woe to me that I did not know your wish before! Woe to me that you did not send for me secretly before! Woe to me for such dear ones as I have lost! 'How are the mighty fallen, and the weapons that were desired have perished!'[118]

---
113 Cf. 2 Kings 1.23.
114 *Ibid.*
115 2 Kings 1.22.
116 2 Kings 1.26.
117 Cf. Eccli. 34.1.
118 2 Kings 1.27.

(81) O Lord, since no one can grant to another more than what he desires for himself, do not separate me after death from those whom in this life I have held most dear. O Lord, I pray that 'where I am, they also may be with me,'[119] that there at least I may enjoy their everlasting union, since here I was unable to enjoy their association longer. I beseech Thee, O highest God, that Thou mayest raise and revive these dearest youths by an early resurrection,[120] that Thou mayest compensate for their unduly short span of life in this world by an earlier restoration. Amen.

---

119 John 17.24.
120 St. Ambrose would seem to be referring here to a view still held by some in his time that there would be a millenial reign of Christ, at the beginning of which the saints would rise again, and at the end of which the general resurrection would take place. But, apart from this passage and one or two others, he adheres definitely to the belief in one general resurrection. Cf. F. H. Dudden, *The Life and Times of St. Ambrose* (Oxford 1935) II 667-668.

SAINT AMBROSE

FUNERAL ORATION ON THE DEATH OF EMPEROR THEODOSIUS

Translated by
ROY J. DEFERRARI, Ph.D.
The Catholic University of America

INTRODUCTION

THE ORATION ON THE DEATH of Theodosius was delivered by the Bishop of Milan, St. Ambrose, on February 25, 395, the fortieth day after the death of the emperor. The date of February 26, often given in handbooks, is an error created by a failure to include the day of his death in this reckoning. The occasion of the eulogy was the memorial service, held before the departure of the funeral cortege for Constantinople.

A loyal and manly friendship had existed between the emperor and the bishop, who, as they worked for a common cause, found their mutual aims and desires to be quite compatible. The man who did so much to make the empire a Christian state was Theodosius, but the chief impulse behind him came from Ambrose.

The task of the eulogist was not merely the preparation of a discourse polished and made perfect according to rhetorical canons. Officially, the task of St. Ambrose was the presentation of a panegyric on the dead emperor; personally it was much more. He had, of course, to give to the dead the tribute customary to his rank, but he had also to reach out to the living and to offer to each group of the varied throng comfort and salutary spiritual advice. The audience which gathered in the basilica was varied and interesting. It consisted of the newly appointed Emperor Honorius, a child of ten; Stilicho, his guardian and regent of the West; the army corps which had come out of the Orient for the last campaign of Theodosius; the Milanese; and that conglomerate array of court officials and visitors that an imperial capital always attracts.

On this occasion, however, the threatening possibilities of the future cast additional gloom over the funeral ceremonies and complicated the orator's emotions still more. The fate of the Roman Empire become a Christian State was now hanging in the balance. The empire as now established was only a century removed from the times of Diocletian and only a generation older than the paganism of Julian. Idolatry was still widespread and constantly trying to recuperate its failing strength. Even more dangerous foes, since they were passing under the name of Christians, threatened the Church from within. Barbarian hordes, which formed a definite part of the Empire, threatened Church and State. Theodosius, by his strength and courage, had been able to sustain the great burden and preserve both. But Theodosius was now dead. The unity of the Empire had been disrupted. To Arcadius, a youth of eighteen, had passed the Empire of the East, to Honorius, a boy of ten, the Empire of the West. Would these young rulers rise to the occasion? It was a solemn moment when Ambrose rose to speak.

Ambrose's anxiety is shown by his repeated appeals to the army, reminding them of the victories of their chief, and exhorting them to show gratitude to their dead ruler by being faithful to his sons. It appears again in the examples chosen from the Bible of the long and prosperous reigns of two youthful kings of Israel.

Then, desiring to impart a moral lesson, Ambrose develops at length an exposition of the virtues of Theodosius, choosing such as are profitable for imitation by the prince and his guardian, in whose hands the reins of the government may well prove the deciding factor either for good or for evil. In this exposition Theodosius stands forth as the exemplar of all Christian rulers. He is shown as the guardian of the Church, distinguished for piety and zeal; as the refuge and father of the poor and erring, magnanimous toward his enemies, faithful to his friends; and, finally, as the sinner, humbled, repentant, and forgiven.

ON THE DEATH OF THEODOSIUS

SEVERE EARTHQUAKES, continual rains, and darkness denser than usual gave notice of this, that our most merciful Emperor Theodosius was about to leave the earth. The very elements, then, were mourning his death. The heavens were veiled in obscurity; the air was shuddering in unbroken gloom; the earth was shaken by tremors and filled with floods of waters. Why should not the universe itself bemoan the fact that this prince was presently to be snatched away, for was he not accustomed to alleviate the hardships of this world when by forgiveness he forestalled the punishment of crime?

(2) And he has indeed departed to receive his kingdom, which he did not lay aside, but, admitted by right of piety into the tabernacles of Christ, he has exchanged it for the heavenly Jerusalem. Having taken his place there, he says: 'As we have heard, so have we seen in the city of the Lord of hosts, in the city of our God,' which 'God hath founded forever.'[1] But he has left behind many deprived of a father's protection, as it were, and, above all, his sons. But they are not destitute whom he left as the heirs of his piety; they are not destitute for whom he gained the grace of Christ and the

---
1 Ps. 47.9.

loyalty of the army, to which he was a proof that God cherishes devotion and is the avenger of treachery.

(3) Recently, then, we lamented the death of this prince, and now we are celebrating the fortieth day, with the prince Honorius assisting at the holy altar. For as holy Joseph performed the burial rites for his father Jacob during forty days, so this son also renders his just due to his father Theodosius. And because some are accustomed to observe the third and the thirtieth day, others the seventh and the fortieth, let us consider what the Scriptural text tells us. When Jacob died, it says, 'Joseph commanded the servant undertakers to bury him, and the undertakers buried Israel, and forty days were completed for him; for thus the days of the funeral rites are reckoned. And Egypt mourned for him seventy days.'[2] Accordingly, the observance which Scripture prescribes is to be followed. In Deuteronomy, also, it is written that 'the children of Israel mourned for Moses thirty days, and the days of mourning were finished.'[3] Both observances, then, have authority because the necessary duty of filial piety is fulfilled.

(4) And so Joseph was good, who furnished the model for filial devotion, whom his father loved, and to whom his father said: 'May my God aid thee, and may he bless thee with the blessing of the earth holding all things because of the blessing of the breasts and of the womb, blessings of thy mother, and because of the blessings of thy father.'[4] Joseph was the good offspring of a devoted father. So he, too, celebrates the fortieth day of his father, Jacob, that great supplantor,[5] and we celebrate the fortieth day of Theodosius, who, after the example of Jacob, supplanted the perfidy of

---
2 Gen. 50.2,3.
3 Deut. 34.8.
4 Gen. 49.25,26.
5 Cf. Gen. 25.25; 27.36.

tyrants,⁶ who put away the idols of the Gentiles. For his faith removed all worship of images and stamped out all their ceremonies. He grieved, too, that the remission of punishment which he had granted to those who had transgressed against him had come to naught,⁷ the opportunity for pardon had been denied him. But his sons will not refuse what their father granted, nor will they refuse, even though anyone should attempt to confuse or disturb them. Those who honor his grants to individuals will not be able to refuse what he granted for all.

(5) The death of so great a prince had in it nothing more glorious, who had already consigned all to his sons: his empire, his power, and the title Augustus. Nothing, I say, more splendid was reserved for him in death than the fact that while the promised mitigation of the necessary payment of the grain tax in some cases was delayed, his successor has become the heir of these indulgences, and the one who wished to prevent this has created ill will for himself. Nevertheless, the crown of so great a favor has not been taken away from Theodosius. And not undeservedly, for if the last wishes of private citizens and the testaments of the dying have permanent validity, how can the testament of so great a prince be considered void? Theodosius is also glorious in this, that he did not make his will in the ordinary manner, for he had no further provision to make for his sons, to whom he had given everything, except to commend them to a relative who was present.⁸ He was obliged to provide by will for all who were

---

6 An allusion to Theodosius' defeat of the usurper Maximus in 388 and of the usurper Eugenius in 394.
7 In a communication to the Senate, Theodosius expressed regret that the death of Flavian, the consul who had sided with the usurpers, had deprived him of the pleasure of granting pardon.
8 Flavius Stilicho, the great general of Theodosius, was married to Serena, niece and adopted daughter of the emperor. Stilicho and Serena were appointed guardians of Honorius when he was appointed joint-emperor in 394.

subject to him or committed to his care, so that he might discharge legacies and designate trusts. He ordered that a law of indulgence which he left in writing be published. What is more worthy than that this law be the last will of the emperor?

(6) Thus the great emperor has withdrawn from us, but he has not wholly withdrawn, for he has left us his children in whom we should recognize him, and in whom we behold and possess him. Let not their age disquiet you. The loyalty of his soldiers is the perfect age of an emperor, for age is perfect where strength is perfect. These characteristics are reciprocal, for the faith of an emperor also is the strength of his soldiers.

(7) You recall, I am sure, what triumphs the faith of Theodosius acquired for you. When, because of the difficulties of the terrain and the hindrance of camp followers, the army was deploying too slowly into combat position and through delay in offering battle the enemy seemed to be charging, the emperor leaped down from his horse and, advancing alone before the line, he cried out: 'Where is the God of Theodosius?' He spoke thus when already close to Christ, for who could have said this except one who knew that he was attaching himself to Christ? By this cry he aroused all, and by his example he armed all. He was already indeed somewhat advanced in years, but robust in faith.

(8) The faith of Theodosius, then, was your victory: let your faith be the strength of his sons. Faith, therefore, adds to age. Hence, even Abraham did not consider age when in old age he begot a son, nor Sara, when she gave birth. And it is not astonishing if faith adds to age, since it anticipates the future. For what is faith except the substance of those things for which we hope?[9] So the Scriptures teach us. Therefore, if faith is the substance of those things for which we

---

9 Cf. Heb. 11.1.

hope, how much the more of those which we see? Good is the faith of which it is written: 'But the just man lives by faith. But if he draws back, he will not please my soul.'[10]

(9) Now, let us not draw back at the expense of our souls, but let us cling to faith for our soul's gain;[11] for in this warfare of faith our elders, Abraham, Isaac, and Jacob, obtained proof, and thus they left us a heritage of faith. Abraham was faithful, who was justified not by works but by faith, since he believed in God.[12] Isaac was faithful, who through faith did not fear the sword of his father as he was about to strike him. Jacob was faithful, who followed in the footprints of his father's faith and, while he was journeying, saw an army of angels and called it the council of God.[13]

(10) Elsewhere, also, that is, in the Books of Kings we read that Eliseus was in Samaria, and suddenly an army of Syrians surrounded and set upon him. Giezi saw them and said to his master: 'O Master, what shall we do?'[14] And Eliseus the Prophet said: 'Fear not, for there are more with us than with them.' And he prayed that the Lord would open the eyes of Giezi. And his eyes were opened and he saw the mountain full of horses and chariots around Eliseus. And Eliseus prayed that God would strike them with blindness. And they were struck, and they entered into the city whither they were going, seeing not at all. Surely, you soldiers who have been surrounded have heard that where there is perfidy there is blindness. Rightly, therefore, was the army of the unbeliever blind. But where there is faith there is an army of angels. Good, then, is faith, which often exercises its power among the dead.[15] Hence, our Adversary and his legions are daily hurled back by the virtue of the martyrs. So I think

---
10 Heb. 10.38.
11 Cf. Heb. 10.39.
12 Cf. Rom. 4.2.
13 Cf. Gen. 32.1,2.
14 4 Kings 6.14-16; cf., also, 4 Kings 6.17-19.
15 Cf. Col. 2.12; Acts 17.31.

that the strings of the cithern are called *fides,* because, although dead, they give forth sound.[16]

(11) Wherefore, we must strive more and more, lest while engaged in the tasks of life we be ungrateful, and let us bestow constant and paternal affection on the children of the pious prince. Pay to his sons what you owe to their father. You owe more to him now that he is dead than you owed to him while he was living. For, if among the children of private citizens the rights of minors are not violated without grave crime, how much more is this true in the case of the children of an emperor!

(12) It may be added: 'Of what an emperor!' Of a pious emperor, of a merciful emperor, of a faithful emperor, concerning whom the Scripture has spoken in no ordinary manner, saying, 'Great and in honor is the merciful man; but to find a faithful man is difficult.'[17] If it is a great thing to find anyone who is merciful or faithful, how much more so an emperor whom power impels toward vengeance, but whom, nevertheless, compassion recalls from taking vengeance? What is more illustrious than the faith of an emperor whom power does not exalt, pride does not elevate, but piety bows down? Of him Solomon admirably says: 'The threatening of an unjust king is like the roaring of a lion, but as dew upon the grass, so also is his cheerfulness.'[18] Therefore, what a great thing it is to lay aside the terror of power and to prefer the sweetness of granting pardon!

(13) Theodosius of august memory thought he had received a kindness whenever he was asked to pardon, and he was more disposed to forgiveness at the time when the emotion of his wrath had been greatest. A token of forgiveness was that he had been angry, and what was feared in others

---

16 Cf. 1 Cor. 14.7. There is a word play in Latin here between *fides* (faith) and *fides* (a cithern).
17 Prov. 20.6 (Septuagint).
18 Prov. 19.12. The word 'unjust' is not found in the Septuagint or Vulgate.

was desired in him, that he be moved to wrath. It was the relief of the accused that, although he had power over all, he preferred to expostulate as a father rather than to punish as a judge. Often we have seen men whom he was rebuking tremble when convicted of crime, and then, when they had despaired, we have seen them freed from the charge. For he wished to win them as a fair judge, not to crush them as a dispenser of punishment, for he never denied pardon to one confessing guilt. If there was anything which the secret conscience concealed, he reserved that for God. Men feared that voice of his more than punishment, because the emperor acted with such modesty as to prefer to attach men to himself by reverence rather than by fear.

(14) It is said that the greatest[19] of the philosophers granted immunity from punishment to those crimes which had been committed through anger, but the divine Scripture says better: 'Be angry and sin not.'[20] It preferred rather to cut off sin than to excuse it. It is better to find praise for mercy in an occasion for indignation than to be incited by wrath toward vengeance.

(15) Who, then, will doubt that he will be a powerful protector for his sons in the house of God?[21] By the favor of the Lord, the Emperor Arcadius is already a robust youth; Honorius now knocks on the door of manhood, a little older than Josias.[22] For the latter, having lost his father, assumed the government and reigned continuously for thirty-one years. He pleased the Lord because, better than the other kings of Israel, he celebrated the Pasch of the Lord and abolished false religious practices. Asa, likewise, though still of immature age when he succeeded to the throne, reigned in Jerusalem

---

19 Cf. Plato, *Laws* 9.7ff.; also, Aristotle, *Nic. Ethics* 7.6.
20 Ps. 4.5.
21 Cf. 1 John 2.1.
22 Cf. 4 Kings 22.1. Josias was eight years old at his accession. At the death of Theodosius, Arcadius was about eighteen and Honorius was in his eleventh year.

forty years.²³ When he was hard pressed by an infinite and innumerable multitude of Ethiopians, he had trust in the Lord that he could be among the few saved. Would that he had been as faithful during his course as he was devout at its beginning! For, one of the few saved and a victor, he afterwards abandoned the Lord and asked aid from the Syrians and summoned physicians to cure a disease of the feet. Since he had received such great indications of divine favor, he ought not to have abandoned his Helper but to have retained Him. Therefore, the physicians did not benefit him, and as an unbeliever he paid the penalty of death.

(16) But their fathers, Abiam and Amon, were both unbelievers.²⁴ Theodosius, however, was filled with the fear of God, was filled with mercy, and we hope that he stands before Christ as a protector of his children, if the Lord be propitious to human affairs. The merciful man is a blessing. While he assists others, he is mindful of himself, and by applying remedies to others he cures his own wounds.²⁵ For he who knows how to forgive realizes that he is human, and he follows the way of Christ who, by assuming flesh, chose to come into this world as a Redeemer rather than as a Judge.

(17) Hence the Psalmist has said beautifully: 'I have loved, because the Lord will hear the voice of my prayer.'²⁶ While this psalm was being read, we heard, as it were, Theodosius himself speaking. 'I have loved,' he says. I recognize his pious voice and I recognize also his testimonies. And truly has he loved who fulfilled his duty diligently, who spared his enemies, who loved his foes, who pardoned those by whom he was entreated, who did not even allow those who strove to usurp his power to perish. That voice is of one

---
23 Cf. 3 Kings 15.10. Cf. also 2 Par. 14.11-12, and 16.3-12.
24 Cf. 3 Kings 15.3; 4 Kings 21.21.
25 Cf. Prov. 11.17.
26 Ps. 114.1.

not partially, but fully perfected in the Law, saying: 'I have loved. For love is the fulfillment of the law.'[27] But let us hear what he has loved. When the kind of love is not mentioned, surely the grace of divine charity is signified, whereby we love what is to be desired above all desirable things.[28] Of this it is written: 'Thou shalt love the Lord thy God.'[29]

(18) Thus the good soul, on departing from earth and filled with the Holy Spirit, when questioned, as it were, by those who hastened to meet it as it rose to the high and lofty regions above, kept saying: 'I have loved.' Nothing is fuller than this, nothing is clearer. Angels and archangels asked repeatedly: 'What have you done on earth?' For God alone is the witness of secret things. The soul kept saying, 'I have loved,' that is, 'I have fulfilled the Law, I have not neglected the Gospel'; that is, 'I have offered myself to death and all the day long I am regarded as a sheep for the slaughter.'[30] 'For I am sure that neither death, nor life, nor angels, nor powers, nor height, nor depth, nor any other creature will be able to separate us from the love of God which is in Christ Jesus our Lord.'[31]

(19) The Lord Jesus also teaches in the Gospel that this commandment of the Law must be observed, when He says to Peter: 'Simon, son of John, dost thou love Me?' And he answered: 'Thou knowest, Lord, that I love Thee.' And He said a second time: 'Simon, son of John, dost thou love Me?' And again he answered: 'Yea, Lord, Thou knowest that I love Thee.' And when asked a third time, said: 'Lord, Thou knowest all things, Thou knowest that I love Thee.'[32] And so his threefold answer confirmed his love and effaced the fault of his threefold denial. And here, if we seek, we find the

---

27 Rom. 13.10.
28 Cf. Prov. 8.11.
29 Deut. 6.5; Matt. 22.37.
30 Cf. Ps. 43.22; Rom. 8.36.
31 Rom. 8.38,39.
32 John 21.15-18.

threefold answer: 'I have loved, because the Lord will hear the voice of my prayer. I have loved since He has inclined his ear to me, that in my day I might call upon Him. I have loved because I have found tribulation and sorrow, and for the sake of my God I have not fled the dangers of hell but have waited that they might seize and find me.'[33]

(20) And beautifully does he say: 'I have loved,' because now he had completed the course of this life. Wherefore, the Apostle also says in the midst of his suffering: 'I have fought the good fight, I have finished the course, I have kept the faith. For the rest, there is laid up for me a crown of justice.'[34] Great is the Lord who has given us the struggle, whereby he who has conquered merits to be crowned. 'I have loved,' he says trustingly, 'because the Lord will hear the voice of my prayer.'[35]

(21) 'I have loved' and therefore 'he has inclined his ear'[36] to me, to raise up the fallen, to quicken the dead. For God does not incline his ear so as to hear corporally but to condescend to us. He deigns thus to hear us and to lift up the substance of our weakness. He inclines himself toward us that our prayer may ascend to Him. He who offers mercy does not need a voice. He did not need a voice who heard Moses, though silent,[37] and He said that Moses cried out to Him, although he did not speak, but was pleading with unutterable groanings.[38] God also knows how to hear blood,[39] for which no voice exists nor tongue is present, but it received a voice by virtue of the sacred Passion. It cried out in martyrdom, it cried out in the parricide which it suffered as a sacrifice.

---

33 Cf. Ps. 114.1-3.
34 2 Tim. 4.7,8.
35 Ps. 114.1.
36 Ps. 114.2
37 Cf. Exod. 14.15.
38 Cf. Rom. 8.26.
39 Cf. Gen. 4.10.

(22) 'I have loved,' he said, and therefore, 'with love I have done the will of the Lord, and I have called upon Him not on a few, but on all the days of my life.'[40] For to call upon Him on certain days and not on all is the mark of one who is proved, not of one who hopes. It is to return the debt of gratitude after the manner of those who abound in wealth and not from a spirit of devotion. And so Paul said: 'Give thanks for all things.'[41] For when do you not have something which you owe to God? Or when are you without a gift of God, since your daily enjoyment of living is from God? 'For what hast thou, that thou hast not received?'[42] Therefore, because you always receive, always call upon God; and since what you have is from God, always acknowledge that you are His debtor. I prefer that you pay your debts rather through love than as one forced to do so.

(23) Do you hear him saying: 'The sorrows of death have compassed me'?[43] 'Still, I have loved the Lord even in the sorrows of death. The perils of hell have found me, not fearing indeed, but loving, but hoping, because no distress, no persecution, no dangers, no sword shall separate me from Christ.'[44] Therefore, he found tribulation and sorrow willingly, knowing that 'tribulation works out endurance, and endurance tried virtue, and tried virtue hope.'[45] As a good athlete, he sought the contest that he might gain the crown, but he knew that this was given to him not through his own strength but by the aid of God. He could not have been victorious had he not called upon Him who helps contenders.

(24) Miserable man enters the contest to be victorious, and he rushes headlong into danger unless the name of the Lord be present with him; unless, when he fears, he prays,

---

40 Cf. Ps. 22.6; Ps. 26.4; Ps. 114.2.
41 1 Thess. 5.18.
42 1 Cor. 4.1.
43 Ps. 114.3.
44 Cf. Ps. 114.3; Rom. 8.35.
45 Rom. 5.3.

saying: 'O Lord deliver my soul.'[46] Hence we have these words of the Apostle: 'But I see a law of my flesh warring against the law of my mind, and making me prisoner to the law of sin, that is in my members. Unhappy man that I am! Who will deliver me from the body of this death? The grace of God, by Jesus Christ our Lord.'[47]

(25) He is victorious who hopes for the grace of God, not he who presumes upon his own strength. For why do you not rely upon grace, since you have a merciful Judge in the contest. 'For the Lord is merciful and just, and our God sheweth mercy.'[48] Mercy is mentioned twice, but justice once. Justice is in the middle, enclosed by a double wall of mercy. Sins superabound. Therefore, let mercy superabound. With the Lord there is an abundance of all powers, for He is the Lord of hosts.[49] Yet there is neither justice without mercy, nor without the exercise of mercy is there justice, for it is written: 'Be not overjust.'[50] What is above measure, you cannot endure, even if it is good. Preserve measure that you may receive according to the measure.[51]

(26) Yet mercy has not impeded justice, because mercy is itself justice. 'He hath distributed, he hath given to the poor, his justice remaineth forever.'[52] For the just man knows that he ought to succor the weak and the needy. Wherefore, the Lord, coming to baptism in order to forgive us our sins because we are weak, said to John: 'Let it be so now, for so it becomes us to fulfill all justice.'[53] Thus, it is clear that justice is mercy, and mercy is justice. For if the mercy of God did not sustain us, how would we survive as infants in the very

---

46 Ps. 114.4.
47 Rom. 7.23-25.
48 Ps. 114.5.
49 Cf. Ps. 23.10.
50 Eccles. 7.17.
51 Cf. Eph. 4.7.
52 Ps. 111.9.
53 Matt. 3.15.

beginning when, issuing from the womb, from warmth into cold, from moisture into dryness, we are cast forth like fishes that a flood of nature, as it were, has cast shipwrecked into this life? Reason is lacking, but divine grace does not fail. Therefore, He Himself guards the little ones, or at least those who humbly confess that they are as little ones.

(27) Good, therefore, is humility. It delivers those who are in danger and raises those who have fallen. This humility was known to him who said: 'Behold it is I that have sinned, and I the shepherd have done wickedly; and these in this flock, what have they done? Let thy hand be against me.'[54] Well does he say this who made his kingdom subject to God and did penance and, having confessed his sin, asked pardon. He attained salvation through humility. Christ humbled Himself to raise up all,[55] and whoever follows the humility of Christ attains the rest of Christ.

(28) And so because Theodosius, the emperor, showed himself humble and, when sin had stolen upon him, asked for pardon, his soul has turned to its rest, as Scripture has it, saying: 'Turn my soul unto thy rest, for the Lord hath been bountiful to thee.'[56] Beautifully is it said to the soul: 'Turn,' that the soul, tired out, as it were, with the daily sweat of its toil, may turn from labor to rest. The horse is turned toward the stable when it has finished its course; the ship to the port, where it is given safe anchorage protected from the violence of the waves. But what is the meaning of the phrase, 'to thy rest,' unless you understand it according to the words of the Lord Jesus: 'Come, blessed of my Father, take possession of the kingdom prepared for you as an inheritance from the foundation of the world'?[57] For we receive, as it were, an in-

---
54 2 Kings 24.17.
55 Cf. Phil. 2.8.
56 Ps. 114.7.
57 Matt. 25.34.

herited possession, the things which have been promised to us, for God is trustworthy[57a] and does not withdraw what he has once prepared for His servants. If our faith endures, His promise likewise endures.

(29) See, O man, the grace of Christ about you. Even while you are harassed on earth, you have possessions in heaven. There, then, let your heart be, where your possession is.[58] This is the rest which is due the just, and is denied the unworthy. Whence says the Lord: 'As I swore in my wrath, that they shall not enter into my rest.'[59] For they who have not known the ways of the Lord shall not enter into the rest of the Lord, but to him who has fought the good fight and has finished his course it is said: 'Turn to thy rest.' It is a blessed rest to pass by the things of the world and to find repose in the celestial fellowship of the mysteries which are above the world. This is the rest toward which the Prophet hastened, saying: 'Who will give me wings like a dove and I will fly and be at rest?'[60] The holy man knows this as his rest, and to this rest he says his soul must turn. Therefore was his soul in its rest, to which he says it must return. This is the rest of the great Sabbath, in which each of the saints is above the sensible things of the world, devoting himself entirely to deep and invisible mystery and cleaving to God. This is that rest of the Sabbath on which God rested from all the works of this world.

(30) Theodosius, now at peace, rejoices that he has been snatched away from the cares of this world and he lifts up his soul and directs it to that great and eternal rest. He declares that he has been admirably cared for, since God has snatched his soul from death,[61] the death which he frequently withstood in the treacherous conditions of this world, when

---

57a Cf. 1 Cor. 1.9.
58 Cf. Matt. 6.21.
59 Ps. 94.11.
60 Ps. 54.7.
61 Cf. Ps. 114.8; Ps. 55.13.

he was disturbed by the waves of sin. And God has snatched his eyes from tears, for sorrow and sadness and mourning shall flee away.[62] And elsewhere we have: 'He shall wipe away every tear from their eyes; and death shall be no more; neither shall there be mourning, nor crying, nor pain.'[63] If, then, death will be no more, he cannot suffer a fall when he is in that rest, but he will please God in the land of the living.[64] For while man is here enveloped in a mortal body subject to falls and transgressions, that will not be so there. Therefore, that is the land of the living where the soul is, for the soul has been made to the image and likeness of God, it is not flesh fashioned from earth.[65] Hence, flesh returns to earth, but the soul hastens to celestial rest, and to it is said: 'Turn, my soul, to thy rest.'

(31) Theodosius hastened to enter upon this rest and to go into the city of Jerusalem, of which it is said: 'And the kings of the earth shall bring their glory into it.'[66] That is true glory which is assumed there, and that is a most blessed kingdom which is possessed there. To this the Apostle was hastening when he said: 'We have the courage, then, and we prefer to be exiled from the body and to be at home with the Lord; and therefore we strive, whether in the body or out of it, to please Him.'[67]

(32) Thus freed from an uncertain struggle, Theodosius of august memory now enjoys perpetual light and lasting tranquility, and in return for what he did in this body he rejoices in the fruits of a divine reward. Therefore, because Theodosius of august memory loved the Lord his God, he has merited the companionship of the saints.

(33) And to conclude my discourse by a kind of per-

---

62 Cf. Isa. 51.11.
63 Cf. Apoc. 21.4.
64 Cf. Ps. 114.9.
65 Cf. Gen. 1.27; 2.7.
66 Apoc. 21.24.
67 Cf. 2 Cor. 5.8,9.

oration, I have loved a merciful man, humble in power, endowed with a pure heart and a gentle disposition, a man such as God is accustomed to love, saying: 'Upon whom shall I rest, unless upon the humble and gentle?'[68]

(34) I have loved a man who esteemed a reprover more than a flatterer. He threw on the ground all the royal attire that he was wearing. He wept publicly in church[69] for his sin, which had stolen upon him through the deceit of others. He prayed for pardon with groans and with tears. What private citizens are ashamed to do, the emperor was not ashamed to do, namely, to perform penance publicly, nor did a day pass thereafter on which he did not bemoan that fault of his. Need I mention also that when he had gained an illustrious victory, yet because the enemy lay fallen in battle he abstained from participation in the sacraments until he recognized the grace of God toward him in the arrival of his children?

(35) I have loved a man who in his dying hour kept asking for me with his last breath. I have loved a man who, when he was already being released from the body, was more concerned about the condition of the Church than about his own trials. I have loved him, therefore, I confess, and for that reason I have suffered my sorrow in the depths of my heart, and thought to be consoled by the delivery of a lengthy discourse. I have loved, and I presume upon the Lord that He will receive the voice of my prayer, with which I accompany this pious soul.

(36) 'The sorrows of death have compassed me, the perils of hell have found me.'[70] For perils affect many, but remedies are found for few. A bishop participates in the perils of all, and he suffers anguish in all sinners. What others suffer he himself endures; in turn, he is freed when others who are beset

---

68 Cf. Isa. 66.2.
69 St. Ambrose is speaking here of the public penance of Theodosius for the massacre of Thessalonica.
70 Ps. 114.3.

with dangers are freed from them. I am crushed in heart because a man has been taken from us whom it is almost impossible to replace. Yet, O Lord, Thou alone shouldst be called upon, Thou shouldst be implored to replace him in his sons. Thou, Lord, the keeper also of little ones in this lowliness,[71] save those hoping in Thee.[72] Give perfect rest to Thy servant Theodosius, that rest which Thou hast prepared for Thy saints. Let his soul turn thither, whence it descended, where he cannot feel the sting of death, where he knows that this death is not the end of nature but of guilt. 'For the death that he dies, he died to sin,'[73] so that there can no longer be a place for sin. And he will rise again, that his life may be restored more perfectly by a renewed gift.

(37) I have loved, and so I accompany him to the land of the living,[74] and I will not abandon him until, by my tears and prayers, I shall lead the man whither his merits summon, unto the holy mountain of God,[75] where there is eternal life, where there is no corruption, no sickness, no mourning, no sorrow, no companionship with the dead.[76] It is the true land of the living where 'this mortal body shall put on immortality and this corruptible body shall put on incorruption.'[77] It is the great repose which fulfills the prayer of the living, a most glorious promise. Therefore, Psalm 114 bears the title 'Alleluia.' And, accordingly, above in Psalm 14[78] we have learned the perfection of man. But while the man represented there may be perfect, he still is subject to sin because he is living in this world. There above is true perfection, where

---

71 Cf. Ps. 114.6.
72 Cf. Ps. 16.7.
73 Cf. Rom. 6.10.
74 Cf. Ps. 114.9.
75 Cf. Ps. 2.6; Ps. 3.5; etc.
76 Cf. Rom. 8.35; Isa. 35.10.
77 Cf. 1 Cor. 15.53.
78 St. Ambrose seems to have in mind Ps. 14 in its entirety. However, the reference could apply very properly to Ps. 114 also.

sin has ceased and the beauty of perpetual rest has shone forth.

(38) We have Psalm 114, because it is the recompense of love.[79] From this the Pasch of the Lord received its law of celebration at the fourteenth moon, since he who celebrates the Pasch ought to be perfect. He should love the Lord Jesus who, cherishing His people with perfect love, offered Himself in His Passion. And let us so love that, if there should be need, we shall not avoid death for the name of the Lord, we shall not have thought for my suffering, and we shall fear nothing, 'for perfect love casts out fear.'[80] Sublime mystery of number, since the Father delivered His only Son for us all when the moon shone with the full orb of its light! For so is the Church, which devoutly celebrates the Pasch of our Lord Jesus Christ. As the perfect moon, she abides forever.[81] Whoever during life fittingly celebrates the Pasch of the Lord shall be in perpetual light. Who celebrated it more gloriously than he who removed sacrilegious errors, closed temples, destroyed idols? For in this was King Josias preferred to his predecessors.

(39) Theodosius, then, abides[82] in the light and glories in the assembly of the saints. There he now embraces Gratian, who no longer grieves for his wounds, for he has found an avenger. Although he was snatched away prematurely by an unworthy death, he possesses rest for his soul. There those two good and generous exponents of devotion rejoice in the common reward for their mercy. Of them it is well said: 'Day to day uttereth speech.'[83] On the other hand, Maximus and Eugenius are in hell, as 'night to night sheweth knowledge.' They teach by their wretched example how wicked it

---
79 In early Christian number symbolism, the Greek letters indicating the number fourteen could signify 'Jesus-Gift.'
80 Cf. 1 John 4.18.
81 Cf. Ps. 88.38.
82 Cf. 1 John 2.10.
83 Ps. 18.3.

is for men to take up arms against their princes. And of them it is admirably said: 'I have seen the wicked highly exalted and lifted up like the cedars of Libanus, and I passed by and lo, he was not!'[84] The pious man passed over from the darkness of the world to eternal day, and the wicked man was no more, for through his wickedness he ceased to be.

(40) Now, Theodosius of august memory knows that he reigns, since he is in the kingdom of our Lord Jesus Christ, and contemplates his temple.[85] Now, indeed, he is conscious of his kingship when he receives Gratian and Pulcheria, his sweetest children, whom he had lost here; when his Flacilla, a soul faithful to God, embraces him; when he rejoices that his father has been restored to him; and when he embraces Constantine. Although Constantine was in his last hours when he was freed by the grace of baptism from all sins, yet, since he was the first of the emperors to believe and left after him a heritage of faith to princes, he has found a place of great merit. Of his times the following prophecy has been fulfilled: 'In that day that which is upon the bridle of the horse shall be holy to the Lord Almighty.'[86] This was revealed by the great Helena of holy memory, who was inspired by the Spirit of God.

(41) Blessed was Constantine with such a mother! At her son's command she sought the aid of divine favor in order that he might take part safely even in battles and not fear danger. Noble woman, who found much more to confer upon an emperor than she might receive from an emperor! The mother, solicitous for her son to whom the sovereignty of the Roman world had fallen, hastened to Jerusalem and explored the scene of the Lord's Passion.

(42) It is claimed that she originally was hostess of an

---
84 Ps. 36.35,36.
85 Cf. Ps. 26.4.
86 Zach. 14.20.

inn, and thus became acquainted with the elder Constantine, who afterwards obtained the imperial office. Good hostess, who so diligently searched for the manger of the Lord! Good hostess, who did not ignore that host who cared for the wounds of the man wounded by robbers![87] Good hostess, who preferred to be considered dung, to gain Christ! For that reason Christ raised her from dung to a kingdom, for it is written that 'He raised up the needy from the earth, and lifted up the poor out of the dunghill.'[88]

(43) Helena, then, came and began to visit the holy places. The Spirit inspired her to search for the wood of the Cross. She drew near to Golgotha and said: 'Behold the place of combat: where is thy victory? I seek the banner of salvation and I do not find it. Shall I,' she said, 'be among kings, and the cross of the Lord lie in the dust? Shall I be covered by golden ornaments, and the triumph of Christ by ruins? Is this still hidden, and is the palm of eternal life hidden? How can I believe that I have been redeemed if the redemption itself is not seen?'

(44) 'I see what you did, O Devil, that the sword by which you were destroyed might be obstructed. But Isaac cleared out the wells stopped up by foreigners, and did not permit the water to lie concealed.[89] So let the ruins be removed that life may appear; let the sword by which the head of the real Goliath was cut off be drawn forth; let the earth be opened that salvation may shine out. Why did you labor to hide the wood, O Devil, except to be vanquished a second time? You were vanquished by Mary, who gave the Conqueror birth. Without any impairment of her virginity, she brought Him forth to conquer you by His crucifixion and to subjugate you by His death. Today, also, you shall be van-

---

87 Cf. Luke 10.35.
88 Ps. 112.7.
89 Cf. Gen. 26.18.

quished when a woman discovers your snares. That holy woman bore the Lord; I shall search for His cross. She gave proof that He was born; I shall give proof that He rose from the dead. She caused God to be seen among men; I shall raise from ruins the divine banner which shall be a remedy for our sins.'

(45) And so she opened the ground and cleared away the dust. She found three fork-shaped gibbets thrown together, covered by debris and hidden by the Enemy. But the triumph of Christ could not be wiped out. She hesitated in her uncertainty. She hesitated, as a woman, but the Holy Spirit inspired her to investigate carefully, because two robbers had been crucified with the Lord. Therefore, she sought the middlebeam, but it could have happened that the debris had mixed the crosses one with another and that chance had interchanged them. She went back to the text of the Gospel and found that on the middle gibbet a title had been displayed, 'Jesus of Nazareth, King of the Jews.'[90] Hence, a sequence of sound reasoning was established and the Cross of salvation was revealed by its title. This is what Pilate answered to the Jews who petitioned him: 'What I have written, I have written,'[91] that is: 'I have not written these things to please you, but that future ages may know them. I have not written for you, but for posterity,' saying, as it were: 'Let Helena have something to read whereby she may recognize the cross of the Lord.'

(46) She discovered, then, the title. She adored the King, not the wood, indeed, because this is an error of the Gentiles and a vanity of the wicked. But she adored Him who hung on the tree, whose name was inscribed in the title; Him, I say, who, as a scarabaeus,[92] cried out to His Father

---
90 John 19.22.
91 *Ibid.*
92 Cf. Hab. 2.11. St. Ambrose often employs the scarab as a symbol of Christ.

to forgive the sins of his persecutors.[93] The woman eagerly hastened to touch the remedy of immortality, but she feared to trample under foot the mystery of salvation. Joyful at heart, yet with anxious step, she knew not what she should do. She proceeded, however, to the resting place of Truth. The wood shone and grace flashed forth. And, as before, Christ had visited a woman in Mary, so the Spirit visited a woman in Helena. He taught her what as a woman she did not know, and led her upon a way which no mortal could know.

(47) She sought the nails with which the Lord was crucified, and found them. From one nail she ordered a bridle to be made, from the other she wove a diadem. She turned the one to an ornamental, the other to a devotional, use. Mary was visited to liberate Eve; Helena was visited that emperors might be redeemed. So she sent to her son Constantine a diadem adorned with jewels which were interwoven with the iron of the Cross and enclosed the more precious jewel of divine redemption. She sent the bridle, also. Constantine used both, and transmitted his faith to later kings. And so the beginning of the faith of the emperors is the holy relic which is upon the bridle.[94] From that came the faith whereby persecution ended and devotion to God took its place.

(48) Wisely did Helena act who placed the cross on the head of sovereigns, that the Cross of Christ might be adored among kings. That was not presumption but piety, since honor was given to our holy redemption. Good, therefore, is the nail of the Roman Empire. It rules the whole world and adorns the brow of princes, that they may be preachers who were accustomed to be persecutors. Rightly is the nail on the head, so that where the intelligence is, there may be pro-

---
93 Cf. Luke 23.39.
94 Cf. Zach. 14.20.

tection, also. On the head, a crown; in the hands, reins. A crown made from the Cross, that faith might shine forth; reins likewise from the Cross, that authority might govern, and that there might be just rule, not unjust legislation. May the princes also consider that this has been granted to them by Christ's generosity, that in imitation of the Lord it may be said of the Roman emperor: 'Thou hast set on his head a crown of precious stones.'[95]

(49) On that account the Church manifests joy, the Jew blushes. Not only does he blush, but he is tormented also, because he himself is the author of his own confusion. While he insulted Christ, he confessed that He was King; when he called Him king of the Jews,' he who did not believe confessed his sacrilege. 'Behold,' they say, 'we have crucified Jesus, that Christians after death may rise again, and, having died, may reign! We have crucified Him whom kings adore; Him whom we do not adore they do adore! Behold, even the nail is held in honor, and He whom we crucified to death is the remedy of salvation, and by an invisible power torments demons! We thought that we had conquered, but we confess that we ourselves are conquered! Christ has risen again, and princes acknowledge that He has risen. He who is not seen lives again.' Now we have a greater struggle; now the battle against Him becomes more furious. We have despised Him whom kingdoms attend, whom power serves. How shall we resist kings? Kings are bowed under the iron of His feet! Kings adore Him, and Photinians deny His divinity! Emperors prefer the nail of His Cross to their own diadem, and Arians violate His power!

(50) But I ask: Why was the holy relic upon the bridle if not to curb the insolence of emperors, to check the wantonness of tyrants, who as horses neigh after lust that they may be allowed to commit adultery unpunished? What infamies

---

95 Ps. 20.4.

do we not find in the Neros, the Caligulas, and the rest, for whom there was nothing holy upon the bridle?

(51) What else, then, did Helena accomplish by her desire to guide the reins than to seem to say to all emperors through the Holy Spirit: 'Do not become like the horse and mule,'[96] and with the bridle and bit to restrain[97] the jaws of those who did not realize that they were kings to rule those subject to them? For power easily led them into vice, and like cattle they defiled themselves in promiscuous lust. They knew not God. The Cross of the Lord restrained them and recalled them from their fall into wickedness. It raised their eyes that they might look toward heaven and seek Christ. They threw off the bit of unbelief. They took the bridle of devotion and faith, following Him who said: 'Take my yoke upon you, for my yoke is easy and my burden light.'[98] Thereafter, the succeeding emperors were Christians, except Julian alone, who abandoned the Author of his salvation when he gave himself over to philosophic error. After him came Gratian and Theodosius.

(52) Prophecy did not lie, then, when it said: 'Kings shall walk in thy light.'[99] They shall walk openly, and especially Gratian and Theodosius before other princes, no longer protected by the weapons of their soldiers, but by their own merits; clothed not in purple garments, but in the mantle of glory. In this world they took delight in pardoning many. How much the more are they consoled in the other life by the remembrance of their goodness, recalling that they had spared many? They now enjoy radiant light, and, possessing far nobler dwellings there than they enjoyed here, they say: 'O Israel, how great is the house of the Lord, and how vast is the place of his possession! It is great and hath

---

96 Ps. 31.9.
97 Cf. Ps. 31.9.
98 Matt. 11.29,30.
99 Isa. 60.3 (Septuagint).

no end.'[100] And they who have endured the greatest hardships converse with each other, saying: 'It is good for a man when he hath borne the heavy yoke from his youth. He shall not sit solitary, and shall hold his peace, because he hath borne a heavy yoke.'[101] For he who has borne the heavy yoke from youth rests afterward. Removed from the throng, he possesses a distinguished place for his rest, saying: 'For Thou, O Lord, singularly hast settled me in hope.'[102]

(53) Lazarus, the poor man, bore the heavy yoke from his youth, and so he rests apart in Abraham's bosom, according to the testimony of the sacred text.[103] Theodosius bore the heavy yoke from youth, since those who had killed his victorious father were plotting against his safety. He bore the heavy yoke, since he endured exile because of filial devotion and since he assumed the imperial power when the Roman Empire was overrun by barbarians. He bore the heavy yoke that he might remove tyrants from the Roman Empire. But, because he labored here, he rests there.

(54) But now let us come to the transportation of the illustrious body. You weep, Honorius, illustrious scion, and give testimony of your filial love by your tears. You are sending the body of your father on a long and distant journey, for it still lacks the honor of a tomb. But the patriarch Jacob, because of the necessity of liberating his people who were being oppressed by the dangers of a great and bitter famine, also left his home, though an old man, and hastened to a foreign land. When he had died, his body, escorted by his son, was brought in the course of some days to the sepulchre of his fathers. And nothing was taken away from his merits; rather, it redounded to his praise that, having suffered the

---
100 Baruch 3.24,25.
101 Lam. 3.27,28.
102 Ps. 4.10.
103 Cf. Luke 16.20.

loss of his rightful home for the sake of his family, he traveled like an exile even after his death.

(55) You weep, also, august Emperor, because you yourself will not escort the honored remains to Constantinople. We are both in the same situation. We all shall accompany them with due sorrow. We should all like, if it were possible, to go with you as an escort for the body. But Joseph went into a neighboring province. Here, many different regions intervene; here, seas must be crossed. Even this would not be laborious to you, did not the public welfare restrain you, which good emperors place before parents and children. Therefore, your father made you emperor, and God has confirmed this, so that you might not serve under your father only, but that you might have command over all.

(56) Do not fear lest the triumphant remains may seem to be unhonored wherever they go. This is not the feeling of Italy, which witnessed his magnificent triumphs, which, freed for a second time from tyrants, acclaims the author of her liberty. This is not the feeling of Constantinople, which for a second time has sent a prince to victory. Although she wished to retain him, she could not. She was indeed awaiting triumphal celebrations at his return and the tokens of victories. She was awaiting the emperor of the whole world, surrounded by the army from Gaul and supported by the might of the whole world. But now Theodosius returns thither, more powerful, more glorious. Choirs of angels escort him, and a multitude of saints accompanies him. Surely, blessed art thou, Constantinople, for thou art receiving a citizen of paradise, and thou wilt possess in the august hospice of his buried body a dweller of the celestial city.

INDEX

INDEX

Aaron, 6, 90, 91, 246, 268
Abraham, 59, 89, 103, 155, 212, 236, 239-243, 310, 311
Abraham's bosom, 17, 295, 331
Absalom, 208, 286
Adad, 72
Adam, 88, 124, 199, 200, 212, 237
Alexander the Great, viii
Ambrose, St., as bishop, 170, 187, 190, 277, 322; closeness to brother, 164, 173, 176-179, 192, 195, 197; as envoy of Valentinian, 278; and Latin funeral oration, xix-xxi; *De bono mortis*, 211 n.; *Expositio in Lucam*, 211 n., 258 n.; *In Psalmos*, 217 n.; *On Satyrus*, 161-259; *On Theodosius*, 307-332; *On Valentinian*, 265-299
Amnon, 286
Anaxagoras, 21, 44 n.
Anthimus, Bishop of Tyana, 75 n.
Antioch, Council of, 133 n.
Antisthenes, x

Arbogast, 263, 264, 276 n.
Arcadius, Emperor, 304, 313
Aristotle, x, 21, 82 n., 313 n.
Arius, 53, 128, 132, 167 n.
Armenians, 41, 42
Asa, 313
astronomy, 9, 35, 47, 235
Athanasius, 66 n.
Athenagoras, xiv, xv
Athens, 14, 38-45
athletes, of God, 14, 30, 32, 317

Babel, Tower of, 85
baptism, 129, 144, 287, 288, 296, 318
barbarians, threat of invasion by, 161, 175, 176, 266, 275, 304, 331
Barnabas, 55
Basil, St., 3, 4, 150, 154, 155; ancestry of, 29-35; as bishop, 51, 59-77; care of sick, 80, 81; charity of, 57-59, 80; comparison of, with others, 88-95; cure of emperor's son, 71-72;

defense of orthodoxy against Valens, 53-56; defense of right of asylum, 73-74; dispute with Eusebius, 51; death of, 95-97; education of, 35-49; eloquence of, 38, 47, 83-85; founder of monastic communities, 80; parentage of, 34; as priest, 38, 49-59; sentence of exile rescinded, 71; struggle against Arianism, 53-56; struggle with Valens and Modestus, 64-72; Trinitarian teaching of, 85-88; virtues of, 56-58, 60-62, 74-83, 95; writings of, 64, 85-88
Basil, the Elder, 34, 36, 37
basilikòs lógos, royal oration, ix, xii
Beseleel, 64
Bion of Borysthenes, x
bishops, inept selection of, 50, 51
Boulenger, Fernand, xvii, xxii
Byzantium, 10, 38, 332

Caesarea, 37, 49, 146
Caesarius, St., brother of St. Gregory, charity of, 21; at court, 10-16; death of, 16, 117; education of, 8-10; eloquence of, 21; learning of, 21; marriage of, 10; occasion of funeral oration on, 3; as physician, 9-12; struggle with Julian, 13-16; as treasurer, 15, 20; virtues of, 8, 9, 12-16
Caligula, 330

Cappadocia, 29, 34, 55, 75, 76
catechumenate, 128
celibacy, 79
Chalane (Babel), 85
charity, 57-59, 80, 81, 108-110, 125, 126, 134, 135, 185, 186; *see also* wealth
chastity, 43, 73, 184, 185, 202, 274
Christ, 7, 14, 24, 36, 53, 60, 79, 81, 82, 87, 114, 121, 129, 164, 174, 279-281, *et passim*; as Archetype, 104; Incarnation of, xiii, 162, 166; as King, 18, 329; as Lover, 114; miracles of, 230-234; as Physician, 111, 113, 140, 214, 314; as Redeemer, xiii, 162, 163, 199, 200, 215, 216, 224, 233-237, 240, 242, 244, 314, 316, 319, 324; Resurrection of, xiv, 214, 232-237, 329; tears of, 165, 166; as Truth, 236, 248, 249, 328; as Word, 5, 13, 25, 54, 59, 93, 150, 212, 271
Cicero, xi, xii, xx, 160, 202 n., 205 n., 255 n., 259 n.
Cleanthes, 21
Clement of Rome, xiv
Cleobulus, 77 n.
communion of saints, xiii, 17, 104
consolatio, vii-x, xvi, xix, xx
consolatory treatise, as literary genre, vii, x-xv

Constantine, Emperor, xv, 325, 326, 328
Constantius, Emperor, 3
contemplation, 80, 211
Crantor, x
Crates, 12, 78
Creed, the, 133 n.
Cross, true, 325-330
Cynics, x, 78 n.
Cyprian, St., xv

David, 19, 23, 36, 63, 65, 71, 84, 86, 92, 110, 128, 137, 152, 167, 206, 208, 210, 212, 215, 225, 236, 249, 255, 259, 272, 286, 288
death, as escape from misfortunes of this world, viii, xiii, xx, 17, 20, 22, 23, 121, 155, 174, 175, 191, 198, 204, 205, 211, 213, 255, 320, 321; happy life follows, viii, 18-20, 22, 23, 117, 121, 155, 191, 239, 321; lot of all men, viii, xii, xvii, 19, 162, 163, 198, 199, 205, 217; natural, spiritual, and penal, 212-213; not an evil, 205-215; origin of, 216; sin as, 211-213, 319, 320; *see also* Christ as Redeemer, emotions, grief, immortality, resurrection
Democritus, x, 21
Demosthenes, Arian agent, 67
Devil, the, 63, 234, 311; outwitted by St. Helena, 326, 327

Diocletian, 304
Diogenes, 78 n.
Dionysius of Halicarnassus, xi
Dudden, F. H., 222 n.
Duff., J. W., 222 n.

education, as human advantage, 135
Elias, 52, 58, 92, 143, 233, 238, 255, 278
Eliseus, 92, 311
Emmelia, mother of St. Basil, 34
emotion, display of, xiii, 5, 6, 18, 96, 97, 116, 126, 165, 168, 193, 194, 200, 202, 267, 284
encomium, as literary genre, vii, ix; pagan, x, xii, xiii
encomium, as laudatory unit of eulogy, ix, xvii, xviii; family, 2-4, 29-34, 103-104, 122-123; physical endowments, 8, 94-95; upbringing and education, 8-10, 35-49, 271-272; life and occupation, 10-12, 49-81, 124-153; moral qualities, xx, 6-8, 12-16, 56-62, 78-83, 104-115, 124-126, 133-143, 179-187, 273-274, 309-310; achievements, 12-16, 49-82, 145-153, 266-267, 275, 309-312; comparison with others, 88-95, 103, 124, 130, 286, 311-314; death and funeral, 16, 95-97, 114-117, 152, 169-170, 264
Enos, 89
Epicurus, 21

epitáphios lógos, ix, xii, xvii, xviii
Esau, 66
Eucharist, Holy, xiii, 113, 114, 119, 126, 180-182
Euclid, 21
Eugenius, Emperor, 264, 309 n., 324
Eusebius of Caesarea, 51, 52, 59, 147-149
Eusebius of Vercelli, 52 n.
Eusebius, Vicar of Pontus, 72
Evagoras of Cyprus, viii
Eve, 111, 124, 328
exhortation, as unit of oration, ix, xvii, xviii, xx, 16-25, 154, 189-195
exordium, as unit, ix, xvii, xix, 5-6, 27-29, 101-102, 119-122, 161-164, 265-271, 307-309
Ezechias, 143

Faustinus, Bishop of Iconium, 4, 112 n.
Flacilla, 325
Flavian, consul, 309 n.
fortune, as fate, xii; as goddess, 148
funeral oration, as literary genre, vii-xxi

Galen, 21
games, pagan, 17, 273
geometry, 9, 47
George of Cappadocia, 66 n.
Giezi, 311

God, 32, 35, 51, 53, 57, 58, 62, 68, 75, 86-90, 111, 119, 122, 123, 126, 127, 132, 169, 186, 187, *et passim*; anger of, 138; as Creator, xiii, xv, 9, 25, 85, 162, 181, 225 n., 234, 235, 244, 275; as Judge, 207; as Lawmaker, 31, 180; providence of, 31, 49, 188, 220, 318
gods, pagan, as ancestors, 30
Gorgonia, St., sister of St. Gregory, charity of, 108-110; date of panegyric on, 4; death of, 114-117; faith of, in Holy Eucharist, 113, 114; marriage, 105, 106, 115; parentage of, 103, 104; physical injury to, 111, 112; virtues of, 104-114
Grata, sister of Valentinian, 264
Gratian, Emperor, 263, 268, 278 n., 288, 294-298, 324, 325, 330
Gregory Nazianzen, St., association with St. Basil, 27, 39-49, 61, 77, 97; and baptism, 144; education of, 8; interest in philosophy, 11; references to own skill in oratory, 5, 8, 16, 17, 27; rhetorical method of, xvii-xix; *On His Father,* 119-156; *On St. Basil,* 27-99; *On St. Caesarius,* 3-25; *On St. Gorgonia,* 101-118
Gregory the Elder, baptism and initiation to priesthood of, 128-130; charity of, 134, 135; comparison with others, 137;

courage in resisting Julian, 145, 146; defense of election of Eusebius, 147-149; family of, 122, 123; founder of church at Nazianzus, 153; illness of, 140-143, 151; marriage of, 124-128; personality of, 6, 8; as priest, 131-153; official competence of, 6; orthodoxy of, 132; and selection of St. Basil as bishop, 59-60, 155; virtues of, 6-8, 103, 104, 133-143, 152
Gregory of Nyssa, St., xvi, xix, 122 n.
grief, Christian attitude toward, 5, 6, 18, 121, 156, 163-165, 191, 199, 213-215; patience in, 201-204, 254; tempered by reason, xiii, 17, 18, 156, 198, 200, 218
Guignet, M., xviii, xix

Helena, St., 325-330
Henoch, 89, 238, 289
Heraclitus, 21
Hero, 21
Herodotus, 221 n.
Hesiod, 124 n., 221 n.
Himerius, x
Hippocrates, 12, 21
Homer, 42, 46, 47, 49, 148 n., 256 n.
Honorius, Emperor, 304, 308, 313, 331, 332
Horace, xi
Hypereides, viii
Hypsistarii, 122

immortality, xiv-xvii, xx, xxi, 21-23, 205, 212, 221, 321; phoenix as symbol of, xiv, xv, 221, 222; true life in, xiii, xvii, xxi, 174, 198, 201; *see also* death
Iphigenia, 33
Isaac, 103, 156, 239-243, 295, 311
Isocrates, viii

Jacob, 66, 90, 239, 242, 290, 295, 308, 311, 331
James, St., 91, 137
Jeroboam, 50
John the Baptist, St., 52, 93
Joseph, 58, 90, 206, 290, 308, 332
Josias, 289, 313
Julian the Apostate, 3, 13-16, 53, 145, 146, 148, 149, 275, 289, 304, 330
Justa, sister of Valentinian, 264

Lactantius, xv, 222 n.
laudatio funebris, vii, xi, xii, xix
laughter, attitude toward, 106
Lawrence, St., 169
Lazarus, 213, 231-233, 242, 295, 331
lector, 187
Leontius, Bishop, 128
Libanius, x
Lucifer of Cagliari, 52 n., 182 n.
Lucretius, xi
luxury, proper attitude toward: cosmetics, 107, 125; dress, 17, 107, 136; food, 20, 45, 109,

136, 185, 273; head dresses, 107; jewelry, 107; land, 20; perfume, 17; slaves, 20; spectacle, 45, 273

Marcellina, sister of St. Ambrose, 159, 160, 168, 169, 176, 179, 193, 194
Martial, xi
martyrs, 30-33, 66, 215, 288, 311, 316
Mary, sister of Lazarus, 233
Mary, Virgin, 166, 283, 328
mathematics, 9, 47
Maximinus, 30
Maximus, Emperor, 263, 278 n., 283, 309 n., 324
medicine, study of, 9, 10, 12, 36, 47
Menander, ix, xvii, xix, 82 n.
miraculous occurrences, 111-114, 140-146, 150-151, 169, 180, 181, 230-234, 326, 327
Modestus, prefect, 67 n.
monody, as literary genre, ix, xvii, xx
Moses, 6, 58, 90, 91, 129, 130, 137, 142, 229, 247, 248, 288, 308, 316
Mysteries, holy, 180, 183
mythology, pagan, 30, 33, 36, 45-48, 51, 227, 228, 256-258

Nabuzardan, *see* Demosthenes
Nazarites, monks, 52, 132, 149
Nero, 330
Nicaea, 16, 128
Noe, 89, 132
Nonna, St., mother of St. Gregory, 16, 21, 116, 155; attitude toward pagans, 126; charity of, 125, 135; conversion of husband, 127, 128; illness of, 143, 144; personality of, 6-8; prayers of, 10, 141; prenatal dedication of Gregory, 127; virtues of, 6, 8, 103, 104, 124-126; vision of, 144-146

Offertory, at Mass, 70
'one soul in bodies twain,' 44, 48, 164, 171, 178
Orders, Holy, 50, 128-130
Orestes, St., 76
Orphism, 225 n.
Ovid, xi, 256 n., 257 n.

Panaetius, x
Paul, St., xiv, xxi, 22, 55, 84, 94, 130, 137, 211, 213, 223, 224, 238, 239, 243, 254, 317
Pericles, viii, ix
Peter, St., 94, 137, 207, 233, 279, 315
philosophy, as life of Christian perfection, 6 n., 35, 49, 125; study of, 47, 52
Phineas, 137
phoenix, xiv, xv, 221, 222
Photinians, 329
Pilate, 73
Pindar, 44

Plato, x, xv, 21, 180 n., 225 n., 255 n., 313 n.
Pliny the Elder, 221 n.
Pliny the Younger, xi
Plutarch, xi
Polybius, xi
Pontus, 29, 30, 34, 36, 52, 54, 72
prayer, ix, xvii, xviii, xx, 25, 98, 99, 118, 144, 163, 195, 214, 288, 289, 299, 317, 323
Propertius, xi
Ptolemy, 21
Pulcheria, daughter of Theodosius, 325
Pyrrho, 21
Pythagoras, xv, 225 n.

Quintilian, xii n.

Rand, E. K., 274 n.
Rebecca, 89
resurrection, of body, xiii, xiv, xvii, 216-259, 285; *see also* immortality
Roboam, 50
Rozynski, F., xix, xx

Sabellius, 53, 132
Samuel, 70, 91, 137
Sara, 103, 155, 310
Saul, 38, 50
Satyrus, brother of St. Ambrose, charity of, 185, 186; closeness of Ambrose to, 164-173, 176-179, 192-195, 197; counsel of, 170, 178; death of, 169, 170; faith of, in Holy Eucharist, 180; as mediator between St. Ambrose and Marcellina, 179; and Prosper, 169 n., 172; shipwreck of, 180, 181; virtues of, 179-187
scarab, as symbol of Christ, 327
Scripture, Holy, xiii, xiv, xviii, xx, xxi, 50, 51, 54, 55, 58, 64, 86, 119, 124, 153, 189, 208, 225, *et passim.*
Quotations from, or references to:
Acts, 94 n., 96 n., 130 n., 137 n., 174 n., 188 n., 233 n., 280 n., 311 n.
Apocalypse, 213 n., 243 n., 244, 253 n., 258 n., 321 n.
Baruch, 331 n.
Canticle of Canticles, 252, 253 n., 267-269 nn., 290-297 nn.
Colossians, 24 n., 182 n., 237 n., 244-246 nn., 279 n., 311 n.
1 Corinthians, xiv n., 18 n., 22 n., 25 n., 31 n., 58 n., 84 n., 98 n., 119 n., 165 n., 191 n., 210 n., 211 n., 219 n., 220 n., 223 n., 224 n., 231 n., 237 n., 238 n., 243-245 nn., 248 n., 249 n., 251 n., 254 n., 259 n., 281 n., 312 n., 317 n., 320 n., 323 n.
2 Corinthians, 22 n., 36 n., 79 n., 98 n., 162 n., 214 n., 236 n., 237 n., 245 n., 248 n., 279 n., 321 n.

Daniel, 93 n., 119 n., 143, 226 n., 273, 274
Deuteronomy, 95 n., 126 n., 308, 315 n.
Ecclesiastes, 19, 20 n., 83 n., 131, 134 n., 209 n., 221 n., 268 n., 318 n.
Ecclesiasticus, 6 n., 211 n., 271 n., 289 n., 292 n., 298 n.
Ephesians, 210 n., 238 n., 245 n., 280 n., 318 n.
4 Esdras, 188-190 nn.
Exodus, 31 n., 32 n., 57 n., 64 n., 71 n., 90-92 nn., 119 n., 129 n., 130 n., 141 n., 143 n., 229 n., 248 n., 293 n., 316 n.
Ezechiel, 22, 212 n., 227, 228-230 nn.
Galatians, 24 n., 137 n., 243 n.
Genesis, 58 n., 85 n., 88-90 nn., 103 n., 124 n., 174 n., 206 n., 212 n., 229 n., 234 n., 236 n., 238-242 nn., 289 n., 290 n., 295 n., 308 n., 311 n., 316 n., 321 n., 326 n.
Habacuc, 327 n.
Hebrews, 64 n., 91 n., 104 n., 289 n., 294 n., 310 n., 311 n.
Isaias, 58 n., 119 n., 130, 134 n., 143 n., 166 n., 226, 235 n., 272 n., 278 n., 294 n., 321-323 nn., 330 n.
James, 75 n.
Jeremias, 19, 55 n., 130, 211, 243 n., 255, 271, 279 n., 291 n.
Job, 19 n., 90, 105 n., 108, 109 n., 137, 153 n., 210, 226, 285, 286
John, 14 n., 68 n., 121 n., 163 n., 166 n., 205 n., 207 n., 215 n., 217, 223 n., 231-233 nn., 236 n., 243, 244, 247 n., 253, 258, 278 n., 281 n., 283 n., 299 n., 315 n., 318, 327 n.
1 John, 313 n., 324 n.
Jonas, 63, 93 n.
Josue, 32 n., 91, 119 n.
Judges, 287 n.
1 Kings, 38 n., 70 n., 91 n., 92 n., 137 n.
2 Kings, 71 n., 92 n., 206-208 nn., 286 n., 297 n., 298 n., 319 n.
3 Kings, 57 n., 72 n., 92 n., 143 n., 209 n., 233 n., 247 n., 255 n., 314 n.
4 Kings, 92 n., 143 n., 233 n., 238 n., 290 n., 311 n., 313 n., 314 n.
Lamentations, 266-271 nn., 278, 331 n.
Leviticus, 245 n., 247 n.
Luke, 57 n., 58 n., 60 n., 64 n., 93 n., 96 n., 114 n., 174 n., 189 n., 199 n., 212 n., 213 n., 233 n., 234 n., 239 n., 243 n., 247 n., 252 n., 268 n., 272 n., 278 n., 281 n., 295 n., 326 n., 328 n., 331 n.
2 Machabees, 93 n.
Mark, 94 n., 137 n., 233 n., 278 n.

Matthew, 15 n., 24 n., 52 n., 57 n., 79 n., 80 n., 93 n., 94 n., 113 n., 166 n., 184 n., 185 n., 187 n., 212 n., 224 n., 230 n., 234 n., 239 n., 242 n., 252 n., 270 n., 271 n., 278-280 nn., 290 n., 315 n., 318-320 nn., 330 n.
Numbers, 119 n., 137 n., 214 n., 229 n., 246 n., 248 n., 249 n.
Osee, 19 n., 112 n.
2 Paralipomenon, 314 n.
1 Peter, 62 n., 239 n.
2 Peter, 23 n.
Philippians, 22 n., 95 n., 111 n., 114 n., 119 n., 213 n., 214 n., 243 n., 279 n., 285 n., 319 n.
Proverbs, 6 n., 57 n., 63 n., 106 n., 120 n., 124 n., 135 n., 187 n., 235 n., 251 n., 272 n., 294 n., 312 n., 314 n., 315 n.
Psalms, xiii, xxi, 19 n., 23-25 nn., 36 n., 55 n., 57-59 nn., 63 n., 65 n., 70, 84-86 nn., 90-92 nn., 96 n., 97, 109 n., 110, 112 n., 115 n., 117, 120 n., 122 n., 125, 128, 136-138 nn., 152 n., 165-167 nn., 176 n., 181 n., 187 n., 207 n., 208 n., 210 n., 211 n., 215 n., 225 n., 226 n., 229 n., 234 n., 236 n., 243 n., 244 n., 250 n., 252 n., 255 n., 258 n., 259 n., 269-272 nn., 280 n., 281 n., 285 n., 289 n., 290 n., 293 n., 297 n., 307 n., 313-326 nn., 329-331 nn.
Romans, 24 n., 66 n., 84 n., 94 n., 162 n., 199 n., 200 n., 211 n., 213 n., 214 n., 215 n., 236 n., 241 n., 246 n., 249 n., 292 n., 311 n., 315-318 nn., 323 n.
1 Thessalonians, 22 n., 25 n., 165 n., 217 n., 231 n., 238 n., 247 n., 285 n., 317 n.
1 Timothy, 119 n., 161 n., 185 n., 203 n.
2 Timothy, 95 n., 316 n.
Titus, 91 n.
Tobias, 265 n.
Wisdom, 15 n., 19 n., 35 n., 46 n., 175 n., 180 n., 209 n., 216 n., 288 n., 289 n.
Zacharias, 325 n., 328 n.

Seneca, xi, xiii
Serena, guardian of Honorius, 309 n.
Sodom, 85
Solomon, 46, 50, 63, 83, 92, 106, 120, 125, 134, 135, 209, 210, 251, 272, 312
soul, and visions in sleep, 192; contemplative joys of, after death, 21, 22; pagan beliefs on, 217, 225, 255, 256; transmigration of, 225, 256; union of, with body, in punishment and reward, 235, 236
Spirit, Holy, 16, 53, 54, 56, 59, 63, 77, 83, 84, 86-89, 95, 105,

115, 129, 132, 142, 147, 150, 187, 231, 245, 249, 255, 279, 315, 327, 330
Statius, xi
Stephen, St., 94, 137
Stilicho, Flavius, 304, 309 n.
Stoics, x
Symmachus, L. Avianius, 176

Tabitha, 174, 233
Tacitus, xii
Taurus, Mount, 76
Tertullian, xv, 256 n.
theater, Greek, 49, 83, 107, 125, 126
Themistius, x
Theodosius, Emperor, 263, 264, 268; achievements of, 309-312; comparison with others, 311-314; date of funeral oration on, 303; disturbance of elements at death of, 307; penance of, 319, 322; removal of body of, to Constantinople, 332; virtues of, 309-310
Theophrastus, x
Thucydides, viii
Thurston, H., 199 n.
tópoi, viii-x, xii, xiii, xviii
transmigration, 225, 256
Trinity, xiii, 53, 54, 73, 85-88, 91, 99, 117, 132, 166, 167, 240

trumpets, allegorical interpretation of, 244-251

Valens, Emperor, 53 n., 64-67; 70, 151 n.
Valentinian I, 275 n., 289
Valentinian II, 263, 264; achievements of, 266, 267, 275; and baptism, 287, 288, 296; comparison of, with others, 286; date of consolatory sermon on, 264; and Gratian, 288-298; mysterious death of, 264; and sisters, 281-288; upbringing of, 271, 272; virtues of, 272-275
Vergil, 169 n., 225 n., 257 n., 297 n.
Victory, Altar of, 274 n.
vigils, 110
virginity, 79, 125, 185
visions, 144-146, 192

wealth, spiritual vs. temporal, xvii, 17, 19, 21, 78, 104, 125, 185

Xenocrates of Chalcedon, x
Xenophon, x
Xerxes, 65

Zeno, x

www.ingramcontent.com/pod-product-compliance
Lightning Source LLC
Chambersburg PA
CBHW032025290426
44110CB00012B/670